Voting Behavior in Indonesia since Democratization

Indonesia is the world's third largest democracy (after India and the USA) and the only fully democratic Muslim democracy, yet it remains little known in the comparative politics literature. This book aspires to do for Indonesian political studies what *The American Voter* did for American political science. It contributes a major new case, the world's largest Muslim democracy, to the latest research in cross-national voting behavior, making the unique argument that Indonesian voters, like voters in many developing and developed democracies, are "critical citizens" or critical democrats. The analysis is based on original opinion surveys conducted after every national-level democratic election in Indonesia from 1999 to the present by the respected Indonesian Survey Institute and Saiful Mujani Research & Consulting.

Saiful Mujani, Associate Professor of Political Science at the Universitas Islam Negeri Syarif Hidayatullah, is the intellectual and creative founder of the most respected political research firm in Indonesia today – Saiful Mujani Research and Consulting (SMRC). A leading pioneer of survey research in Indonesia, Professor Mujani also founded the Indonesian Survey Institute, serving as its director from 2004 to 2009. In addition to being the former director of research and development for Metro TV (the first and still most highly regarded Indonesian news channel), Mujani regularly appears on Metro TV as well as TVOne and SCTV. He also writes for the top national newsweekly *Tempo* and newspapers including *Kompas*, *Media Indonesia*, and *Koran Tempo*. His academic publications include articles in the *American Journal of Political Science*, *Comparative Political Studies*, *Journal of Democracy*, *Asian Survey*, and *Japanese Journal of Political Science*, and he (along with coauthors Dr. Liddle and Thomas Pepinsky) was awarded best paper by the American Political Science Association for its 2009 Annual Conference.

R. William Liddle, now Professor Emeritus at Ohio State University, has devoted his entire academic career to research, observation, and analysis of the politics of Indonesia as the country transitioned from a dictatorship to the established democracy it is today. Recognized for his expertise in the field, Professor Liddle has long served as a source, across the globe, for understanding the politics of Indonesia – writing for the international and Indonesian media (including *The New York Times*, *The Wall Street Journal*, the Jakarta daily *Kompas*, and Indonesian newsweekly *Tempo*), appearing on television and radio programs in the US (*PBS News Hour*), Europe, Australia, and Indonesia, and consulting for US government agencies. He is especially proud of the 2008 publication of a book of essays in his honor: *Dari Columbus untuk Indonesia: 70 Tahun Profesor Bill Liddle dari Murid dan Sahabat* ("From Columbus for Indonesia: 70 Years of Professor Bill Liddle from Students and Friends").

Kuskridho Ambardi is Senior Lecturer at Universitas Gadjah Mada and current Executive Director of the Indonesia Survey Institute (Lembaga Survei Indonesia). Recognized as an outstanding scholar, Ambardi has published numerous scholarly articles including "Indonesia's New Democracy: Who Controls Political Parties?" in *Journal of Asia*, Korea. He has also presented papers and participated in many seminars and workshops, including at the Rajaratnam School of International Studies (Singapore, 2010), the Association for Asian Studies (Hawaii, 2011), and the Centre for Democratic Institutions, Australian National University (Canberra, Australia, 2011). Ambardi is a member of the Indonesian National Research Council (Dewan Riset Nasional, 2015–2018). As a public intellectual, he also writes influential columns for the Jakarta daily *Kompas* and newsweekly *Tempo* and appears regularly as a resource person on Indonesian national television channels.

Voting Behavior in Indonesia since Democratization

Critical Democrats

SAIFUL MUJANI

Universitas Islam Negeri Syarif Hidayatullah

R. WILLIAM LIDDLE

Ohio State University

KUSKRIDHO AMBARDI

Universitas Gadjah Mada

CAMBRIDGE
UNIVERSITY PRESS

CAMBRIDGE
UNIVERSITY PRESS

University Printing House, Cambridge CB2 8BS, United Kingdom

One Liberty Plaza, 20th Floor, New York, NY 10006, USA

477 Williamstown Road, Port Melbourne, VIC 3207, Australia

314-321, 3rd Floor, Plot 3, Splendor Forum, Jasola District Centre, New Delhi - 110025, India

79 Anson Road, #06-04/06, Singapore 079906

Cambridge University Press is part of the University of Cambridge.

It furthers the University's mission by disseminating knowledge in the pursuit of education, learning and research at the highest international levels of excellence.

www.cambridge.org
Information on this title: www.cambridge.org/9781108421799
DOI: 10.1017/9781108377836

First published 2018

A catalogue record for this publication is available from the British Library

Library of Congress Cataloging in Publication data
NAMES: Mujani, Saiful, author. | Liddle, R. William, 1938– author. | Ambardi, Kuskridho, author.
TITLE: Voting behavior in Indonesia since democratization : critical democrats / Saiful Mujani, R. William Liddle, Kuskridho Ambardi.
DESCRIPTION: New York : Cambridge University Press, 2018. | Includes bibliographical references and index.
IDENTIFIERS: LCCN 2017053764 | ISBN 9781108421799 (alk. paper)
SUBJECTS: LCSH: Voting – Indonesia. | Elections – Indonesia. | Political participation – Indonesia. | Democratization – Indonesia. | Indonesia – Politics and government – 1998–
CLASSIFICATION: LCC JQ778 .M857 2018 | DDC 324.9598–dc23
LC record available at https://lccn.loc.gov/2017053764

ISBN 978-1-108-42179-9 Hardback
ISBN 978-1-108-43233-7 Paperback

We dedicate this book to our wives:
Baikuniyah
Wanda Carter
Santi Kusumasari
and our children:
Putri Matahari, Berlian Khatulistiwa, and Jagad Alit
Dallas, Craig, Caitlin, and Adam
Marsa Daniswara and Hafid Sasayuda

Contents

Figures

Tables

Acknowledgments

This book is the product of nearly two decades of research conducted by the authors on Indonesian voting behavior since the restoration of democracy in 1999, after a hiatus of nearly half a century since the last democratic election in 1955. Our primary data come from eight national, individual-level, scientific surveys that we conducted ourselves: the first just after the first democratic parliamentary election in 1999 and the last after the most recent parliamentary and presidential elections in 2014.

An undertaking of this magnitude would not have been possible without the robust support, generous contributions, and enthusiastic participation of many others. We would like to begin by thanking Paul Beck and Ned Lebow, whose assistance was critical to the success of our first survey in 1999. At that time, none of us had any experience in conducting public opinion surveys and there were no country experts to whom we could turn, since Indonesia had been a dictatorship for more than three decades.

Paul Beck, at the time chair of the political science department at Ohio State University, helped us in two ways: by giving us a crash course in the basics of political survey research, and by writing compelling letters of support to potential funding agencies, including the National Science Foundation, from which we received a grant of USD 25,000 (#9975671). Matching funds were provided by Ohio State's Mershon Center for International Security Studies, whose director was then Ned Lebow. Ned also provided us with graduate research assistance, office space, and opportunities to present our findings to the Mershon and Ohio State scholarly communities. That assistance has continued to this day, under the leadership of subsequent Mershon directors Richard Herrmann and Craig Jenkins.

In Indonesia, our first survey was carried out in collaboration with colleagues at the Political Science Laboratory of the Faculty of Social and Political Sciences at the University of Indonesia in Jakarta. We especially appreciate the leadership at the Laboratory of Valina Singka Subekti, Eep Saefulloh Fatah, and Sri Budi Eko Wardani.

The 2004 and 2009 surveys were conducted by the Lembaga Survei Indonesia (LSI, Indonesian Survey Institute), founded in 2003. We are grateful for the support of our founding researchers: Djunaedi Hadi Sumarto, Heri Akhmadi, Theodore P. Rachmat, Oentoro Surya, and Joyo Winoto. Crucial outside funding for LSI, making possible a series of surveys conducted between 2003 and 2006, was provided by JICA (Japan International Cooperation Agency). We thank in particular Takashi Shiraishi, then at Kyoto University, for his early belief in LSI's promise, and JICA's staff in Jakarta. We are also grateful to Asian Barometer, under the leadership of Yun-han Chu, for collaboration with LSI in 2009.

We have been blessed by the presence of many skilled researchers at LSI over the years. We are especially grateful to Denny J. A., who was with us until 2005, and to Iman Suhirman, Adam Kamil, Wahyu Prasetyawan, Deni Irvani, Dudi Herlianto, M. Dahlan, Hendro Prasetyo, Burhanuddin Muhtadi, Rizka Halida, Nur Widiyati, and Zezen Zaenal Mutaqin.

For funding and implementation of the 2014 surveys, we thank Saiful Mujani Research and Consulting (SMRC), in particular Grace Natalie, Jayadi Hanan, Sirajuddin Abbas, and Ade Armando. Conducting an extensive series of national surveys at both LSI and SMRC would not have been possible without the hard work of our field coordinators and supervisors in the regions, plus the hundreds of researchers and interviewers from Aceh at the northwest corner of Indonesia to Papua in the southeast, a distance of more than 3,000 miles. Though we lack space to list their names, they are the backbone of our enterprise, making possible the collection of data from the far corners of the archipelago, often including reaching respondents in barely accessible sites determined by our random sampling procedures. We are very grateful to them all.

The 2004, 2009, and 2014 surveys also benefited from our collaboration with the Comparative National Elections Project (CNEP), centered at Ohio State and led by Richard Gunther and Paul Beck.

We are grateful to the Indonesian publisher Mizan, which encouraged our work at an early stage and in 2011 published our preliminary analysis, based on Indonesia's first three democratic elections (1999–2009), as *Kuasa Rakyat*.

Two anonymous readers for Cambridge University Press showed us how to better connect our analysis of the Indonesian data to current debates in the scholarly literature on comparative electoral behavior.

Final responsibility for the accuracy and quality of our analysis and interpretation of our data rests of course with the authors. *Semoga berkenan*, we hope the reader is pleased.

Introduction: Indonesia and Critical Democracy

INDONESIA'S DEMOCRATIC HISTORY

Democratic participation by Indonesian citizens in choosing members of Parliament, provincial and local legislatures, the president and regional executives is still a rare event in modern Indonesian history. The first parliamentary election was held in 1955, about ten years after the proclamation of Indonesian independence, and was judged democratic by observers (Feith 1957). When Parliament was dissolved in 1959 by decree of Indonesia's founding father, President Sukarno, returning the country to its Revolution-era 1945 Constitution, the era of parliamentary democracy was over.

Under the 1945 Constitution, the formal governmental system combined elements of parliamentarism and presidentialism. In this mixed system, sovereign authority was held by a People's Consultative Assembly (MPR, Majelis Permusyawaratan Rakyat). The president as head of state and government was selected by and responsible to the Assembly. After dissolving parliamentary democracy, President Sukarno labeled the mixed governmental system Guided Democracy, but it was in fact a form of authoritarianism. During Guided Democracy, there were no elections.

President Sukarno was removed from power in 1966 by Army General Suharto, whose authoritarian New Order government ruled for the following thirty-two years. A second parliamentary election was held in 1971. Elections were then held quinquennially under Suharto's New Order regime until 1997, but did not fulfill basic democratic conditions (Anderson 1996; Liddle 1996a, 1996b). They were instead a mechanism for political mobilization and legitimation by which the New Order sought to justify its own continuation. Through the electoral domination of the state party Golkar (Golongan Karya, Functional Groups), the Suharto government tried to demonstrate that its authoritarianism was supported by a popular majority. Because the New Order manipulated these elections, however, we cannot use the results to measure regime support or to assess the characteristics of the Indonesian voter.

Suharto resigned in May 1998 and was succeeded, following the Constitution, by his vice president, Bacharuddin Jusuf Habibie. A top priority of the Habibie government was to hold, within a short time, a new general election that fulfilled genuine democratic norms. Just over one year later, in June 1999, this demand was realized. Most observers and participants agreed that this election was conducted democratically. Political rights to hold opinions and to associate were recognized and protected for all citizens. Indonesians were free to form, join, and support the political parties of their choice. There was freedom for party leaders to campaign, mobilize, and influence citizens. Like mushrooms in the rainy season, hundreds of new parties were born, though in the end only 48 were awarded a place on the ballot by the independent General Election Commission (KPU, Komisi Pemilihan Umum).

The parliamentary elections of 1999, 2004, 2009, 2014 and the 2004, 2009, and 2014 direct presidential elections, like the parliamentary election of 1955, can be used to measure the extent to which the government was supported by the people. Unlike Suharto's manipulated New Order elections, all of these post-Suharto elections have been genuinely democratic and thus suitable for examination by political scientists who study comparative modern democratic voting behavior (International Foundation for Electoral Systems 1999, 2005, 2010, 2015; National Democratic Institute 1999, 2004).

CRITICAL DEMOCRATS

Indonesian democracy is less than two decades old and still in the process of consolidation (Liddle and Mujani 2013; Linz and Stepan 1996). Constitutionally, the preconditions of democracy were achieved by a series of amendments to the Constitution adopted between 1999 and 2002. Attitudinally, as measured by public opinion polls, most Indonesians quickly came to regard democracy as the best form of government for themselves. Behaviorally, most conflicts among citizens are now resolved through the democratic process.

It is true that within Indonesia some have questioned the democraticness of post-New Order elections as well. The 1999 election was marred by the failure of the General Election Commission to officially confirm its results. Then-President B. J. Habibie took over the process, declaring that the election was over and confirming that its results were legitimate. Habibie's action, in accordance with the election law, saved the country from uncertainty, even though at the time his own party, Partai Golkar (Functional Groups Party), the old state party under the authoritarian New Order, had been soundly defeated by PDIP (Partai Demokrasi Indonesia Perjuangan, Indonesian Democracy Party of Struggle), the main opposition party at the time, led by Megawati Sukarnoputri. In so doing, Habibie performed a considerable service for a democratizing Indonesia.

The 1999 election was closely watched from abroad because it marked the first general election since the overthrow of Suharto's authoritarianism. Foreign observers and commentators generally agreed that the 1999 election was conducted democratically. The democraticness of subsequent parliamentary and presidential elections has been more problematic, certainly in the view of defeated parties and politicians, but also to nonpartisan observers, especially Indonesians. Much of their criticism has been aimed at the General Election Commission, though they have failed to provide enough evidence to convince the respected Mahkamah Konstitusi (Constitutional Court) (Samadhi and Warouw 2009; Aspinall and Mietzner 2010; Hadiz 2010; Winters 2011).

Less disputed has been the concern, which the authors share, that in terms of civil liberties, especially the freedom to hold and practice religious beliefs, Indonesia is not yet fully free. In this Muslim-majority country, the Muslim world's largest and its longest established democracy, "National and local governments have repeatedly failed to protect religious minorities from violence and discrimination, and exhibited bias in investigations and prosecutions" (Freedom House 2016). The lack of religious freedom has become one of the most important sources of citizen dissatisfaction not with democracy itself as a principle but with its practice. The Constitution clearly guarantees freedom of religion but state authorities have often failed to implement it.

In addition to the religious issue, prodemocracy Indonesian citizens have many other concerns about democratic performance, which will be described and analyzed in the chapters to follow. It is these individuals whom we label critical democrats.

A POLITICAL ECONOMY EXPLANATION

What are the sources of the emergence of critical democrats? In *Democratic Deficit: Critical Citizens Revisited* (2011), Pippa Norris begins by asking if contemporary democratic states are "experiencing a major legitimacy crisis?" (p. 3). The question arises because of extensive empirical evidence, from the United States and other postindustrial socie-ties, of low or falling voter turnout and declining party loyalties, widely accepted indicators of civic disengagement. Indonesia, though only a democracy since 1999, is also experiencing falling turnout and declining loyalties.

Norris' answer, based on the analysis of fifty countries worldwide, is measured. She begins by showing that, "contrary to the prevalent view, *public support for the political system has not eroded consistently across a wide range of countries around the world ...* " (her italics, here and below). Nonetheless, "*in many countries today, satisfaction with the performance of democracy diverges from public aspirations,*" a condition that she labels a "democratic deficit."

In her earlier work, *Critical Citizens* (1999), Norris had identified "the phenomenon of 'critical citizens.' This group aspires to democracy as their ideal form of government, yet at the same time they remain deeply skep-tical when evaluating how democracy works in their own country" (p. 5). In the Indonesian case, we have also found significant evidence for a democratic deficit and for critical citizens, whom we label "critical democrats."

Finally, "*The most plausible potential explanations for the democratic deficit suggest that this phenomenon arises from some combination of growing public expectations, negative news, and/or falling government performance*" (p. 5).

In the Indonesian case, we believe that a political economy explana-tion, based on voters' evaluations of government performance in an era of growing public expectations, best fits our data. It is superior to the two main alternatives in comparative electoral behavior theory, the socio-logical and psychological models, whose variables we also include in our surveys and analysis in this book. According to the sociological model, voting behavior is determined by such characteristics as social class, religion, and ethnic/regional/linguistic affiliation. In the case of Indonesia, these variables have changed little in the nearly two decades of democracy, but support for democracy has been relatively dynamic and the partisan map has changed dramatically. Every national election has given birth to new parties with significant support, indeed to the extent that the dominant party has changed every time! In 1999 PDIP was the top vote-getter, while five years later it was Golkar, supplanted by Partai Demokrat in 2009, and finally PDIP again in 2014. The same is true for presidential candidates. The social background of successful presidential candidates has varied from election to election, while the social factors themselves have remained relatively constant.

Psychological factors, especially those connected with party identification or party ID, are also poor explainers of Indonesian behavior. In the literature, the concept of party ID was conceived to explain why patterns of party support were relatively stable over long periods of time as had been experienced in the US (Campbell, Converse, Miller, and Stokes 1960), not to explain rapid changes in party voting as has occurred in democratic Indonesia.

In contrast, the political economy model claims that political attitudes and behavior such as democratic support, voting, and partisan choice are much affected by the dynamism of political economy factors. We believe this model best explains the very dynamic patterns of change in regime support and performance, voting, and partisan choice that we have observed.

Support for democracy is influenced by evaluations of democratic performance that are in turn shaped by governmental performance, especially connected to the economy. Voting is affected by voter calculation, and partisan choice is explained by the assessment of incumbent performance and current economic condition.[1] We see these evaluations as the best explanation for the emergence of critical democrats in Indonesia, which take the form of critical assessments of democratic performance, declining voter turnout, and openness to change in partisan choice.

Why has voting turnout declined, why has identification with parties or party ID not strengthened, why is party choice not stable, why are there more and more parties, and why are presidential candidates only loosely associated with parties? These are the questions that this book answers with the argument that Indonesians are critical democrats, an argument that depends heavily on a political economy or rational choice explanation.

---

[1] The classic rational choice theorists are Downs (1957), Olson (1965), and Riker and Ordeshook (1968). More recently, Fiorina (1981), Kiewiet (1984), and Lewis-Beck (1998) have introduced measures for voters to evaluate their own and the national economic condition, both retrospectively and prospectively.

CHAPTER OVERVIEW

Chapter 2 offers citizen evaluations of Indonesian democracy in general, introducing the argument that in the fifteen years between democratization and our most recent surveys, Indonesians have become critical democrats. This chapter constitutes the foundation for the following chapters, assessing whether the elections held to date are or are not accorded democratic legitimacy by the citizenry. In addition, we offer in this chapter an analysis of the prospects for Indonesian democracy, seen from the citizens' point of view. Factors that may help strengthen or weaken democracy are explored through analysis of the attitudes and behavior of the citizens themselves.

Chapter 3 presents the historical context of Indonesian voting behavior, covering both the level of participation in parliamentary and presidential elections and the choice of parties and candidates for Parliament and candidates for the presidency. Our examination of this behavior is placed in comparative party theory, macroinstitutional political, and historical contexts.

Chapter 4 offers an analysis of the extent to which sociological factors influence Indonesian voting behavior. Principal attention is given to three factors: religion, ethnicity and regionalism, and social class. These three factors have long been regarded as highly significant, if not central, to understanding Indonesian voting behavior by most scholars as well as political practitioners. We attempt to evaluate their importance in a more systematic way. At the end of this chapter we discuss the limitations of the model for explaining the behavior of a relatively dynamic electorate in a sociologically relatively stable country.

Chapter 5 analyzes how rational or political economy factors help explain the relatively rapid changes in Indonesian voting patterns. Attention is focused on perceptions: concerning participation in elections as an obligation, concerning the purpose of participating in elections, concerning the probability that the party or candidate of one's choice is likely to win or lose, and concerning the probability that others will not participate in elections. All these perceptions are evaluated as to the extent to which they can explain citizens' choices to vote in a parliamentary or presidential election. To explain party or candidate choice, we look at evaluations of the condition of the economy and the performance of the government. To what extent do these factors explain political choices in the parliamentary and presidential elections?

At the end of Chapter 5 we raise the possibility that voters' rationality is shaped by psychological factors. Chapter 6 presents the results of our research on these factors. We focus on the exposure of the voter to political advertising through the mass media, the level of identification of the voter with a political party (party ID) and his or her evaluation of the personal qualities of party leaders and presidential candidates. The results of our multivariate analysis, incorporating sociological, psychological, and rational factors, are reported in this chapter to demonstrate the extent to which the influence of those factors remains significant, allowing us to reach some conclusions about which are more or less important and more or less directly influence voting behavior.

Chapter 7 recapitulates our most important findings and discusses their significance for our understanding of Indonesian voting behavior and Indonesia's place in the literature on comparative voting behavior. Hopefully, the study also has practical value, providing input to policy makers concerned to improve the quality of democratic life in Indonesia and in democracies elsewhere.

2

The Emergence of Critical Democrats

Support for Democracy and Criticism of Its Performance

In modern democracies, the citizenry determines who will rule via elections. They are the final arbiters of the competition to determine which of the contestants acquires authority over them. Indeed, their voice is important not only in determining who rules, but also in determining whether the selection process is conducted in a democratic fashion or not, freely and fairly or not. Their judgment provides the democratic legitimation of parliamentary and presidential elections.

In the Indonesian case, many domestic observers have paid insufficient attention to this aspect of democratic politics, as discussed in Chapter 1. They have failed to evaluate just how democratic Indonesian elections have been in the eyes of the voters themselves. Accordingly, this chapter will present the voters' judgments on the elections that have already been conducted. In our surveys, citizens were asked to evaluate the degree of democraticness of the parliamentary or presidential election in which they had just participated.

Before describing the results of our exit polls and postelection surveys, we will offer an analysis of the depth of citizens' commitments to the value of democracy in general, and of how they judge the practice of democracy thus far. Understanding the degree of popular commitment and evaluation of democratic performance at the macro level is important, because in the final analysis elections have meaning only in the context of democratic legitimation by the citizenry itself.

COMMITMENT TO DEMOCRACY

Democratic legitimacy is the extent to which citizens positively value their government. Voting behavior has a democratic meaning if that behavior occurs in the context of democratic political competition. Competitive democratic politics in turn has meaning only if most citizens decide that democracy is a good, or at least better, regime than possible alternatives for their country.

In studies of democracy conducted throughout the world, one effective way of finding out how meaningful democracy is in a particular country is by asking the people themselves if they value democracy as a preferred and desirable regime (Norris 1999). In Indonesia studies like this are still rare. They have recently begun to appear especially in the public opinion surveys that were conducted by Liddle and Mujani (2007), Mujani (2007), and the Indonesian Survey Institute (LSI, Lembaga Survei Indonesia) since the 2004 election.

As in the World Values Survey, these national surveys ask voters the extent to which they agree or disagree with the view that democracy is the best system of government for Indonesia.[1] In addition, different surveys used different questions to measure the preferences of citizens regarding democracy: whether they judge democracy to be the most desirable form of government even though it is not perfect, whether in certain circumstances a nondemocratic government is preferable, or whether they are indifferent to forms of government and believe that democracy and nondemocratic governments are the same. Figure 2.1 displays the results of our main series of surveys, conducted after national elections, showing the level of support for the opinion that democracy, even though not perfect, compared to other forms of government, is the best system of government for Indonesia.[2]

In general, a majority of Indonesian voters agree or agree strongly with the view that democracy is the best government for Indonesia. The level of appreciation reached its peak in 2004 but has remained high to the present.

[1] In the 1999 survey the wording was: Democracy is a better system than the nondemocracy of the New Order. For 2004–14, the wording was changed to: compared with other forms of government, even though it's not perfect, democracy is the best system of government for our country: agree (strongly agree or agree) disagree (disagree or strongly disagree).

[2] 1999 is the survey data after the 1999 parliamentary election, 2004a is the data after the parliamentary election of that year, 2004b after the presidential election round one, 2004c after the presidential election round two, 2009a after the 2009 parliamentary election, 2009b after the 2009 presidential election, 2014a after the legislative election, and 2014b after the presidential election. All similar tables in this book follow this format.

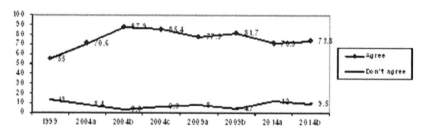

FIGURE 2.1 Democracy is the best form of government for Indonesia (%)

Conversely, those who hold the opposing position are well below a majority and have remained few over time.[3]

In addition, respondents were asked if they always prefer democracy as the best system of government for Indonesia even though it is not perfect, if in certain circumstances they agree that a nondemocratic form of government is acceptable for Indonesia, or if forms of government, democratic or not democratic, are no different or not important for them. Toward these three alternatives, a majority of eligible voters consistently say that democracy is always the preferred system of government even though it is not perfect. Far fewer say that in certain circumstances a nondemocratic government is acceptable. This support has tended to decline in the last five years even though the majority always prefer democracy.

In the Asian Barometer Wave 2 Survey, commitment to democracy as the best form of government, though measured differently, is relatively high in Indonesia at 73.5 percent, at least if compared to other Asian democracies such as Japan (70.4 percent), Korea (47.9 percent), the Philippines (55.3 percent), and Mongolia (40.3 percent). The Asian Barometer measured democratic legitimacy more deeply. Citizens were asked how democratic they wanted Indonesia to be.

Table 2.1 shows that adult Indonesian citizens, or those who have the right to vote, in general want Indonesia to be "very democratic," and believe that democracy is suitable for Indonesia. This attitude is quite consistent from 2004 to 2014. The country's democratic condition today is judged not to have achieved this level but is nonetheless regarded as democratic, while the previous New Order is regarded as not democratic and for that reason not desirable.[4] This attitude can be

---

[3] In Figure 2.1, the total percentage is not 100 percent because "don't knows" were not included in the figure.

[4] The survey question was accompanied by a request to the respondent to place his or her response on a scale of 1–10, where 1 indicates the strongest desire for Indonesia not to be a

TABLE 2.1 *Descriptive statistics of evaluation of democracy and its practice (score 1–10), 2006 & 2014b*

	2006		2014b		
	Mean	Std. Deviation	Mean	Std. Deviation	Interpretation
Indonesia during Suharto's time: Dictatorship-democracy	4.68	2.636	4.32	2.722	Dictatorship
Indonesia under President Yudhoyono: Dictatorship-democracy	6.96	1.954	7.57	1.637	Democracy
Desire for democracy in Indonesia: Strongly oppose – strongly desire	8.46	1.766	8.34	1.693	Strongly desire
Suitability of democracy for Indonesia: Completely unsuitable – completely suitable	7.88	1.942	8.31	1.770	Suitable

Source: Asian Barometer Wave 2, and after the 2014 Presidential Election Survey.

read even more clearly in our 1999 survey where most people did not want to return to a regime like the New Order. These findings indicate the great depth and breadth of the commitment of Indonesian society to democracy.

What do Indonesians understand about democracy as a system of government? In the Asian Barometer survey, the important meanings of democracy identified by Indonesians were diverse, and can be grouped into two categories: political freedom and prosperity combined with equality in economic life. Indeed, Indonesian society is quite divided on these two understandings, even though a few more respondents defined democracy as political freedom, including free elections, freedom of

democracy, the strongest view that democracy is not suitable for Indonesia, and the strongest view that the government of Suharto previously or of Yudhoyono during his incumbency is not democratic. Conversely, the closer to 10 indicates the more the respondent desires democracy, believes that democracy is suitable for Indonesia, and regards the government of Suharto or Yudhoyono as democratic.

speech, and freedom to criticize government policy implementation. Comparable interpretations of democracy are found in other Asian countries like Japan, Korea, and the Philippines. This demonstrates that most Indonesians understand democracy accurately, because the universal common meaning of democracy is in fact political freedom, not economic prosperity or equality, even though the latter can influence the former.

That the condition of the economy can influence democracy was long ago demonstrated by modernization theory (Lipset 1959; Przeworski and Alvarez 2000), but development or prosperity are not themselves democracy. In Southeast Asia, Singapore is known as a country with an advanced economy and a high level of prosperity, but democracy experts do not place it among the group of democratic countries (Freedom House 2016). At the same time, the Philippines, whose level of prosperity is far below Singapore's, is considered a democracy. The reason is simple: Political and civil freedom are much better in the Philippines compared to Singapore even though economically the Philippines is much poorer than Singapore.

It is also important to point out that most Indonesians take a positive attitude toward the practical value of democracy. When asked if there is a form of democratic government that is capable of resolving various problems that confront the nation, 84 percent answer positively (compared to 78.5 percent in Japan, 68.6 percent in Korea, and 60.9 percent in the Philippines). So optimism about the value of democracy is a characteristic of Indonesian society and is higher than in a number of other Asian democracies.

DEMOCRATIC PERFORMANCE

How well are Indonesia's governments doing when it comes to promoting democratic values? Our first survey in 1999 explored this question, especially in terms of popular understanding of political freedom. Large majorities of Indonesians at that time believed that freedom of speech (75.4 percent), freedom to form and join a political party (79.9 percent), and political freedom in general (87.1 percent) are better or much better since democratization the previous year.

A series of surveys since 1999 have examined in depth the extent to which Indonesians are or are not satisfied with the implementation or the practice of democracy in national life. Figure 2.2 shows that at the beginning Indonesians were less than satisfied but subsequently there

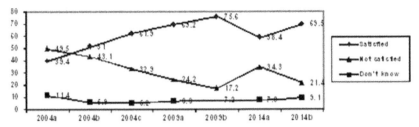

FIGURE 2.2 Satisfied or not satisfied with the implementation of democracy in Indonesia (%)

has been a tendency for very satisfied or satisfied enough responses to increase.[5]

FREE AND FAIR

Democratic performance can also be measured by the extent to which the elections were free and fair. The Indonesian equivalents are honest and just (*jujur* and *adil*, often shortened to *jurdil*), direct (*langsung*), and secret (*rahasia*). How honest, just, direct, and secret are the parliamentary and presidential elections that have been conducted up until now?

In our survey after the 1999 election, people evaluated its honesty and level of justice. A huge majority (86.4 percent) said that the election was more or much more just and honest than the New Order elections. In subsequent surveys, Indonesians have also judged the elections in which they themselves have participated as democratic or very democratic. Worth noting, however, is the level of quality in their judgments in 2009 and 2014, compared to 2004. In the most recent years, a greater number considered the presidential election more democratic than the legislative election (in 2009, 87 percent to 67 percent; in 2014, 78 percent to 64 percent).[6] The main takeaway, however, is that large majorities of citizens

---

[5] The question read: How satisfied or dissatisfied are you with the implementation of democracy in our country until now: satisfied (very or satisfied enough) and dissatisfied (less satisfied or not at all satisfied).

[6] How honest and just was the election of members of Parliament (DPR) or president conducted a few days ago (2004a, 2009a, 2009b, 2014a, 2014b): democratic (very or sufficiently honest and just), not democratic (less or not at all honest and just); how democratic or not democratic was the presidential election recently conducted: democratic (very democratic without problems, democratic with a few problems) not democratic (democratic with many problems, not democratic).

agreed that both the parliamentary and the presidential elections were carried out in a very or sufficiently democratic fashion. This does not mean that the elections were problem-free, of course, but only that most Indonesians believed them to be democratic.

Most Indonesians have a positive commitment toward democracy. They define democracy primarily as political freedom, are optimistic that democracy is capable of solving the problems confronting society, judge that the implementation of democracy in Indonesia up to the present is reasonably good, that freedom is much greater than during the New Order, and specifically perceive that parliamentary and presidential elections have been carried out in an honest, just, direct, and secret way.

This relatively high popular rating of Indonesia's democratic performance does not vary much from expert opinions concerning Indonesian democracy, defined as civil and political freedom as reported in a regular fashion by Freedom House (2016). Before democratization in 1999, Indonesia was described as an Unfree country. Several years later, Indonesia's status rose to Partly Free. From 2006 to 2013, the country was labeled fully Free, only slipping back into the Partly Free category in 2014 as a result of a 2013 law restricting the activities of nongovernmental organizations.

In Southeast Asia, Indonesia is now much more democratic than Singapore, Vietnam, Cambodia, Laos and Burma, and more democratic than Malaysia and Thailand. In 2015, only the Philippines, the first country in the region to become a democracy, held as high a rank as Indonesia. At the same time, it is important to note that in Indonesia in the last five years commitment to democratic principles and positive evaluations of democratic performance have declined slightly as the civil liberty component has weakened.

Which Indonesians have the highest commitment to democracy, and who perceives that the implementation of democracy in Indonesia up to now is good or good enough? There are still citizens who express tolerance toward nondemocratic forms of government, and there are those who are not convinced that democracy is the most suitable system for Indonesia. Moreover, there are still many who define democracy as economic prosperity, many who are pessimistic that democracy can solve Indonesia's problems, many who evaluate democratic performance up to the present as unsatisfactory, and, finally, many who deny that elections in Indonesia have been conducted in a democratic manner.

What accounts for these differences, and what kinds of people are in each category? Is there a connection between evaluations of democratic performance and support for democracy as the best system compared with others, that a citizen has the right to differ from the majority view, that the government must be supervised by representatives of the people, and that there must be honest and just competition to select the holders of important public offices like members of Parliament and the president, and so on?

COMMITMENT TO DEMOCRACY, DEMOCRATIC PERFORMANCE, AND GOVERNMENT PERFORMANCE

Support for democracy, according to many scholars, is influenced by how democracy is implemented in a society. Citizens will support democracy if they evaluate its practice positively (Clarke, Dutt, and Kornberg 1993; Mishler and Rose 1997; Bratton, Mattes, and Boadi 2004). Further, democratic practice is evaluated positively if government performance is also evaluated positively. In other words, the better the performance of a democratic government in the eyes of the citizen, the more likely that citizen will be to positively evaluate it. The normative commitment of a citizen to democracy can therefore weaken if democratic practice is lacking, and this evaluation will further weaken if the performance of the government is evaluated negatively.

There is also a scholarly view, however, that commitment to democracy is not strongly influenced by how democracy is implemented in a country because citizens separate the two and do not fault normative democracy itself even if they evaluate its practice negatively. In this view, support for democracy is thought not to be influenced by how governmental performance is evaluated. Democracy becomes consolidated when its existence is not influenced by the rise and fall of support for governmental performance (Linz and Stepan 1996).

Bivariate analysis (Table 2.2) of data from our 2009 and 2014 parliamentary surveys shows that for Indonesians democratic performance has a significant connection with commitment to democracy. Disappointment with how democracy is implemented or practiced in daily political life influences commitment to democracy. People will tend to fault democracy itself if it is not implemented well. They do not simply idealize democracy but connect that ideal with the way it is realized in daily life.

TABLE 2.2 *Correlations (Pearson's r) of several factors with commitment to democracy and democratic performance, 2009a & 2014a*

	2009a		2014a	
	Commitment to Democracy	Democratic Performance	Commitment to Democracy	Democratic Performance
Democratic performance	.089**	–	.117**	–
Voted	.007	.144**	−.006	.109**
Represented in Parliament	.000	.118**	−.001	.044
Chose Partai Demokrat	−.004	.132**	.021	−.011
Government performance	.050*	.323**	.065**	.365**
Party ID	.101**	−.089**	.076*	.006
Political engagement (Discussion, media information, and interested)	.114**	−.155**	.091**	−.122**
Social capital	.061*	.026	.028	.013
Education	.172**	−.166**	.129*	−.205**
Urban residence	.041	−.133**	.023	−.188**
Religiosity	.065*	.079**	.006	−.030
Age	.010	.203*	−.039	.097**
Male	.068**	−.012	.020	−.035

**P<.01, *P<.05

That relationship pattern is relatively consistent after including several economic and political factors, including political engagement, and several demographic factors in the multivariate analysis (Table 2.3).[7]

---

[7] Prodemocracy is an index constructed of three variables: democracy as the best form of government (1=strongly disagree, 4=strongly agree), it's better to have just one political

TABLE 2.3 *Regression of commitment to democracy, 2009a & 2014a*

	2009a			2014a		
	B	Std. Error	Beta	B	Std. Error	Beta
Constant	2.512***	.093		2.313***	.102	
Democratic performance	.088***	.024	.123	.119***	.025	.136
Political engagement (interested plus information plus political discussion)	.028***	.011	.089	.028	.018	.046
Party ID	.030*	.012	.077	.023	.013	.047
Government performance	.055	.039	.046	.025	.015	.048
Social capital	-.019	.019	-.032	.059	.052	.030
Education	.036**	.011	.108	.018**	.004	.143
Urban residence	-.004	.023	-.006	-.002	.017	-.004
Religiosity	.017	.012	.048	-.016	.012	-.036
Age	-.001	.001	-.043	.001	.001	.023
Male	.023	.022	.034	.001	.016	.001
N	1038			1501		
R-square	.054			.045		

***P<.001, **P<.01, *P<.05

party to rule (1=strongly agree, 4=strongly disagree), elections as a way of choosing members of Parliament and the Regional Representative Council should be done away with so that the government can rule and conduct its own oversight (1=strongly agree, 4=strongly disagree). The total score for the three variables is divided by three to make an index scaled 1–4. Democratic performance is an index constructed of a number of variables: satisfied with the way democracy works until now (1=not at all, 4=very satisfied), how democratic is Indonesia now (1=not at all, 4=very democratic), how free and fair is the election conducted by the government(1= not at all, 4=very free and fair), how often do people fear to practice their religion or beliefs (1=very often, 4=never), criticize the government (1=very often, 4=never), associate or organize (1=often, 4=never), and government violates the Constitution (1=very often, 4=never). And to what extent do you agree that freedom of opinion is allowed even though it conflicts with general opinion as long as it doesn't violate the law (1=strongly disagree, 4=strongly agree). The total score of all of these variables is divided by eight to form an index scaled from 1 to 4.

This means that the existence of Indonesian democracy as a normative system is threatened if the democratic actors do not practice it effectively. Conversely, Indonesian democracy will strengthen if the actors do practice it effectively.

Evaluation of democratic performance is apparently strongly influenced by the degree to which the citizen evaluates governmental performance in overcoming major problems confronted by the society, particularly involving the economy, corruption, security and order (Table 2.4).[8] If citizens evaluate governmental performance positively, they will also tend to evaluate democratic performance until now positively, and in turn have a commitment to democracy, believe that democracy is the best system compared to others.

Conversely, if governmental performance is evaluated negatively, democratic performance will also be evaluated negatively, and in turn normative democracy will be evaluated negatively as well. Consequently, it will lose legitimacy in the sense of popular support. In that situation democracy becomes vulnerable to antidemocratic behavior, both from elites and from ordinary citizens.

The pattern of the relationship between commitment to democracy, evaluation of democratic performance, and evaluation of governmental performance is relatively consistent, not considering other factors (Table 2.3 and Table 2.4). Citizens tend to evaluate democratic performance positively if governmental performance is also good, regardless of whether or not they are interested in politics, have or do not have political information, feel close to a party or not, are involved in social activities (that is, possess social capital) or not, vote or not, are highly educated or not, are young or old, or live in the village or the city. In sum, governmental performance has a strong impact on democratic performance.

POLITICAL PARTIES

In addition, politically, there is a possibility that citizens evaluate both normative and actual democracy more positively because they feel represented in national politics when the party that they chose wins seats in

---

[8] Governmental performance is an index that is constructed of a number of variables each of which is scaled 1–4 (1=very negative, 4=very positive): national economic condition, national political condition, the state of the rule of law, satisfaction with the performance of the president, the performance of the government in eradicating corruption, reducing poverty, reducing unemployment, and regulating prices so that basic commodities are affordable for most citizens.

TABLE 2.4 *Democratic performance regressions, 2009a & 2014a*

	2009a			2014a		
	B	Std. Error	Beta	B	Std. Error	Beta
Constant	2.922***	.078		2.392***	.076	
Political engagement (interested plus information plus political discussion)	-.057***	.014	-.129	-.034	.019	-.049
Party ID	-.038*	.016	-.068	.022	.013	.040
Governmental performance	.467***	.047	.284	.208***	.014	.347
Participation	.007	.019	.014	.059	.053	.039
Choosing Partai Demokrat	.039	.034	.039	-.062*	.028	-.051
Represented in Parliament	.069	.039	.069	.007	.041	.006
Education	-.031*	.015	-.066	-.011**	.004	-.079
Urban	-.058*	.028	-.061	-.070***	.017	-.104
Religiosity	.013	.015	.026	-.024	.013	-.047
Age	.007***	.001	.177	.001	.001	.050
Male	.013	.028	.014	-.007	.016	-.011
N	1064			1501		
R-square	.204			.188		

***P<.001, **P<.01, *P<.05

Parliament or when their presidential candidate wins. Conversely, there is a possibility that citizens will evaluate democracy less positively because they feel unrepresented in national politics since the party of their choice lost or has no seats in Parliament or their presidential candidate lost, leading to a feeling that they are not adequately represented.

A second possibility has to do with the influence of the number of votes won by parties. The more votes won by the voters' party or presidential candidate, the more positively they will evaluate democracy. In this scenario, democracy apparently does not benefit those who have lost, but only those who have won, so that those who have lost or won fewer votes feel that democracy limits their ability to achieve their goals. They become disenchanted with democracy.

Our data show that in the Indonesian case participation in elections, representation in Parliament, and party choice apparently have no connection with commitment to democracy. Those who do and do not vote, who do or do not have representatives in Parliament, whose party has won the most votes or not, do not differ much in their democratic attitudes. They all have a high commitment, over 90 percent, to democracy as the best system of government even if they did not vote, have no representatives, and belong to a party that received few votes in the last election.

It is also true that support for democracy is relatively high for all party voters. The same is true for evaluations of democratic performance and election implementation. Whatever party is chosen, the citizen evaluates democracy positively, and also the carrying out of honest and just elections.

To be sure, one can see a significant difference in the evaluation of democratic performance according to partisan choice, but as we will explain below that difference is not significant after weighing other factors (Table 2.4). What appears to be a difference is in fact not partisan choice but other factors, especially governmental performance plus dimensions of political engagement including political information, political discussion, and interest in politics.

Both partisan voters whose parties won the most votes and voters whose parties won the least votes are apparently not influenced by this factor in their evaluation of the implementation of democracy, whether good or bad. All of these findings indicate that citizens in general are fair in their judgments: They do not fault the rules of the democratic game or the way in which those rules are enforced when they lose in the political competition.

POLITICAL ENGAGEMENT AND THE CRITICAL DEMOCRAT

Political engagement – including level of exposure to political news in the mass media, interest in politics, intensity of discussing political or governmental issues, and party identification – has a significant impact on commitment to democracy. The more engaged politically, the stronger the citizen's support for normative democracy. This pattern confirms several previous studies concerning the relationship of political engagement or civic culture with the democratic system itself (Almond and Verba 1963; Verba, Schlozman, and Brady 1995).

What is of greater interest here, however, is the significant negative influence of political engagement on evaluations of democratic performance. Citizens who receive a great deal of political information from the mass media tended to feel unsatisfied with democratic performance. Similarly, those who more intensively discussed and are more interested in politics tended to be more negative in evaluating democratic performance. However, the tendency is weakening. The negative impact of political engagement on democratic performance over the last five years has not been significant. The indicator of Norris' critical citizen (1999, 2011) or what we have labeled the critical democrat is not consistently associated with political engagement having taken into account education and rural-urban cleavage.

EDUCATED URBAN VOTERS AS CRITICAL DEMOCRATS

The presence of critical democrats may also be seen in the tendency for citizens who are more educated to have a stronger commitment to normative democracy (Table 2.2). Several studies in addition to Norris have discovered a relationship between education and democracy. In general, the higher the level of education, or more broadly the socioeconomic level of a country, the more likely the country will be democratic (Lipset 1959; Przeworski and Alvarez 2000). More specifically, education becomes important for democracy because education is believed to constitute a social institution where the individual students within it are socialized in the values of freedom and equality, basic components of democracy (Putnam 1993; Nie, Junn, and Stehlik-Barry 1996; Shin 1999).

As in the case of political engagement, education also has a tendency to negatively influence evaluations of democratic performance (Table 2.4). The higher the level of a citizen's education, the more likely that citizen will have a commitment to democracy. Higher levels of education are also associated with negative evaluations of democracy because citizens see a gap between the ideals and practice of democracy.

A similar finding characterizes the attitude of the urban resident toward democracy. In terms of commitment to normative democracy, the rural-urban difference does not matter, but the urban resident tends to evaluate the implementation of democracy negatively. Urban residents are more critical. They tend to demand greater freedom and equality in governmental democratic performance.

This is not only because in general their education level is higher and because they have more political information through the mass media, but also because of more fundamental differences between individuals who live in rural and urban areas. Even though level of education is high, rural citizens tend to be less critical, more quickly satisfied with what has already been achieved, and for that reason more likely to be positive in evaluating democratic performance.

This is visible in the multivariate analysis where the urban-rural residential difference continues to be significant in influencing evaluations of democratic performance apart from the factors of education or political engagement (Table 2.4). This pattern occurs perhaps because level of education, income, and type of employment are not enough to explain the rural-urban difference. In Durkheimian language, the mechanical solidarity of rural residents may have a more complex effect than the organic solidarity of urban residents. Mechanical solidarity tends to reflect a conception of social order that is more harmonious, emotional, and hierarchical and does not readily lead to demands for greater freedom and equality, which represent the basic elements of democracy (Durkheim 2014).

Conversely, organic solidarity tends to reflect a conception of social order that is more functional, rational, more open and more egalitarian. It leads to greater social and political demands for openness, freedom, and equality, the bases of a democratic order. So it is understandable if urban residents tend to be more negative or critical than rural residents regarding the implementation of democracy (Mujani 2007).

The critical democrat phenomenon is also connected to age groups. Senior citizens tend to be more positive in evaluating democratic performance compared to younger citizens, apart from other factors (Table 2.4). This pattern occurs because, at least according to one study, older citizens accept more readily a settled order. Younger citizens, on the other hand, tend to want change and improvement and are thus critical of that which has already been achieved, including the implementation of democracy (Sullivan, Pierson, and Marcus 1982; Sullivan, Shamir, Walsh, and Roberts 1985; Shin 1999). In Indonesia's democratic history, opposition to the authoritarian New Order was driven primarily by activists, especially students, so it is logical if they are more inclined to make demands for democratic improvement and to be more critical. However, the impact of age groups on democratic performance has weakened over time. Compared to 2009, the distinction between youth and senior citizen status in 2014 no longer matters for democratic performance.

Putting together the tendency for a positive and significant relationship between commitment to democracy and level of political information, level of interest in and frequency of discussing public issues, level of education, and urban citizens, with democratic performance, there emerges what we have called the critical citizen or critical democrat in post-New Order Indonesia. These individuals are democrats who persistently demand improvements in the daily performance of their democracy.

CONCLUSIONS: DEMOCRATIC SUPPORT AND THE EMERGENCE OF CRITICAL DEMOCRATS

To this point we can conclude that support for democracy as the best form of government for Indonesia, compared with other governmental systems, is very high. Citizens in general feel that today's democratic system is better than the New Order authoritarian regime. A majority of citizens understand democracy as political freedom, but a significant number also identify it as economic equality and the fulfillment of the people's economic needs. Citizens also judge that with regard to social and political freedom conditions now are better than during the New Order.

Positive evaluations of democratic performance, that is, how well the government has implemented democracy to date, are not as high as the commitment to democracy itself. Nonetheless, there is a tendency in the last decade and a half for citizens to evaluate the practice of democracy as continually improving. They state that elections, the vehicle through which political freedom is expressed, have been conducted freely and fairly. Analyses of parliamentary and presidential elections in subsequent chapters, for this reason, are founded in democratic legitimacy, and do not reflect the opinions, attitudes, or behavior of citizens who are not free.

Support for or commitment to democracy is linked to how democracy is practiced. Commitment to democracy strengthens when evaluations of democratic performance are also strong, and conversely weakens when citizens judge democratic performance to be weak. The strengthening of democracy as the best political system will thus increase as the government practices democracy in accord with popular wishes. Conversely, Indonesian democracy will weaken, will lose support, if the government's democratic practice is poor.

The primary source of popular evaluation of democratic performance is the performance of the government itself. The better the performance of the government especially with regard to the economy and the justice sector the more positive the citizen's evaluation of democratic performance.

And conversely, the more negatively a citizen evaluates governmental performance the more negative his or her evaluation of democratic performance, and finally also the weaker the commitment toward democracy itself.

It is in the pattern of the relationship between commitment to democracy, evaluation of democratic performance, and evaluation of governmental performance that we see signs of the emergence of the critical democrat. The evidence is the combination of a positive commitment toward democracy but a negative evaluation of democratic performance. Critical democrats are shaped by political information that they receive via the mass media, their interest in public issues, their feelings of closeness to parties, involvement in social activities, and more significantly having a higher education and being more urban. They have a high commitment to democracy but are very critical of its implementation. They demand better democratic practice and governmental performance, and if those hopes are not fulfilled eventually they will question the existence of democracy itself. Democracy weakens and suffers from the erosion of public support.

3

Participation and Choice

In comparative electoral behavior studies, two basic connected components receive the most attention: political participation and political choice. Participation is related to voters' involvement in choosing candidates or parties and other related forms of participation, especially the act of voting itself. Choice is connected to the candidates or parties that are chosen.[1] This chapter examines both of these components. They represent the dependent variables that will be explored in the subsequent chapters as in other voting behavior studies.

POLITICAL PARTICIPATION

In this study, political participation is limited to two dimensions: voting and activities connected to election campaigning. More specifically, activities connected to campaigning are limited to attendance at rallies or open gatherings held by a party, parliamentary or presidential candidate in 1999, 2004, 2009, and 2014. In addition, for the 2009 and 2014 elections, we included a number of items connected to campaigning, that is, assisting and financially supporting a party and persuading others to choose a party or candidate.[2] Other forms that are considered unconventional are not included, not because we consider them unimportant, but because this

---

[1] For the relevant theoretical literature, see Verba and Nie (1972); Verba, Nye, and Kim (1978); Kaase and Marsh (1979); Parry, Moyser, and Day (1992); McDonough, Shin, and Moises (1998); Verba, Schlozman, and Brady (1995); Brady (1999).
[2] See the Appendix for variables and indicators.

book only forms a part of our larger analysis of Indonesian voting behavior.[3]

Because the life of Indonesian democracy has been so short, scholars have not yet had the opportunity to systematically study political participation. There are some relevant studies, but they are limited to partisan choice as opposed to political participation. In addition, most of those studies are based on more limited national or aggregate data, and for that reason cannot explore deeply the characteristics of political participation in Indonesia (Liddle 1973, 6).

Voter Turnout

In the history of independent Indonesia, voter turnout in democratic elections is still a rare event; it has occurred only seven times. The first parliamentary election was conducted in 1955, the second more than four decades later in 1999, the third in 2004, the fourth in 2009, and the most recent in 2014. Four democratic presidential elections have been held: the two-round (initial plus runoff) elections in 2004 and the one-round elections in 2009 and 2014. During the authoritarian New Order, elections were held six times between 1971 and 1997 before Suharto resigned from office in 1998.[4] These elections were not meaningful from a democratic perspective.

In the first democratic election in 1955, voter turnout was 87 percent of all citizens who had the right to vote (Feith 1957), Figure 3.1.[5] According to the General Election Commission, fifty-five years later, in the 1999 election, voter turnout was even better at 93 percent. In the next two legislative elections, in 2004 (2004a) and 2009 (2009a), it declined to 84 percent and then 71 percent, before rising to 75 percent in 2014 (2014a).[6]

---

[3] For unconventional forms of political participation in the post-New Order period, see Mujani (2007).

[4] Nonetheless there have been a number of studies of parliamentary elections during the New Order, for example Mallarangeng (1997) and Gaffar (1992). Even though from a democratic perspective these elections had no value, seen in terms of the need for legitimacy of the authoritarian regime they did have some scholarly interest.

[5] In this study the percentage of voter turnout is the total number of actual voters divided by the total number of registered voters. "Invalid" voters are also a part of the study of participation because citizens who cast an invalid vote have nonetheless exercised their right to vote.

[6] Malik, Husni Kamil. 2013. "Pemutahiran Data Pemilih dan Penyusunan Daftar Pemilih." www.dpr.go.id/doksetjen/dokumen/mingwan-seminarKisruh-DPT-Golput-atau-diGolput-kan-1432262112.pdf, accessed April 4, 2017; Komisi Pemilihan Umum (KPU). 2014.

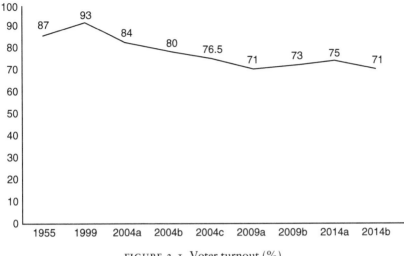

FIGURE 3.1 Voter turnout (%)

In the 2004 presidential election the turnout was about 80 percent in the first (2004b) and 76.5 percent in the second round (2004c). In the 2009 single round presidential election (2009b), it declined to 73 percent and in 2014 to 71 percent (2014b).[7] The secular trend, with the one exception of the 2014 parliamentary election, has thus been for a decline in the level of participation in both legislative and presidential elections since democratization began with the fall of Suharto's New Order.

The level of turnout in Indonesia is relatively high when compared to all other countries in the world at the same period.[8] The number of nonvoters has risen but is still below the world average. In other words, until now voter turnout has not been an issue in democratic Indonesia, though of course we have to pay attention to the secular trend which has been relatively steep.

The generally high level of voter turnout in Indonesia is not a surprise. High levels of turnout are often found in countries that have just become

Buku Data dan Infografik Pemilu Anggota DPR dan DPD RI 2014, vi, 27. See also International IDEA: www.idea.int/data-tools/question-view/521

[7] Komisi Pemilihan Umum (KPU). 2004. *Pemilu 2004 dalam Angka dan Gambar Peristiwa*, 5, 124, and 129; *Komisi Pemilihan Umum* (KPU). 2014. *Buku Data dan Infografik Pemilu Presiden dan Wakil Presiden 2014*, 44.

[8] See www.idea.int/sites/default/files/publications/voter-turnout-trends-around-the-world_0.pdf

democracies, or whose election history has not been democratic. In the United States, voter turnout is lower than the world average and has been declining for some time. Compared to other industrial democracies like Great Britain or Germany, America does indeed have a problem (Lijphart 1999). In several countries voting is required by law; citizens who do not vote typically pay fines. These laws have been passed because the tendency of citizens to not vote has worsened over time, for example in Australia and the Netherlands.

If not anticipated and addressed, the turnout level in Indonesia will probably continue to decline, but hopefully remain within range of the world average of about 65 percent. The level of voter turnout is an indicator of the quality of democracy: the higher the turnout, the higher the level of democratic performance. This level is in turn connected to the legitimacy of election results and the level of support for government. The more citizens who participate in elections, the greater the support or legitimacy for the subsequent government.

Why do some citizens not vote? In Indonesia, according to our surveys, most don't vote for technical reasons. They are not registered, are ill, in the process of moving to a new address, have other pressing business on election day, and so on. The proportion of citizens who do not vote because they think elections have no value, that there is no candidate or party that represents their aspirations (alienated or pessimistic voters in the language of electoral behavior studies), varies from election to election.

The 2014 legislative election produced the most significant number of alienated citizens: 39.4 percent of those who did not vote. In Indonesian political history, alienated voters were labeled the "white group" (*golongan putih* or *golput*) during the New Order because they punched the empty or white part of the ballot. They protested undemocratic elections, which they dismissed as not in their own interests or the interests of the nation. This was an important issue at the time because it threatened to destabilize the authoritarian regime.

Elections during the New Order were designed for the sole purpose of obtaining popular legitimacy for the authoritarian regime, and for that reason Liddle (1996b) called them a "useful fiction," useful in the sense of creating the impression that the regime did in fact have popular support. Nonetheless it is important to examine the level of nonparticipation. Does the voter turnout model help us to understand Indonesian turnout? This issue will be addressed in subsequent chapters.

Participation in Campaigns

Turnout is only one of many forms of election-oriented action or political participation. Campaign activities are another. Participating in campaign activities before an election perhaps reflects better the attraction of the citizen to politics. Someone who participates in a campaign, or some other form of campaign activity, will very likely have a greater desire to influence a candidate, a party, or other voters with his or her preferences (Verba, Schlozman, and Brady 1995). Citizens who are involved in a party campaign very likely have a strong desire to lend their support to that party and conversely to avoid providing support to other parties.

There is also the possibility, however, that campaign involvement is better understood as mobilization than participation. A citizen can attend the program of one party on one day and another party on another day, because there is more than one party that is encouraging him or her to attend. Attendance at a campaign activity can therefore not easily be identified as a form of support for one and rejection of another party.

We do not yet know definitively how many Indonesians participate in activities connected to campaigning. Roughly, the level of participation can be ascertained via the citizen's admission that he or she has or has not participated. In several surveys, there are items about campaigns conducted just before elections: attending a campaign rally for a party or individual candidate; helping a party or a candidate by leafleting, wearing party and candidate symbols; persuading others to support a particular candidate or party; and even sending money to a party.

According to the findings of a 2002 survey, three years after the 1999 parliamentary election, about 30 percent of the respondents said that they had once attended a campaign event (a rally, open party meeting, or a parade) in the 1999 campaign season. The same proportion also reported that they had worn party insignia at party events or put them in their home or car. About 13 percent distributed party brochures, photos, and so on (Mujani 2007). This proportion was about the same as participation in persuading others to choose a certain party. These items all form a single factor in a factor analysis, in accord with the finding of previous studies that campaign activity is a dimension of political participation (Verba and Nie 1972).

In our surveys conducted just after the 1999 and 2004 parliamentary elections, the number of participation items was limited to just the single item of ever attending or participating in a party or candidate's campaign

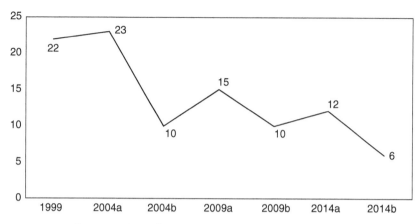

FIGURE 3.2 Ever participated in campaign activities before the parliamentary or presidential elections (%)

in the form of an open meeting or mass rally. In the surveys conducted after the 2009 and 2014 parliamentary and presidential elections, several additional participation items were included: voluntarily assisting a party, a success team, or a candidate during the campaign period, including displaying pictures, posters, signs, and similar material; persuading others to choose a particular party or candidate; and contributing money to a party, success team, or candidate.

Figure 3.2 shows that viewed in terms of these campaign indicators, the level of mass participation varies considerably. There is a significant difference in the level of participation between the legislative and presidential campaigns starting in 2004. This difference is probably connected to the difference in the frequency of campaigning in the two types of election. In the legislative campaign, the frequency of campaigning door to door or attending public meetings was much greater because it involved many more contestants than in the presidential election. There were thousands of candidates for legislative office but only a few for the presidency. The frequency and geographical reach of the legislative election in the form of party meetings was thus much higher and greater.

The possibility of a connection between the contestant and the number of campaigns was also visible in the difference in the level of participation in the first and second round presidential elections in 2004. In the first round, there were five contesting pairs of presidential/vice presidential candidates, while in the second round there were only two. Face-to-face meetings in the second round were obviously fewer, and were affected by the law against open campaigning.[9] The level of citizen participation in the first round of the presidential election was therefore higher than in the second round.

This pattern also appeared in 2014. Participation in campaigns in the parliamentary election was higher than in the presidential election. In the presidential election, there were only two pairs of candidates while in the parliamentary elections there were thousands of contestants. The presidential contestants were also fewer than in the first-round presidential election in 2004 and 2009. The power to mobilize the masses was therefore also lower, as was the level of participation in or exposure to the campaign.

In addition, in the 2009 and 2014 elections the level of participation in campaign events was lower than in 1999 or 2004. In the latter two elections, the percentage of citizens who reported that they had once attended a campaign event was above 20 percent, while in the 2009 election it was only 15 percent, despite the fact that the number of parties participating in the 2009 election was greater.

The secular trend continued in 2014. In addition to attending party and candidate campaign events, in the 2009 and 2014 elections some citizens reported that they had provided assistance to a party, success team, or legislative or presidential candidate. The number of those who had, on at least one occasion, provided assistance was modest even in 2009, 8 percent before the legislative election and 6 percent before the presidential election, but declined slightly in 2014 to 7 percent and 4 percent respectively.

In addition, in 2009 about 7 percent prior to the legislative election and 8 percent prior to the presidential election reported that they had attempted to persuade others to vote for a particular party or candidate. The comparable figures for 2014 were virtually identical. Citizens everywhere do not generally engage in this kind of activity, so it is understandable if the proportion is relatively small. Nonetheless, the 7–8 percent figures are reasonably impressive, when we remember that most Indonesian citizens do not fulfill the criteria for engaging in such activity, especially psychological requirements like the attitude that elections and winning them are important and the self-confidence that one can influence others.

---

[9] Formally the General Election Commission did not provide an opportunity for campaigning in the second round of the presidential election. This did not mean, however, that face-to-face campaigning did not occur. It did, but usually indoors.

Giving money to a party, legislative, or presidential candidate is a type of participation in which still fewer Indonesians are involved. Across the two election years, only 1 percent report that they have ever given money for political purposes. Donating money to a party or candidate requires not only psychological but financial preparedness as well. Voters must feel that elections and their results are important, they must be interested in politics, and must have enough money to feel capable of donating.

The difference in level of campaign event participation between legislative and presidential elections is also tied to a difference in the use of mass media. In legislative campaigns, the proportion of citizens who follow media reports is smaller than in presidential elections. This is actually an indication that the frequency of campaign reporting in the media itself is lower than in presidential campaigns.

This fact is in turn tied to a basic characteristic of legislative campaigns, which rely heavily on party symbols and slogans and have many more candidates spread throughout the country, making it easier for them to campaign by holding events and engaging in other partisan activities. The larger quantity and the geographical spread of these activities help citizens to be exposed to campaigns. Despite these facts, it remains the case that the ability of a party or candidate to reach more than 100 million voters in 1999 and more than 185 million voters in 2014 was limited.

At the same time, the number of contestants in a presidential election is much more limited and the direct reach of a presidential campaign is comparably limited. A presidential candidate will use the mass media with the greatest reach, especially television, as the best means to reach the most people. Indeed, presidential candidates can use the mass media effectively to increase support for their political party. A comparative study found that the mass media, especially TV, are a factor that contributes toward the presidentialization of legislative elections, in which candidates influence voting for members of Parliament through their media campaigns (Mughan 2000). In the Indonesian case, exposure to campaigns via TV was high when we first measured it for the parliamentary election of 2004 (83 percent) and increased to 92 percent in the presidential election of 2014.

Exposure to radio increased from the parliamentary election of 2004 (29 percent) to a high of 47 percent in the second-round presidential election of 2004, but has since declined to 16 percent. With exposure to newspapers, after a drop from a high of 46 percent in the 2004 second round presidential election to a low of 25 percent in the 2009 presidential election, there was a modest climb to 31 percent in the 2014 presidential election.

Viewed in terms of the information that flows from the party or candidate to the viewer, the low level of participation in direct campaigning is compensated for by the intensity with which citizens follow campaigns in the mass media, especially TV. Even though watching TV or reading the newspaper is an activity, participants are basically passive. What occurs is a one-way influence from the contestant to the voter, not the other way around. For that reason, following a campaign via the media reflects mobilization by the contestant rather than participation by the citizen.

There is also voter mobilization through direct contact with the candidate or a member of his or her success team. The extent, however, is small compared to the participation that occurs in the form of attendance at campaign events. Eighteen percent of voters in 2004 and 2009, but only 13 percent in 2014, reported that they were contacted by a candidate or a member of his or her success team or party to vote for a particular candidate or party. Those who report having been contacted for the same purpose during a presidential campaign are many fewer, in the single digits. This also shows that contestants and members of success teams who are active in presidential campaigns are fewer than in legislative campaigns.

Most Indonesian citizens vote, but on average, through seven elections from 1999, about 25 percent do not. The number of citizens who participate directly in campaigns is much smaller. Why do some citizens vote and others not, some citizens participate in campaign activities and others not? This problem will be discussed in subsequent chapters.

POLITICAL CHOICE

For which party or candidate do citizens vote? In this section, we present the aggregate data on partisan choice for the parliamentary elections of 1999, 2004, 2009, and 2014 and on choice of presidential/vice presidential candidates in 2004, 2009, and 2014 to provide a dynamic picture of party strengths and changes in the presidential elections. In addition, we provide a succinct description of each party and presidential candidate, who represent the dependent variables that we will explain in the following chapters.[10]

[10] In the general election for members of Parliament and regional legislatures in 2009 and 2014, a semi-open system was used in which voters could choose the name of a candidate or the name of a party or both, as long as the candidate chosen came from the party

The party description will follow the typology of Larry Diamond and Richard Gunther (2001). Most Indonesian parties fit into their electoralist category, which is further divided into three subtypes: "catchall, which gain votes through broad and eclectic issue appeals and candidate image"; "programmatic, which gain votes through articulation of programmatic (and/or ideological) appeals"; or "personalistic, which gain votes through emphasis on the personal charisma of the party leader, particularistic benefits, and activation of clientelistic linkages" (p. 11).

As we shall see, most Indonesian parties are catchall or personalistic. Few are even in part programmatic, the most desirable subtype in normative democratic theory. It is arguably programmatic parties that are most able to be held accountable by the voters for the policies and programs they enact and implement.

Why are few Indonesian parties programmatic? Because most Indonesian voters, as our survey data over a decade and a half show, are primarily attracted to leaders, not programs or indeed parties themselves. The clearest case is that of Susilo Bambang Yudhoyono, who founded a party in 2001 purely as a vehicle for his successful presidential candidacy in 2004. But evidence is also provided by leaders such as former President Megawati Sukarnoputri, largely responsible at least from 1999 to 2009 for the strength of her party, and current President Joko Widodo, who drove much of the support for that same party in 2014. Abdurrahman Wahid, also an ex-president, and Amien Rais, a presidential candidate several times, were also largely responsible for the initial support for their parties in the 1999 parliamentary elections.

Choice of Party or Candidate for Parliament

For the general elections of 1955, 1999, 2004, 2009, and 2014, Table 3.1 shows the percentages of votes and seats obtained by each party reported by the General Election Commission. In those five elections, there have been many changes in party names. Despite the name differences, some scholars have observed that the political parties from 1999 to 2014 for the most part have been the same in terms of *aliran* (cultural and socioeconomic political streams), and so represent a continuation of the 1955

chosen. In a series of simulations before the election, no significant difference was found between a closed system (only choosing the party) and the semi-open system actually used. We found the same results in exit polls that we conducted. For that reason in this analysis, we do not differentiate between party and candidate choice.

TABLE 3.1 *Votes won by parties in democratic elections in Indonesia, 1955, 1999–2014 (%)*

Party	1955 Votes	1999 Votes (seats)	2004 Votes (seats)	2009 Votes (seats)	2014 Votes (seats)
PNI/PDIP	22	34 (33)	18.5 (20)	14 (17)	19 (19)
PKI	16	–	–	–	–
Golkar	–	23 (26)	22 (23)	14 (19)	15 (16)
Demokrat	–	–	7 (10)	21 (26)	10 (11)
NU/PKB	18	13 (11)	11 (10)	5 (5)	9 (8)
Masjumi	21	–	–	–	–
PPP		11 (13)	8 (11)	5 (7)	7 (7)
PAN		7 (7)	6 (10)	6 (8)	8 (9)
PK/PKS		1	7 (8)	8 (10)	7 (7)
Gerindra	–	–	–	5 (5)	12 (3)
Hanura	–	–	–	4 (3)	5 (3)
NasDem	–	–	–	–	7 (6)
Others	23	14 (8)	20 (9)	28 (0)	2 (0)
Total		100.0	100.0	100.0	100.0

Sources: Feith 1957, Komisi Pemilihan Umum 2004, 2014. Vote percentages rounded.

election, in which these streams were first observed (Feith 1957; Geertz 1960; King 2003). PDIP (Partai Demokrasi Indonesia Perjuangan, Indonesian Democracy Party of Struggle) is considered a continuation of PNI (Partai Nasional Indonesia, Indonesian National Party), PKB (Partai Kebangkitan Bangsa, National Awakening Party) a continuation of NU (Nahdlatul Ulama, Awakening of the Traditional Scholars), and so on (King 2003).

It is unclear, however, how Partai Golkar (Functional Groups Party), Partai Demokrat (Democratic Party), PPP (Partai Persatuan Pembangunan, Development Unity Party), PAN (Partai Amanat Nasional, National Mandate Party), Gerindra (Partai Gerakan Indonesia Raya, Greater Indonesia Movement Party), Hanura (Partai Hati Nurani Rakyat, People's Conscience Party), and Partai NasDem (National Democratic Party), which received significant support in 1999 and/or subsequent elections, are related to the parties that participated in the 1955 election.

King (2003) claims that Partai Golkar, PPP, and PAN represent a continuation of Masjumi, the main party representing modernist or reformist Islam in the 1950s. But we observe relatively large differences in percentages of votes for Partai Golkar, PPP, and PAN in the elections of 1999, 2004, 2009, and 2014. The totals are about 42 percent in 1999, 34 percent in 2004, 25 percent in 2009, and 30 percent in 2014. By contrast, Masjumi's strength in 1955 was only about 20 percent. The numbers clearly do not correspond.

A better interpretation is that there is indeed some continuity but there are also significant changes. Many Partai Golkar voters come from communities that were previously strong Masjumi regions, the regions outside Java plus Jakarta and West Java. Many PPP voters come from the Masjumi modernist Muslim tradition, especially in West Java and Sumatra, but many also come from the old Muslim traditionalist NU party, especially in East Java, Central Java, and South Kalimantan. PAN voters probably come from the urban areas where Masjumi support was strong.

PDIP in the 1999 election won 34 percent of the vote, many more than PNI in 1955 (22 percent). In addition to their cultural connection to the old PNI, PDIP voters in 1999 are also believed to have been the descendants of PKI (Partai Komunis Indonesia, Indonesian Communist Party) voters in 1955 (King 2003). In the 2004 election, PDIP's vote shrank to 18.5 percent and further to 14 percent in 2009, before rising again to 19 percent in 2014. The more recent numbers are closer to the PNI 1955 vote. These latter numbers are not, however, consistent with the combined PNI and PKI vote in 1955, which was 38 percent.

It is clear, then, that there has been significant change in the distribution of voter support, deviating from the once-popular *aliran* model. These changes are in our view primarily the result of the political parties' policy of the authoritarian New Order government. We know that the parties contesting the 1955 election differed from those in the first New Order election in 1971. Two of the largest 1955 parties, PKI and Masjumi, had been banned and therefore did not participate in 1971. The aspirations of Masjumi supporters were accommodated in a new party, Parmusi (Partai Muslimin Indonesia, Indonesian Muslims Party), while PKI was not accommodated. PKI and all affiliated organizations were forbidden to participate in political and social life in Indonesia after 1965–6, when hundreds of thousands of its members and leaders were killed or incarcerated (Crouch 1978; Cribb 1990).

Prior to the second New Order election in 1977, the government simplified the party system. The ten political parties of 1971 were combined into three: PPP, PDI (Partai Demokrasi Indonesia, Indonesian Democracy Party), and Golkar. PPP was created to represent the Muslim stream, and PDI to represent the nationalist stream, including non-Muslim voters (Protestants, Catholics, and Balinese Hindus). Golkar was created by the government to represent "functional groups" as a way of bypassing the long tradition (dating to the colonial era) of political parties in Indonesia. Golkar (the term Partai Golkar, Golkar Party, has only been used since 1999) was promoted by the government not as a political party but as an alternative, in the corporatist tradition, to political parties.

PPP was established to accommodate the pious Muslim stream that had previously been represented in Masjumi and later in Parmusi, plus NU and two very small parties, PSII (Partai Serikat Islam Indonesia, Indonesian Islamic Association Party) and Perti (Persatuan Tarbiyah Indonesia, Indonesian Muslim Education Party). PDI was created to accommodate the nationalist stream of voters who had previously supported PNI, plus Protestant and Catholic parties. Most Hindu Balinese had voted for PNI in 1955. During the New Order, elections were held seven times. Golkar always won with an absolute majority above 60 percent. For three decades, genuine political parties, as forces to channel the interests of voters from below, were paralyzed.

The 1999 and subsequent elections demonstrated the hollowness of Golkar's claims to be a majority party. In the post-New Order period, support for Golkar has declined drastically, from above 60 percent to only 23 percent in 1999, 22 percent in 2004, 14 percent in 2009, and 15 percent in 2014. At the same time, new parties with significant support arose, especially Partai Demokrat, which won 7 percent in 2004, 21 percent in 2009, more than either Golkar or PDIP in the latter year, and 10 percent in 2014. Another example is Gerindra, which won 5 percent as a new party in 2009 and more than doubled its support to 12 percent in 2014.

To understand this behavior, it is important to pay attention to the macro context and the political institutions within which parties and voters act. Individual voters can only select from the available choices even when they are free to choose, and those selections are constrained by institutions, especially the elections and parties law revisited prior to every election. We now offer a brief excursion into this institutional and historical context for each of today's parties.

PDIP (Indonesian Democracy Party of Struggle)

In Diamond and Gunther's (2001, p. 11) categorization, PDIP is basically a catchall party, whose electoral strategy makes "broad and eclectic issue appeals." At the same time, it contains some elements of a personalistic party, which emphasizes "the personal charisma of the party leader" and of a programmatic party, which "gains votes through articulation of programmatic (and/or ideological) appeals."

PDIP is generally regarded as the continuation of the PNI first established by Sukarno, Indonesia's charismatic founding father and first president, in 1928. After Indonesia became independent, and in 1955 conducted its first democratic election, PNI was one of the major players. In the 1955 election PNI received more votes, although well below a majority, than any other party (22 percent).

The platform or ideology of PNI was nationalism, with emphasis on the interests of the lower classes, in Indonesian (originally Javanese) called *wong cilik*, little people, connoting lower classes, the poor, the uneducated population. In this respect, there was a similarity between PNI and PKI. The slogan that PNI was the prolittle people party, also referred to as *kaum Marhaen*, (Marhaenists, after a poor farmer identified by Sukarno in a famous speech), influences PDIP to this day.

Perhaps paradoxically, PNI was supported by an ancient class of Javanese *priyayi*, aristocrats, including the Dutch and early independence-era civil servants who often modeled themselves on the Javanese aristocracy. The anthropologist Geertz (1960) observed that the cultural orientation of many nominally Muslim PNI supporters was in fact influenced by *priyayi* culture, that is a tendency toward Hinduism and syncretism, a blend with local customs and including a heavy dose of mysticism. They were "identity card" Muslims but their religious practices included many pre-Islamic religious traditions, especially Hinduism.

Seen in terms of the ideological conflict of the 1950s, especially the conflict between Islam and Pancasila,[11] focused on the debate surrounding the Constitution of 1945, PNI was the largest party opposing an Islamic state, which was supported by Masjumi, NU and several armed social movements. On this score, PNI was aligned with PKI.

---

[11] Pancasila, or Five Principles, is a state doctrine enshrined in the preamble to the Indonesian Constitution. Its first principle is Belief in the Oneness of God, which has been interpreted since 1945 as the main ideological justification for religious pluralism in opposition to the Islamic state proposed by Muslim party leaders.

In 1959, President Sukarno dissolved the Constituent Assembly, an elected body debating a permanent constitution, and took power for himself. He then pushed for the dissolution of the party system but was only partially successful. Masjumi and the small democratic socialist PSI (Partai Sosialis Indonesia, Indonesian Socialist Party) were banned on the ground that their leaders were charged with involvement in separatist movements (Noer 1973). PNI and PKI were among the parties that remained active.

Under Sukarno's authoritarian regime in the early 1960s, Indonesian politics was much influenced by three forces: Sukarno himself, supported by PNI, plus PKI and the national armed forces, led by the army (Crouch 1978). Other parties did not play a major role. During this period, Indonesian national politics was deeply constrained by the conflict between PKI and the army, which ended with the victory of the army under the command of Major General Suharto in 1965. The influence of Sukarno and PNI immediately declined, and PKI was banned, hundreds of thousands of its leaders and members were killed or arrested and imprisoned for decades.

The victory of the army over Sukarno and PKI is the starting point of Suharto's New Order. PNI was permitted to participate in the 1971 election, winning 12 percent of the vote. It was then absorbed into the PDI (Partai Demokrasi Indonesia, Indonesian Democracy Party) created at the order of the Suharto government in 1973 as a fusion of preexisting nationalist and Christian parties. Across the several New Order elections, PDI won its most votes in 1992, when Megawati Sukarnoputri and other members of the Sukarno family joined PDI. Nonetheless the subsequent internal conflict within the party and the intervention of the government after Megawati was selected national party leader led to a sharp drop in PDI support in the 1997 election. Megawati became a symbol of opposition to Suharto and the New Order. In 1997, when Megawati was no longer leading the party, PDI obtained only 3 percent of the vote. This was the lowest percentage in the history of PDI before Megawati established the PDIP at the end of the New Order.

Leading up to the 1999 election, the first democratic election since 1955, most PDI activists chose to be loyal to Megawati, who formed a new party, the PDIP, with Megawati as its national chair. The 1999 election was a stage on which Megawati and PDIP were the star players. The new party demolished the previous impression of popular support for Golkar. PDIP won a strong plurality (34 percent), a much higher percentage than PNI in 1955 (22 percent) and 1997 (3 percent), the last

New Order election, not to mention Golkar (22 percent) and other parties in the 1999 election (see Table 3.1).

After winning a plurality of votes and seats in the 1999 election, PDIP became the governing party even though Megawati herself at the beginning was only elected vice president. According to the not yet democratically amended Constitution, the president was chosen by the MPR (Majelis Permusyawaratan Rakyat, People's Consultative Assembly), a kind of super-Parliament above the DPR (Dewan Perwakilan Rakyat, People's Representative Council) or Parliament. In its first session after the 1999 elections, the MPR did not choose Megawati as president even though her party had won the most popular votes. The winner instead was Abdurrahman Wahid, from PKB, only the third party (with 13 percent) after PDIP (34 percent) and Partai Golkar (23 percent).

At that moment, Wahid was the more skilled politician than Megawati. By 2001, however, opposition within the DPR led to his impeachment by the MPR. The membership of the MPR at the time consisted of all of the members of the DPR plus additional delegates from the regions and other groups. The conflict between the president and the DPR ended with the dissolution of the DPR and the issuing by Wahid of a presidential decree that the country was in a state of emergency.

Unfortunately for President Wahid, but fortunately for the country's embryonic democracy, the decree was not implemented by the army and the national police. Instead, the MPR voted to remove the president from office. In accordance with the Constitution's rules for succession, the MPR then automatically appointed Megawati president in 2001. In this way PDIP finally fully became the governing party.

The quality of governance of Megawati and the ruling PDIP could now be evaluated by the voters. If the voters' evaluation was negative, PDIP should have been thrown out of power. As will be elaborated below, the performance of Megawati's government did not in fact fulfill the expectations of the public, at the time very high, and her party was defeated in 2004. The PDIP vote plunged from 34 percent (1999) to 18.5 percent (2004).

Because Megawati was the incumbent president in 2004 and the challenger in 2009, the case of PDIP in those years affords us a unique opportunity to discover the extent to which the political economy or rational choice model is capable of explaining Indonesian voting behavior. Of course, we will also test the influence of sociological factors – the standard explanatory model – and psychological factors, especially leadership as indicated at the beginning of this section.

Golkar (Functional Groups) and Partai Golkar (Functional Groups Party)

Partai Golkar is a more purely catchall party than Golkar, with no charismatic leaders and little programmatic commitment. Other than PDIP, it is also the party that has experienced the most dramatic decline since democratization. Though it is often said that Partai Golkar won the 2004 election because it received the most votes, support for the party marginally declined from 1999 (23 percent) to 2004 (22 percent). In the 2009 legislative election, Golkar experienced a further erosion in support, this time more sharply, from 22 percent (2004) to 14 percent (2009). It recovered only to 15 percent in 2014.

The relative victory of Golkar in 2004 is closely tied to two other developments. First, the sharp decline for PDIP (34 percent in 1999 to 18.5 percent in 2004); second, the increasing fragmentation of the party system as measured by seats in Parliament. In the 2004 legislative election there were two new parties with significant support, Partai Demokrat and PKS. In the 2009 election there were two more new parties with a large number of seats, Gerindra and Hanura. These two parties plus Partai Demokrat attracted many voters who had previously supported Partai Golkar in 2004, a pattern that continued in 2014.

Nonetheless, the ability of Partai Golkar to maintain itself despite powerful anti-Golkar sentiment at the beginning of the democratic period is worth noting. Its survival capacity is in part the product of its institutionalization. The initial formation of Golkar as an alliance of various functional organizations was intended by the army to balance an increasingly aggressive communist party, whose growth was cut off in 1965. Two years later, under the guidance of President Suharto and several army generals, several of these functional organizations were reactivated. Still under the name Sekber Golkar (Sekretariat Bersama Golongan Karya, Joint Secretariat of Functional Groups), it won the first New Order election in 1971 with considerable help from the army and the civilian bureaucracy, including intimidation of opposition leaders at all levels of society.

In 1973 Golkar was restructured yet again. This time it was consciously divided into three main components or tracks which were at the same time instruments for the representation of three important New Order groups: the armed forces, the civilian bureaucracy, and Golkar itself, meaning the politicians holding its key offices. This new development signified the institutionalization of Golkar as a political party (in function, if still not in name).

Golkar's leadership structure paralleled the military and civilian bureaucratic structure. Military officers and civilian bureaucrats often doubled as Golkar leaders in the provinces, districts, and municipalities (Boileau 1983). The benefits were only enjoyed by Golkar, while PPP and PDI were not permitted to develop similar strategies. In addition, there were a number of policies about the conduct of elections that gave implicit advantages to civilian officials at every level.

After 1973, Golkar developed a corporatist structure designed to include, at least formally, various employment or functional groups in society like fishers workers, and farmers. The effort to incorporate these various social groups was not limited to those based on economic class. Youth, women, and artists were incorporated into Golkar. Golkar even reached out to pious Muslims (Suryadinata 1992). This effort continued to the beginning of the 1980s, when business groups were brought in.

Golkar's strategy to embrace all of these groups demonstrates that the organization was developing as a "catchall" party. Golkar quite consciously did not privilege any single social group, but targeted quite different groups based on class, religion, and profession. Indeed, the two most antagonistic classes in modern industrial societies, workers and business owners, were formally accommodated within Golkar.

The fall of the New Order regime in 1998 had a powerful impact on Golkar. Many observers and activists were convinced that Golkar would disappear after the 1999 election. The pressure was indeed extremely strong. In East Java, for example, Golkar's office building was burned by rioting masses. Golkar functionaries faced challenges and ridicule when they visited the regions, especially on Java and Bali. Many pro-democracy activists demanded that Golkar be dissolved (Tandjung 2008; Azwar 2008).

The 1999 election was a heavy test for Golkar, which it survived but at greatly reduced strength. The party's survival is due in large part to choices made by its leaders, especially then chair Akbar Tandjung, to adjust to new times, including changing the name to Partai Golkar. Golkar now genuinely defines itself as a party, not a "functional group" or a "joint secretariat" without ideology.

Trained and experienced as a political activist when a student leader and deeply networked within Golkar, Akbar Tandjung proved himself a skilled politician in the first Partai Golkar congress after 1998. Akbar and his colleagues were able to tame the forces of the army which at that time supported a retired army general to take over its leadership. This was the first time in its history that Golkar was led by a non-Javanese (Tandjung is from North Sumatra) with a background as a student leader and an Islamic one at that. After the 1998 congress, many Golkar leaders chose to retire, while others left and formed new parties.

Leadership success in Partai Golkar by pious Muslims who came from outside Java continued in the party's 2004 Bali Congress. Jusuf Kalla, from South Sulawesi and with a Muslim student organization background, took over the Golkar leadership from Tandjung. Several other prominent members of the Golkar elite during Kalla's time were also from outside Java. Whether by design or by accident, members of President Yudhoyono's first cabinet in 2004–9 from Partai Golkar were all from outside the Javanese subculture. A similar pattern characterizes the current Golkar leadership.

This demographic shift has very likely had an impact on the pattern of support obtained by Golkar, which is more dominant outside the Javanese ethnic subcultural area, and also probably on the growing strength of the connection between Partai Golkar and pious Muslim voters. Moreover, we can speculate that, in a society that is still influenced by regional and ethnic sentiment, the geographic shift of Golkar elites and voters from the Javanese to the non-Javanese subculture has created new problems in recruitment of national leadership in the era of direct presidential elections. Partai Golkar no longer has figures who stand out in the eyes of the voters, and it lacks emotional ties with the largest subculture, the ethnic Javanese.

Sociologically speaking, pious Muslim culture and regionalism have arguably become important factors in shaping the voting pattern of Golkar voters. How true is this hypothesis? We will see in subsequent chapters.

Islamic Parties

If the *aliran* or political stream argument is correct, the effect of pious Islam as a cultural category on voting for Partai Gokar is probably not as strong as voting for Islamic parties like PPP and PKS, or parties that are thought to be based on Islamic social organizations like PKB (NU) and PAN (Muhammadiyah). However described, in their sociological and historical context, these parties are more Muslim than Partai Golkar.

Several parties entered the electoral arena carrying the flag of Islam in 1999. From the ten parties that declared themselves Islamic, only three were able to win more than 1 percent of the votes and seats in Parliament: PPP, PBB (Partai Bulan Bintang, Crescent Moon and Star Party), and PK, the forerunner to PKS. On the face of it, these three parties apparently were continuing the Islamic party tradition that had been represented in the 1950s by Masjumi and NU.

What voters did they primarily target in the parliamentary election? The answer is straightforward: They were all aiming at the Muslim majority. At the same time, and perhaps most interestingly, they each applied a different approach to those voters.

PPP (Development Unity Party). PPP is really more an "elite" than an "electoralist" party in the Diamond and Gunther scheme. Elite parties are divided into "local notable" and "clientelistic" subtypes. The former "gain votes through appeals to local interests and authority of local notables," while the latter, which better describes PPP, "through hierarchical structure linking local to national leaders and through exchange of particularistic benefits" (Diamond and Gunther 2001, 10). As an avowedly Islamist party, at the same time it contains programmatic elements.

PPP emphasizes its historic continuity in the long tradition of Islamic politics in Indonesia. Campaigning during the parliamentary election of 1999, PPP decried the political marginalization of the Islamic community, especially during the New Order. It will be recalled that PPP was an imposed New Order fusion of Islamic parties in 1973. In Suharto's grand strategy of party simplification, PPP was first designed as a container for parties based on religion. Included were the Catholic and Protestant parties. In its final form, however, PPP contained only four Islamic parties: NU, Perti, PSII, and Parmusi. With these four components, PPP was reminiscent of Masjumi when it was first formed during the Japanese occupation as a confederation of previously autonomous Muslim elements. Non-Muslim religious parties preferred to unite with the new nationalist party, that is, PDI.[12]

NU and Perti were parties that rested on traditional Muslim communities based in Java and West Sumatra. Their leaders and constituents had the flexibility to accommodate local cultural practices in their religious rituals. As parties, neither NU nor Perti pursued an agenda of religious purification. They were very different from PSII and Parmusi, two parties whose constituents were modernist or reformist Muslims whose agenda is indeed Islamic purification.

---

[12] The Catholic and Protestant parties rejected, indeed threatened to dissolve themselves, if they were forced to join the Islamic parties in PPP. They believed that compromise with PNI, the main nationalist party in the new PDI, would be easier, and that ideologically they were closer to PNI's views on religion and politics.

Nonetheless, the internal dynamic of PPP, both during the New Order and today, has not revolved around traditional versus modern orientations within Islam as ideology, but instead has been an organizing principle to distribute offices within the party and seats within Parliament. To the outside, PPP presents itself as a container for the aspirations of the Islamic community. The party symbol chosen at the time of the original fusion was an Islamic symbol, a picture of the holy Ka'bah in Mecca, Islam's most sacred site, but the Suharto government forced it to adopt the less controversial or less-clearly-Islamic star.

In electoral competitions during the New Order, PPP and PDI were always the losers. The policy of "monoloyalitas" to Golkar for civil servants of course benefited the ruling party and disadvantaged PPP and PDI, because the number of civil servants in Indonesia is so large. In addition, civil servants are often spokespeople in their regions who become a reference group for village-level voters when they decide for which party to vote. Moreover, a 1985 political parties law required all parties and social organizations to adopt Pancasila as their sole doctrine. The effect was to distance PPP leaders from followers.

Organizationally as well, PPP and PDI were forbidden (unlike Golkar) to establish leadership branches in the subdistricts (two administrative levels below the province) and below. Nonetheless, PPP's long history of being known as the main representative of Islamic politics encouraged its leaders to reaffirm their position before the 1999 democratic election by restoring the Ka'bah as their logo and ballot symbol.

PBB (Crescent Moon and Star Party). PBB is a programmatic electoralist party, programmatic in the sense that it is committed to the establishment of an Islamic state in Indonesia. Modestly successful in the 1999 and 2004 elections, it failed to reach the electoral threshold for parliamentary representation in 2009 or 2014.

Like PPP, PBB defines itself in terms of historical continuity. Indeed, PBB claims to be the direct legatee of Masjumi, the largest Islamic party in the 1950s. It is not accidental that PBB adopted a basic component of the Masjumi logo, the crescent moon and star, and that at the same time the founders and supporters of PBB called themselves the "crescent moon and star family." The site where PBB declared its formation in 1998 also affirmed its self-image. The declaration was made in front of thousands of supporters at the Al Azhar mosque, Jakarta. Al Azhar has long been known as a breeding ground for pious modernist Muslims, where a number of former Masjumi leaders plan and organize their proselytization (*dakwah*) activities.

PK (Justice Party) and PKS (Prosperous Justice Party). As a pro-syariah Islamic party, PKS is a programmatic electoralist party, but also contains some catchall elements. The Justice Party was a new Islamic party created for the 1999 elections, in which it won 1.4 million votes, gaining it seven seats in Parliament. It did not, however, pass the threshold of two percent stipulated in the election law. Under the unusual threshold provision of that law, which allowed the party to hold seats from 1999 to 2004 but not to contest in 2004, it changed its name to Prosperous Justice Party to compete in 2004.

Like PBB, PK chose the Al Azhar mosque for its initial declaration, indicating that PKS also targets modernist pious Muslims. This similarity is not surprising, since the key figures in the two parties come from the same Islamist culture. The two parties chose different electoral strategies, however. PBB tried to take advantage of the prestige of Masjumi from the 1950s, while PK was more oriented to the present.

PK relied on support from young pious Muslims and recruiting on university campuses, its sociological base. PK was an outgrowth of the *tarbiyah* (Arabic: education) social movement that had spread on campuses, especially the major secular university campuses, since the 1980s. They were campus-based Islamic activists who were not affiliated with the preexisting Muslim student organizations. In the beginning, they were considered apolitical. The movement began on the campus of the Bandung Institute of Technology (ITB, Institut Teknologi Bandung), Indonesia's best technical university. It subsequently spread to many secular state universities via campus mosques.

The movement entered campus politics through competition for offices in student government. It was also effective at fundraising, unlike many similar organizations. At the same time, its leaders had no intention of becoming a political movement, let alone a party (Damanik 2002). Nevertheless, when the New Order ended, and the opportunity to enter the political arena opened wide, a number of *tarbiyah* movement activists decided to form a political party.[13]

In relating this history of the formation of PK, we can identify its social base, which is a relatively small group that is oriented toward Islam and whose activists are much better educated than the society in general. This pattern is mirrored in the level of votes obtained in the first democratic

---

[13] Before this decision was taken, the national leaders of the movement conducted a survey of their comrades across several cities and universities, in order to determine whether they should become a political party (Damanik 2002).

election, which is also small, about 1.4 million voters of a total of 89 million cast. Failing to reach the threshold, PK was excluded from the next election. The creation of PKS was thus a pragmatic response to the desire for the PK community to participate in the upcoming election. It also signified the beginning of a change in the approach used by the party.

For the 2004 parliamentary election, PKS played down its image as an Islamist party. Its desire to formalize *syariah* in national law was dampened, as we see in the position the party took when the Constitution was being amended. While PPP and PBB hardened their commitment to turning Indonesia into an Islamic state, PK rejected this dichotomous choice and proposed the alternative of a state in which adherents to each religion practiced in Indonesia could follow their own religious law.

This alternative was not free of ambiguity. It gave the impression that PK was distancing itself from Islamic conservatism, while at the same time offering a new formulation that it hoped would still be acceptable to its conservative constituency. In the 2004 election, PK, now named PKS, also did not conduct a typically Islamic campaign, but instead stressed its commitment to a "clean and caring" government, signalling a desire to appeal to a wider range of constituencies, even non-Islamic ones. Did this change in strategy become a determining factor in voters' decisions in 2004 and later elections?

PKB (National Awakening Party). PKB is an elite party like PPP, and also like PPP contains some elements of dominance of local notables and clientelism. Founded in 1998, it represents the hopes of leading traditional religious scholars and teachers (*kiai* in Indonesian, *ulama* in Arabic) and ordinary members of NU (Nahdlatul Ulama, Awakening of the Traditional Religious Scholars and Teachers) to have their own political party.

NU is a socioeducational religious organization founded in 1926. In the 1950s NU entered the modern electoral world, first joining Masjumi, then withdrawing to declare itself an independent political party in 1952. In 1955, it was the fourth largest party in number of votes. At the beginning of the New Order, NU was still a political party and participated in the 1971 elections, winning 18.4 percent of the vote, about the same as it had won in 1955. As discussed above, in 1973 NU became one of the primary components of PPP, the party forced on the Islamic community by Suharto.

In the 1977 and 1982 elections, still during the New Order, NU remained within PPP before leaving the party and declaring itself a non-political organization in 1985. In the organization's national congress that year, its leaders (headed by Abdurrahman Wahid, who would later become the first democratic-era president) declared that NU was returning to its original conception or mission as a socioeducational religious organization. NU then withdrew from the political world for nearly two decades, reemerging after the fall of the New Order and the opportunity offered by genuinely democratic elections.

As an NU creation, PKB's prospects were limited by the organizational reach of NU. NU constituted a captive market for PKB, with clear limits as to who would be attracted to the party. In religious terms, the party's appeal is confined to that segment of the Indonesian Muslim community which is traditional, meaning that it adheres to the Syafi'i jurisprudential school, one of four classical schools of interpretation within Sunni Islam, and also that it is friendly to local culture. Second, as NU is centered in east and central Java, the support base of PKB is also mainly restricted to that region.

At least initially, PKB did not aspire to be a closed or exclusive party. Abdurrahman Wahid, longtime NU leader as well as founder of PKB and subsequently president of Indonesia, and other leaders proclaimed that PKB was not an Islamic or religious but rather an inclusive party. This inclusivity in principle seems not to have been enough to attract voters from other groups, however, whether from the non-NU Muslim community or from non-Muslims. At the same time, the decision to become an inclusive party drove a number of traditional NU leaders to decide not to support PKB, founding NU-based parties of their own.

In sum, the sociological base of PKB voters throughout the party's history is probably mostly shaped by pious traditional Muslim culture, membership in NU, regional residence in Java, acceptance of the guidance of a traditional religious leader, rural residence, and lower social class origins. In social class terms, but not the other characteristics mentioned, PKB voters are similar to PDIP voters.

PAN (National Mandate Party). PAN is a catchall electoralist party with some programmatic and personalistic elements. Both PAN, founded in 1998, and PKB are supported by mass Islamic organizations: PKB by NU and PAN by Muhammadiyah. If NU brings together a segment of the Muslim community with a traditional orientation and is village based, Muhammadiyah brings together Muslim modernists who mostly live in cities. In the Indonesian context, the term modernist refers to the back-to-the-Qur'an reform movement that began in the Middle East in the last quarter of the nineteenth century. While Sunni Muslims, they abjure adherence to any of the four classical schools of jurisprudence. They also oppose local cultural adaptations which have long been a point of pride for many traditionalists.

At the level of its formal organization and leadership, Muhammadiyah does not require or encourage its members to vote for PAN. For its part, PAN, under the leadership of its first chair and still most influential leader, Amien Rais, also did not want PAN to limit itself to the Muhammadiyah support base. At the same time, in the regions many Muhammadiyah members became PAN leaders, partly for practical reasons and partly because they were close to Amien, a former chair of Muhammadiyah.

This practical reason was also tied to the availability of human capital within Muhammadiyah. The non-Muhammadiyah Jakarta leaders of PAN did not have a comparable reach that would have enabled them to staff party branches throughout the country. The personal, even charismatic, appeal of Amien was an additional factor that attracted members and leaders of Muhammadiyah in the regions to become local leaders of PAN.

At the beginning, in the months before the 1998 founding of PAN, Amien Rais was involved in the formation of MARA (Majelis Amanat Rakyat, People's Mandate Council), a group highly critical of the political process in Indonesia after the fall of Suharto. MARA itself was a collection of public leaders from various religious and regional backgrounds. It was inclusive, which later became the organizational model for PAN. MARA embraced many groups; PAN wanted to define itself as an inclusive party that also embraced many religious, regional, and social class groups.

PAN was declared a political party in the national sports stadium in Jakarta. If the choice of a location to announce its existence is an indicator of the orientation of a political party, PAN was proclaiming that it wanted to be considered an open party. Like spectators at a soccer game who come from every direction and group, PAN wanted to contain everyone. In his inaugural speech, Amien stressed that PAN was an inclusive party and would not give any group a special position, including Muslims. On many subsequent occasions, he compared PAN to Indonesia as a whole that consists of many ethnic, religious, and cultural groups.

Of course, PAN's choice to present an image as an inclusive party carried its own advantages and risks. There was a possibility of expanding the voter base, at first thought to be limited to Muhammadiyah members, but on the negative side, PAN might lose a significant portion of its initial supporters from Muhammadiyah. The fear was similar to that in PKB with regard to NU, that a large number of members of Muhammadiyah would leave PAN at the moment it declared itself an inclusive party.

In sum, sociologically, PAN voters were most likely to be pious Muslims, urban residents, and more educated members of the middle class. Psychologically, the leadership of Amien Rais was a strong influence.

Partai Demokrat (Democratic Party)

Partai Demokrat or PD is a personalistic electoralist party with some catchall elements. It was founded in 2001 at the direction of Susilo Bambang Yudhoyono, whose personal history is culturally and socio-logically pluralist. Yudhoyono is a retired army general with Javanese cultural roots. His first and second party chairs had similar cultural roots, and several members of the initial governing board of the party were non-Muslims. Therefore, the party is believed to be sociologically closer to Partai Golkar and PDIP than to PAN.

None of the founders of Demokrat had emerged from the movement against Suharto or had any activist background, political or social. Most were academicians without deep roots in society. Demokrat was to be sure not a party that had emerged from a social organization, like a labor union, or from any religious group. It was established as a political vehicle to support Yudhoyono as a candidate for president in 2004. The party should therefore be considered identical with its founder, even though formally he is the chair of the party's supervising board, not the general chair who conducts the party's daily business.

The closeness of Partai Demokrat to Yudhoyono has convinced many people that his personal appeal is the main factor persuading voters to choose the party. Underlying this conviction is the presumption that Yudhoyono is well known and highly regarded as a capable national leader. What is the origin of this conception, recalling that he is not a mass organization leader, not a top-level government official, and not an anti-Suharto democratic activist like Amien Rais? In our view, Yudhoyono is well known because of early and intense exposure by the mass media so that the public feels that it knows him well and likes what it sees.

This media exposure is in turn connected to two important political events. The first involved his unwillingness to back President Wahid who asked him as Coordinating Minister for Politics and Security to carry out a presidential decision placing Indonesia in a state of emergency after the president had been impeached by the MPR in 2001. Instead, Yudhoyono withdrew from Wahid's cabinet. Public sentiment at that time, as reflected in the media and in Parliament, supported Wahid's impeachment. Yudhoyono's attitude then became a part of the public desire for him to step down.

After Megawati replaced Wahid as president, she asked Yudhoyono to once again become Coordinating Minister for Politics and Security. This was the second event. As the 2004 election approached, Yudhoyono no longer felt that he could support Megawati's policies and resigned as Coordinating Minister. His resignation was widely covered in the media, and public opinion was supportive.

Because Yudhoyono played such a central role in the politics leading up to the 2004 election, it is widely believed that positive perception of the quality of his leadership was the primary factor determining the Demokrat vote. His drawing power was apparently confirmed again in the 2009 legislative election when Demokrat was the one party to substantially increase its vote, rising 200 percent, from about 7 percent in 2004 to 21 percent in 2009. Moreover, for the 2009 election, the additional factor of public support for his performance as president also probably helps to explain Demokrat success. Similarly, the decline in support for Demokrat in 2014 (to 10 percent) is probably attributable to the fact that he was no longer a candidate for president, having reached his two-term limit. These hypotheses will be analyzed in subsequent chapters.

Partai Gerindra (Greater Indonesia Movement Party) and Partai Hanura (People's Conscience Party)

Gerindra and Hanura are personalistic electoralist parties with some catchall elements. These parties were established by retired army officers: Gerindra by retired Major General Prabowo Subianto and Hanura by retired General Wiranto. Both had been active in Partai Golkar until 2004, when they campaigned to be nominated as Golkar's candidate for president. Like Demokrat, both parties are primarily electoral vehicles for their leaders.

Gerindra, founded in 2008, presents a nationalist face, meaning both secular (as opposed to Islamic) and populist, in the sense that the party claims to represent a specifically Indonesian identity and interests based on the needs of the common people. Gerindra's organizational strategy has been to embrace social groups usually categorized as lower class, especially farmers, fishers, and workers. Somewhat surprisingly, in the 2014 election, Gerindra also reached out to Islamist voters. Hanura, founded in 2006, is on the secular side of the religious debate but otherwise has no clear class-related ideological identity. It is seen primarily as the presidential campaign vehicle of General Wiranto.

Partai NasDem (National Democratic Party)

Partai NasDem is a personalistic electoralist party with some catchall elements. In the 2014 election, Nasdem was the only new party to win a sufficient number of votes to pass the electoral threshold and obtain parliamentary seats. It was founded in 2011 and is led by Surya Paloh, a former Partai Golkar figure, in reaction to his defeat in a leadership struggle within Golkar. Like Golkar, Nasdem's program is nationalist, secular, and catchall. Its voters are not segmented by social class, ideology, or religion. They are, however, concentrated outside Java, particularly in North Sumatra and Aceh, Paloh's region of origin.

Choosing the President

In Indonesia's current version of presidential democracy, the president is directly elected, unlike the previous quasi-parliamentary system where the president was chosen by the super-parliamentary MPR or People's Consultative Assembly. Direct presidential election occurred for the first time with the two-round election of July and September 2004. This change represented a reaction, though delayed by a few years, to the 1999 election of the first democratic president, Abdurrahman Wahid, by the Assembly.

Institutional Context

Before the era of direct presidential elections, the Indonesian Constitution specified the indirect election of the president by the Assembly, a kind of super-parliament whose main responsibility was to elect the president and vice president. This was true from the beginning of Indonesian independence in 1945 through the parliamentary election of 1999. Because it was the Assembly which chose the president, and since most of the members of the Assembly in the post-New Order period were also members of Parliament, the political parties represented in Parliament determined who would become president of Indonesia.

During most of Suharto's New Order, half of the Assembly members were members of Parliament who represented political parties, Golkar, regions, functional groups, and the armed forces and police. The nonparty delegates were not chosen in elections but appointed. An additional half of the Assembly members were directly appointed. In practice President Suharto had veto power over these appointments, as he did for nominations for seats in the ostensibly popularly elected Parliament. This veto power extended to candidates of PDI and PPP as well as his own state party, Golkar.

By the time of the election of the president in 1999, during the early years of democratization, the regional and group delegations no longer existed. The armed forces and police were, however, still represented in Parliament and thus the Assembly. Their voices were therefore still a part of the calculations made by presidential contestants in 1999.

After the 1999 parliamentary election, the strongest force in the Parliament/Assembly was the PDIP, controlling about 33 percent of total seats. PDIP was followed by Partai Golkar with 26 percent, PPP 13 percent, PKB 11 percent, and PAN with 7 percent. The remainder was divided among several minuscule parties. Even though PDIP had won the largest number of seats, it commanded much less than a majority in a highly fragmented Parliament and Assembly. Critically, this fragmentation occurred in a context in which there were no laws or institutional rules requiring that the president must be from the political party with the most seats in the Assembly. PDIP, even though it controlled the most seats, could not automatically make its leader, Megawati, president.

In the event, the force that did determine the selection of the first democratic president was a coalition of parties that did not include PDIP. Abdurrahman Wahid from PKB, with fewer than half the number of seats of PDIP, was nonetheless chosen as the first democratic Indonesian president. Megawati and other PDIP leaders turned out to be less politically skilled than the leaders of other parties, especially PAN's Amien Rais, the chair of the Assembly at that time, and Golkar's Akbar Tandjung, who chaired Parliament. The selection of Amien as Assembly chair and Akbar as chair of Parliament, when those bodies were first convened after the 1999 election, also demonstrated PDIP's weakness.

In the presidential contest, a coalition self-labeled as the Central Axis, consisting mainly of PKB, PPP, and PAN, played the principal role, defeating PDIP in the Parliament/Assembly. The selection of Amien and Akbar was the outcome of bargaining between this coalition and Golkar. In the coalition, the party with the most votes was PKB, and at the time anti-Golkar sentiment within the PKB elite was very strong. The way out to which all could agree primarily benefited PKB. The presidential candidate put forward in the end to compete with Megawati was not Amien Rais, despite his leading role in bringing down Suharto, and also not

Akbar Tandjung or some other Golkar figure, who were tainted by their New Order history, but rather Abdurrahman Wahid, leader of PKB.

The choice of Wahid to oppose Megawati made political sense. PKB had at that time not won any of the major legislative posts, Wahid was the party leader considered closest to Megawati, and he was a powerful symbol of opposition to the still-strong New Order forces. The attitude of PDIP might have been different if Amien, Akbar, or the sitting President B. J. Habibie, Suharto's last vice president, had been the candidate of the PAN/PPP/PKB coalition. There was also the possibility that the coalition would have split if PPP was not given a share of power. Hamzah Haz, chair of PPP, the party that had won the third most votes in the Parliament/Assembly, had not been given a position at that time. But he was not chosen as presidential candidate because of the perception of the key Central Axis players that Wahid was more capable of neutralizing PDIP and Megawati than Hamzah.

If the choice of Amien Rais, Habibie, or Akbar Tandjung had been forced on the coalition, PKB and PPP might have withdrawn and joined with PDIP. But Amien as the key figure in the coalition was a savvy politician who fully understood the consequences of promoting himself as a presidential candidate. The intraelite conflict would have hardened, and he might well have been denied the position of Assembly chair. The ability of the fragmented elite to reach a consensus on its most basic personnel choices would have come into question.

Even though the near-blind Wahid was probably not fit to become president, he was nonetheless regarded as the most politically qualified of the available candidates, especially in the context of the competition with Megawati. In an effort to dampen PDIP's anger, Megawati was quickly elected vice president. Had they been less politically astute, Golkar and the coalition might well have forced a different vice presidential candidate, like Hamzah Haz from PPP or Susilo Bambang Yudhoyono from the armed forces, who had declared their willingness to become vice presidential candidates. The choices of Wahid as president and Megawati as vice president perhaps remind us that democracy is not a perfect system to choose leaders, but it may be the best way to mediate elite conflict.

After the 1999 parliamentary election, Indonesia had a president who was chosen in a democratic way but by the members of the Assembly, not by the people directly. If the Constitution had been different, for example if it had stipulated that the president be chosen directly as is the case today, it is possible that Wahid and perhaps even Megawati would not have become presidents of Indonesia.

The effect of political institutions can also be seen in the presidential elections held in 2004, 2009, and 2014. In the Constitution as amended between 2002 and 2004, the president is chosen directly by the people. This provision limits the room for elite political maneuvering. Calculating mass politics is much more complex than calculating elite politics in Parliament and the Assembly. Good parliamentary politicians like Amien Rais now found wholly new challenges that forced them to change their strategies.

Strategic adjustment due to political institutional changes was also undertaken by Susilo Bambang Yudhoyono. Before Yudhoyono decided to run for the presidency in 2004, he consulted public opinion pollsters. Before the 2009 election, he regularly requested the Indonesian Survey Institute to conduct surveys for him, discussing the findings for his campaign strategizing.

These changes in the institutional context also shaped the behavior of party elites in contemplating presidential and vice presidential nominations. They could no longer rely solely on the electoral strength of their parties, but had to pay direct attention to the probability of success of a presidential candidate. The party remained important, not as an effective voter-mobilizing machine, but because of the constitutional provision that only parties can nominate presidential candidates. If the reformed Constitution had stated instead that individual citizens may nominate themselves, the political elite might well have abandoned the parties in the presidential election.

Every presidential candidate and supporting party plans a strategy to win elections. In practice, most adopt a two-pronged strategy, starting with the development of a coalition of supportive parties, followed by a strategy for choosing the vice president. Every strategy that is chosen by presidential campaign teams implies hypotheses that can be tested empirically by political scientists. Religious affiliations, regional and ethnic backgrounds, personal leadership qualities, and professional backgrounds of the presidential and vice presidential candidates are all potentially important factors. In the following section, we examine the campaign strategies formulated by each of the success teams. We then conceptualize these strategies in the form of propositions that can be tested and finally actually test them.

The Candidate Pairs

Given the criteria for eligibility stipulated in the law, all parties that passed a threshold in 2004 (at that time 2.5 percent of the legislative vote) were able to nominate their own candidate. Alternatively, a party that failed to reach the threshold was required to form a coalition with other parties until the threshold was reached. Prior to the 2009 presidential election, the law was changed to restrict nominations to parties with at least 20 percent of the DPR seats or 25 percent of the popular vote. That law was retained in 2014.

A. The 2004 Presidential Election

Megawati Sukarnoputri and Hasyim Muzadi

Why were these candidates nominated in 2004 by a coalition consisting of PDIP and PPP? Megawati was of course a popular name in the months leading up to the 2004 presidential election. She was the incumbent president, the daughter of Indonesia's founding father and first president Sukarno, and had been known as a prominent nationalist figure since her youth. She had been active in PNI's university student affiliate, then a member and ultimately leader in PDI, which subsequently became PDIP.

Her political career started at the branch level, where she became chair of PDI for the Jakarta region from 1987 to 1992. She served in Parliament, but her activities there did not bring much media attention. Megawati's popularity first rose when PDI formulated a new strategy for the 1992 parliamentary election, raising the banner of nationalism and promoting the name of Sukarno as a campaign gimmick.

Her subsequent rise was shaped by a series of events that defined her role on the national stage. First, her 1993 election as national PDI chair produced an overreaction from the New Order government. Suharto was unwilling to accept Megawati and decided to reinstall the previous chair. PDI supporters demonstrated in her defense, leading to an armed commando attack on PDI national headquarters in Jakarta, controlled by Megawati's forces. This event signaled the birth of a PDI splinter group, now the PDIP, and consecrated Megawati as the principal icon of the resistance.

The 1998 fall of the New Order catapulted PDIP from its splinter party position to become the largest competitor, with the highest vote percentage in the 1999 election. By 2004, however, PDIP began its decline, winning only the second most votes after Golkar. Entering the 2004 presidential competition, with shrunken political capital of less than 20

TABLE 3.2 *Presidential/vice presidential pairs and their supporting parties, 2004, 2009, and 2014*

Candidate Pair	Support Coalition	Party Electoral Strength (percent)	Presidential Election Result (percent)
First Round 2004:			
Megawati* – Hasyim Muzadi**	PDIP, PDS	21	27
Wiranto* – Salahuddin Wahid**	Golkar, PKB	32	22
Susilo B. Yudhoyono* – Jusuf Kalla**	PD, PBB, PKPI	11	34
Amien Rais** – Siswono Yudho Husodo*	PAN, PKS, *PBR*, PNBK, PNI	20	15
	Marhaen, PPDI, PSI, PBSD		
Hamzah Haz** – Agum Gumelar*	PPP	9	3
Second Round 2004:			
Megawati* – Hasyim Muzadi**	PDIP, Golkar, PKB, PPP, PDS	60	39
Susilo B. Yudhoyono* – Jusuf Kalla**	Demokrat, PBB, PKPI, PAN, PKS	23	61
2009			
Jusuf Kalla – Wiranto	Golkar, Hanura	20	12
Susilo B. Yudhoyono – Boediono	Demokrat PKS, PAN, PKB, PPP	60	61
Megawati – Prabowo Subianto	PDIP, Gerindra	20	27
2014			
Prabowo Subianto – Hatta Rajasa	Gerindra, Golkar, PAN, PKS, PPP, PBB	59	47
Joko Widodo – Jusuf Kalla	PDIP, PKB, NasDem, Hanura, PKPI	41	53

Notes about presidential candidates:
*Leader of a nationalist party or a public figure identified as nationalist.
**Leader of an Islamic party or a public figure identified with a strong pious Muslim background.
From the five pairs, only three individuals come from non-Javanese ethnic groups: Jusuf Kalla (Bugis/South Sulawesi), Hamzah Haz (Banjar/South Kalimantan), and Agum Gumelar (Sunda/West Java)
Supporting party:
  Underlined: nationalist/secular party
  Italics: Islamic party
  Bold: party based on the Muslim community
Source: www.kpu.or.id; *Tempo*, July 12–18, 2004.
Percentages rounded.

percent of the votes, Megawati had to build a coalition with another party. The questions were, which party, and who was the best vice presidential candidate? Was it better, in terms of maximizing votes in the presidential election, to forge a coalition with a strong party or a strong individual leader?

Megawati's initial political capital was her position as the incumbent, which made her a widely recognized figure. Nonetheless, the PDIP's earlier failure to win the presidency for her meant that the party was highly attentive to the need to quickly amass support for her as a presidential candidate. Many more variables had to be considered by Megawati and her team in 2004 than 1999. If PDIP leaders had wanted to form a coalition based on the most ideological consistency and the greatest opportunity for victory, they should have joined with Golkar. Both are nationalist parties, and more importantly, their combined popular vote was more than 40 percent. A pairing of a presidential and vice presidential candidate from these two parties would only need about 10 percent more of the electorate to win in the first round.

In the event, Golkar put forward its own presidential candidate. As the largest party, the Golkar elite felt that it made political sense for them to put forward their own candidate. At the same time, Megawati as the incumbent president was unwilling to become the vice presidential candidate on a Golkar-PDIP ticket. The possibility for Golkar and PDIP to form an ideologically connected or even a pragmatic minimum winning coalition was thus frustrated.

Megawati and PDIP were forced to look for a candidate outside Golkar. The choice fell to Hasyim Muzadi, at that time the chair of NU. Why Hasyim? Megawati and the PDIP's electoral mapping apparently began by dividing the electorate on the basis of religion. PDIP and Megawati are well-known secular nationalists, so they perceived that they needed a vice presidential candidate from the Muslim side. The obvious alternative was to maintain the duet of Megawati and incumbent Vice President Hamzah Haz, a PPP leader who also happened to be an NU figure. In Megawati's calculation, however, there were two ways to win votes from the Muslim community: the party track and the social organization track.

In the end, the choice fell to the largest religious organization, Nahdlatul Ulama. The choice of NU chair Hasyim was an attempt to win support from NU voters. Further, the largest NU base is in East Java, the second largest province in Indonesia. Megawati and PDIP hoped to win significant support from NU voters in East Java.

The Megawati camp was confident that the combination of two leaders representing the largest political cultural groups, secular nationalists and pious traditional Muslims, could aggregate enough support to win. Regionalism was not a consideration. Both Megawati and Hasyim are Javanese, so their coalition did not incorporate the other major division in Indonesian political life, between Javanese and non-Javanese ethnic groups. The civilian-military gap – which some still consider important – was also not bridged, as neither had served in the military.

The prospects for this strategy relied upon a dubious assumption about NU voters, that they would support their chair. The formal leadership of Hasyim Muzadi at the top of the national organization was considered more influential than the nonformal leadership which characterizes much of the organization at lower levels. As we will see below, another presidential candidate would also take as his running mate a prominent NU figure. Further, we need to be aware that PKB, the party formally created by NU, gave its support to still another presidential candidate.

NU is a socially traditional organization with more communal, informal, and personal relationships among its members and between them and its leaders, especially the *kiai* or *ulama*. NU *ulama* are independent figures; they have influence on their communities arguably as strong as the influence of the NU chair, who lives far away in Jakarta. In any event, we need to test empirically, which we do in the following chapters, whether the PDIP failure to take account of this characteristic of NU did or did not have an impact.

Wiranto-Salahuddin Wahid

The Wiranto-Salahuddin pairing was a joining of military and civilian figures, also of a secular nationalist and a prominent Muslim. Wiranto's military credentials were strong. A 1968 graduate of the national military academy, he began his career as a second lieutenant, rose steadily within the officer corps, and finally became a full general in 1997. Along the way he held many important positions as a troop commander, territorial officer, and within the armed forces hierarchy.

In 1996–7 Wiranto served as Commander of Kostrad (Komando Cadangan Strategis Angkatan Darat, Army Strategic Reserve Command), a position once held by Suharto, and was Army Chief of Staff from 1997 to 1998. Finally, he was appointed Minister of Defense and Security and Armed Forces Commander in the last year of Suharto's rule. He maintained these latter positions through the democratic transition under President Habibie, the 1999 parliamentary election, and the election of Abdurrahman Wahid as president. After retirement and during the democratic transition period, he held the civilian position of Coordinating Minister for Defence and Security from 1999 to 2000. During and after the transition, Wiranto was alleged to have a close relationship with several Islamic social organizations in Jakarta, upon whom he is said to have called to stage street demonstrations, but he is much better and longer known as a politician with a nationalist military background.

The party with which he attempted to win the presidency was Golkar, which had just won the 2004 legislative election. He advanced his candidacy through the mechanism of a national Golkar convention, defeating four other candidates, including Akbar Tandjung, the Golkar general chair at that time. Despite these strengths, Wiranto faced a situation and choices that were about the same as Megawati's. His initial political capital, the electoral base of Golkar and his own popularity, did not guarantee that he could easily win the presidency. He had to build a coalition, and he had to choose a vice president. This strategic step was crucial to enable him to advance beyond the first round of the presidential election.

With his military background, Wiranto's best choice for a running mate was probably a civilian. As a nationalist, he could have chosen a vice presidential candidate from the Islamic camp or at least one with impressive Islamic credentials. Alternatively, with an eye to embracing voters on Java and outside Java at the same time, the Javanese Wiranto could have chosen a vice presidential candidate from outside Java. Equally important, at least if we recall the dominant public discourse at that time, was the criterion of winning the support of a substantial political party, in addition to Golkar, or other group in society. Considering all of these factors, the process of choosing a vice presidential candidate was more complex than it appeared to many.

Wiranto chose Salahuddin Wahid, brother of former President Abdurrahman Wahid. Personal closeness was one reason. When Wiranto, as Armed Forces Commander, faced charges of human rights violations after the independence referendum in East Timor, the National Commission for Human Rights investigative team was led by Salahuddin Wahid. The team found that Wiranto was not responsible for significant violations of human rights.

Another reason was that PKB, the official NU party, had already decided to form a coalition with Golkar. PKB had developed alternative scenarios, that if Abdurrahman Wahid could not be nominated again as a presidential candidate, Salahuddin Wahid would be their candidate, for either the presidency or the vice presidency.

Salahuddin himself, though neither an NU nor a PKB activist, had "blue NU blood" in his veins as the grandson of one of the founders of NU. Salahuddin's first national experience came in 1998–9, when he was a member of the New Order Parliament for one year. He was then vice chair of the National Commission for Human Rights starting in 2002. Primarily because of his blue NU blood, plus his position as a formal representative of PKB, Salahuddin Wahid had positive value as Wiranto's vice presidential candidate.

The coalition that was built by Golkar with PKB, and Wiranto's choice of Salahuddin Wahid, has a logic similar to that of Megawati and PDIP. Wiranto and Golkar's mapping of the electorate was also based on the division between nationalist and Muslim voters. Both teams believed that the joining of forces of these two great cultural camps would carry them to victory. Where Megawati relied on the NU organizational network, with Hasyim as NU chair, Wiranto relied on the party organization of PKB and the Islamic cultural status of Salahuddin. Which NU relationship would prove to be more effective in determining, or at least shaping, the political behavior of NU voters?

Yudhoyono-Kalla

Before declaring themselves presidential/vice presidential running mates, Susilo Bambang Yudhoyono and Jusuf Kalla had been members of Abdurrahman Wahid's cabinet. They had very different backgrounds, however. Yudhoyono was a career soldier, while Jusuf Kalla was a successful trader and business person in his native South Sulawesi.

In 1973, Yudhoyono was the best student in his graduating class at the national military academy. In 1995, he was territorial commander in Yogyakarta and from 1996 to 1998 was Commander of the South Sumatran regional command. As an active military officer, his highest position was Chief of Staff of the Armed Forces with the rank of lieutenant general in 1998. A year later, he was required to retire from active military service after being appointed minister by President Wahid. Finally, President Megawati appointed him to the civilian position of Coordinating Minister for Politics and Security.

Jusuf Kalla, Yudhoyono's vice presidential candidate, was best known as a regional business person. Born in 1942, he spent his early years expanding a business inherited from his father. From 1985 to 1998, he was general chair of the South Sulawesi Chamber of Commerce. He entered politics in 1999 when he joined the Abdurrahman Wahid's government.

In partisan terms, the electoral strength of Yudhoyono-Kalla was weak. Its main pillar was Partai Demokrat, a new party that had won only 7 percent of the vote in the legislative election that had just been held. Kalla, though from Partai Golkar, was not the party's official candidate. On paper, therefore, and according to the conventional wisdom at the time, their prospect of victory was not large. What was the political calculation that underlay their campaign?

Public opinion surveys carried out at that time were Yudhoyono's main reason, as stated in interviews, to choose to run. In these surveys, the name of Yudhoyono was always one of the top five, often first or second. The decision to become a team took several factors into consideration. In the eyes of Yudhoyono and Partai Demokrat, the proposed ticket spanned all of the categories being considered by the various candidates: nationalist-Islam, Java/non-Java, and civilian-military.

Yudhoyono, like other generals, was known as a nationalist. Jusuf Kalla could be considered to represent the Muslim community, even though his identity as an Islamic figure was not as strong as Hasyim Muzadi, Salahuddin Wahid, or Amien Rais. Kalla came from a strongly Islamic cultural area, South Sulawesi, while his wife is from West Sumatra, a similar region. As a student, Kalla had been active in the most important Muslim student organization of the time, HMI (Himpunan Mahasiswa Islam, Islamic University Students Association). He could therefore be considered to represent Muslims, or at least, could help to ward off Islamic resistance to the team.

Even more important, the Yudhoyono-Kalla ticket incorporated the two major sides of the regional division in Indonesia, Java and non-Java. The Javanese Yudhoyono represents the largest ethnic group in Indonesia, while Kalla is an ethnic Bugis from South Sulawesi. Kalla's wife's ethnic Minangkabau origins also strengthened his claim to represent the non-Javanese outer islands of Indonesia. In a radio interview, Yudhoyono remarked that Jusuf Kalla's non-Java origin was a positive factor in choosing him.

Another differentiating characteristic, military versus civilian, was also considered an asset. Military and civilian are of course not natural social groups, but rather different styles of leadership, one more closed, hierarchical, and disciplined, the other more open, inclusive, and prone to negotiation. Styles of leadership are potentially important factors coloring voting behavior.

There was one more factor underlying the optimism of Yudhoyono and Kalla. Kalla once claimed that Indonesian voters tend to look at the individual candidate more than the party. It was probably this understanding that encouraged him to withdraw from the Golkar presidential nominating convention. If true, his insight implied that there would be a great deal of vote-splitting in the presidential election. Vote-splitting occurs when voters choose one party in the parliamentary election, but give their votes to a presidential candidate from another party in the presidential election held a few months later. A high percentage of vote-splitting will benefit tickets nominated by small parties. To what extent is the strategy constructed by Yudhoyono-Kalla verified by the empirical evidence?

Amien Rais-Siswono
Among the 2004 presidential candidates, Amien Rais had the most solid Muslim credentials. He had long been known as a prominent Muslim intellectual, and had been deeply involved in 1991 in the formation of ICMI (Ikatan Cendekiawan Muslim Indonesia, Indonesian Muslim Intellectuals' Association), the principal lobby for modernist Muslim interests in the last decade of the Suharto regime. Equally important, he had been a member of the governing board of the large socioeducational Muslim organization, Muhammadiyah, since 1985, and was general chair from 1995 to 2000.

Amien experimented by forming an open party, PAN, which helped him to win support across the Muslim community, including traditionalists and liberals as well as modernists. His experimentation also helped him somewhat to soften his long-perceived sectarian image as a fierce defender of Muslim, particularly modernist, interests against secular nationalism and other religious groups.

Despite these efforts, Amien was well aware that he could not completely escape his own sectarian past and tried to soften it further with his choice of a running mate. As a civilian, he weighed various possibilities from the military. He also considered picking a running mate from outside Java because he himself was born in central Java of an Arab-Javanese family. In addition, he weighed the possibility of picking someone with a nationalist background.

Amien's initial political capital was small. His National Mandate Party drew only 6.4 percent in the 2004 legislative election, a percentage far too low to make him a strong presidential candidate, though high enough for PAN to nominate him. Amien then turned to Muhammadiyah for support. As the second-largest Muslim organization in Indonesia, it could of course be counted on to add more votes, hopefully enough for Amien to make it to the second round.

PAN and Amien then approached PKS, the best known and most respected Islamic party at the time. PKS leaders did not unambiguously support Amien, however. Their initial decision was not to enter the presidential election arena at all, but instead to claim the high moral ground in anticipation of an ideologically pure PKS candidate in 2009. In the end, however, this position succumbed to internal party pressure to support some candidate rather than none, and Amien was clearly preferable to the secular Megawati.

With Muhammadiyah's direct support, Amien Rais was widely seen as the strongest presidential candidate representing the Muslim community. The need for a vice presidential candidate led him to choose a nationalist in hopes of forming a winning coalition. Who had the most credibility to fill this role? Amien first tried to find a military candidate but finally settled on Siswono Yudohusodo, a prominent businessman with a long track record as a nationalist politician and New Order government official. Amien also calculated that victory in the presidential contest would be determined by the appeal of the presidential, not the vice presidential, candidate. The role of the vice president was secondary, adding some votes from a different camp but not determinative.

In the final analysis, the strategy of all these candidate pairs was the same. The term "catchall party," introduced earlier, is also appropriate to describe the catchall pairing of candidates in Indonesian presidential politics.

Hamzah Haz-Agum Gumelar

Compared to other candidates, PPP's Hamzah Haz was slow to decide. His initial political capital was relatively large, because he was the incumbent vice president and chair of the fourth-largest party in the parliamentary election. The apparent reason for Hamzah's delay was that he was waiting for a signal from Megawati. During that period, Megawati and her team were calculating and recalculating how to find the best vice presidential candidate, the one who would add the most votes to her ticket.

As described above, Megawati in the end chose Hasyim Muzadi. But the long delay had an unfortunate impact on PPP. In the words of a PPP chair, the party was made hostage to the process. PPP was also taken captive by Golkar, which was in the process of choosing a running mate for Wiranto. Wiranto's exploration of possibilities had led him to ask if

Hamzah Haz would be willing to be his vice presidential candidate. But Wiranto was still waiting to hear from Salahuddin Wahid. If Salahuddin did not accept, Hamzah Haz would become the alternative.

Because of being held hostage to two internal party decision-making processes that PPP leaders could not control, the time that was available became much shorter, including of course the time to calculate and choose their own vice presidential candidate. When they finally decided to nominate Hamzah Haz for president, they had to very quickly choose a vice presidential candidate as well.

A number of names were already on Hamzah's list. In the end, he chose retired army General Agum Gumelar. The calculation was that Agum was known as a military figure with a nationalist orientation so that he could add votes from that side of the spectrum to a Muslim presidential candidate. The logic of Hamzah and PPP, as we see, was the same as that of the others, that is, how to embrace nationalist and Islamic groups at the same time.

In the final analysis, there was only a single pattern of political recruitment for president and vice president in 2004. All the players calculated sociological factors, especially differences of religion or religious orientation, regionalism or ethnicity, professional background, and partisan strength. Another way to put this is that they were all imprisoned by these sociological and partisan factors.

The five pairs that we have described contested the 2004 presidential election. There were surprises. Yudhoyono-Kalla, with the least party support, about 10 percent, won the most votes (34 percent), defeating Megawati-Hasyim who won 27 percent even though their combined party strength was much greater. Wiranto was in third place (24 percent) even though he had the greatest party support. Amien, supported by PAN and PKS, only won 14 percent, and Hamzah brought up the rear with only about 6 percent of the voters. Because none of the teams won more than 50 percent, a second round was held as required by the Constitution.

The candidates who contested the runoff were Yudhoyono-Kalla and Megawati-Hasyim. The defeated parties from the first round formed coalitions with one or the other of the victorious candidates. The parties that had supported Amien-Siswono, especially PAN and PKS, joined the Yudhoyono-Kalla camp, while Golkar, PKB, PPP, and several small parties joined Megawati-Hasyim. The strength of the Megawati-Hasyim voting bloc in terms of number of supporting parties was greater than 50 percent, a seemingly solid majority. In the event, Yudhoyono-Kalla won the second round decisively, 60.2 percent to the 39.8 percent of Megawati-Hasyim.

B. The 2009 Presidential Election

In 2009, the candidate pairs changed and also the way in which they were formed, especially in the case of Yudhoyono-Boediono, which was to become the victorious team. Sociological factors were no longer as determinative. Psychological factors and pure political calculations played a bigger role in determining candidate selection in 2009.

Yudhoyono-Boediono

The incumbent President Yudhoyono's decision to join with Boediono overturned the sociological assumptions that had become the basic doctrine of Indonesian electoral politics. Yudhoyono set aside the Java-outside Java and nationalism-Islam dichotomies. His calculation was more psychological, in the sense that he believed his own appeal as a candidate was enough to win the hearts of a sufficient number of voters. He also believed, and stated publicly, that voters prefer candidates who are perceived to be competent, have integrity, are clean, honest, and well mannered.

Approaching the election, Yudhoyono announced his vice presidential criteria: capability or competence to govern, acceptability to the voters, a consistent record of integrity, straightforwardness, freedom from legal and moral stains in conducting the public's business, and loyalty or capacity to work with the president, including not creating conflict with the president. Approaching the deadline for vice presidential selection, four names were considered seriously: Jusuf Kalla, the incumbent vice president, Aburizal Bakrie, a prominent businessman, party leader, and government official, Boediono, an economist and central banker, and Kuntoro Mangunsubroto, the respected head of the Aceh Reconstruction and Rehabilitation Agency created after the 2004 tsunami. Yudhoyono chose Boediono.

In the process of nominating Boediono, there were strong negative reactions from several quarters. Most fascinating, Amien Rais, the influential PAN leader, complained that the choice of Boediono didn't fit the classic normative model of Indonesian politics, in which the national leadership must reflect religious and regional diversity, pious Islam and syncretism, Java and non-Java. Amien's way of thinking was typical of many, and in fact was also part of Yudhoyono's calculations. But the public opinion surveys showed that the classic model was no longer important; Yudhoyono believed in the results of the study and, on that basis, chose Boediono as his running mate.[14]

Before and during the campaign, there were a number of attempts to undermine Boediono, especially in connection with the issues of religion, regionalism, and economic ideology. Perhaps most potentially damaging was the accusation that Boediono, an economist and graduate of the prestigious Wharton School in the United States, was a "neoliberal" responsible for impoverishing the people. But the majority of parties who had seats in Parliament continued to support the Yudhoyono-Boediono team. After Partai Demokrat, PKB, PPP, PAN, and PKS formally added their support.

Jusuf Kalla-Wiranto

After Golkar named Kalla its presidential candidate, a strategic problem arose for the party. With which party or parties should Golkar coalesce in order to defeat Yudhoyono? Golkar and PDIP had each won only 14 percent of the parliamentary vote while the minimal percentage to nominate a candidate was 20 percent. Moreover, most of the large parties had already joined Yudhoyono's coalition. Among the parties with parliamentary representation, only four were left: Golkar and PDIP, Hanura (4 percent), and Gerindra (5 percent).

Golkar took the initiative to form a coalition with PDIP. That initiative failed because PDIP wanted Megawati to become its presidential candidate and Golkar wanted Kalla. In the end, Golkar went back to Wiranto, its 2004 presidential candidate. The votes for his party, Hanura, were far below Golkar's. So, in the end, Golkar and Hanura nominated their two top leaders as their presidential and vice presidential candidates respectively.

By their campaign teams, Kalla-Wiranto were considered to best reflect the diversity of Indonesia of all the candidates. Many educated people, including many public intellectuals, agreed. Interestingly, this near-consensus ran against the tendency to that point in the post-Suharto democratic period for public intellectuals to oppose wealthy candidates and candidates thought to be responsible for the violence and repression of the last days of the New Order in May 1998.

The success team for Kalla-Wiranto believed in the vote-getting power of primordial sentiments. Kalla and Wiranto were also considered decisive

---

[14] In addition to the public record, the information in the above paragraphs about Yudhoyono's views comes from our direct discussions with him.

leaders, and therefore antithetical to the notoriously indecisive Yudhoyono, and as well bridged the syncretism-pious Islam and Java-outer island gaps. Finally, Kalla represented pious Muslims and outer islanders, Wiranto religious syncretists, and Javanese.

In their campaign, Kalla-Wiranto paid close attention to socioreligious networks. They approached the NU and Muhammadiyah chairs for photo opportunities. Religious symbols were obvious on their posters. They posed their wives in Muslim headscarves on their advertising posters and billboards, with Muslim schools and students in the background. In public speeches, Wiranto claimed, against the common perception of his syncretist background, that both his and Kalla's wives regularly wore the headscarf.

The point was to draw a contrast with Yudhoyono and Boediono, neither of whose wives wore a scarf. Wiranto was convinced that religious symbolism weighs heavily in voters' choices in presidential elections. Emphasizing his own Islamicness was a way of persuading the voters that Yudhoyono and Boediono were not as good Muslims. The mobilization of religious sentiment was so pervasive that Yudhoyono and Boediono had to confront many rumors. A pamphlet circulated claiming that Boediono's wife was a Christian. Of course, their campaign team acted quickly to refute that story.

Megawati Sukarnoputri-Prabowo Subianto

Megawati and Prabowo's coalition consisted of her PDIP and his Gerindra. In their attacks on the incumbent, Yudhoyono, the pair took a populist, propoor line rather than one based on religious, regional, or civilian-military cleavages. Both Megawati and Prabowo are from the same subculture, Javanese and syncretist, although some observers argued that they are more representative of the whole of the archipelago than Yudhoyono-Boediono. Prabowo's mother comes from Manado, North Sulawesi, and is Christian, while Yudhoyono and Boediono are both from East Java, indeed from a subregion of East Java once part of the Mataram kingdom, which was strongly influenced by Hindu and local mystical and syncretistic culture, in contrast to the more Islamic coastal areas of Java.

Bringing Megawati and Prabowo together was difficult. Prabowo approached Megawati after the parties from which he hoped to win support refused him. On Megawati's side there had also been problems. After she failed to form a coalition with Golkar, Megawati had no other choice but to accept Prabowo in order to fulfill the minimum quota for the presidential nomination.

From inside PDIP many opposed an invitation to Prabowo. Even though both candidates and their parties claimed to be economic populists, Prabowo was considered a controversial figure and once an enemy of PDIP. He is a retired army officer and onetime son-in-law of President Suharto and was considered personally responsible for severe violations of human rights, including the alleged murder of anti-Suharto dissidents. He had been forced to step down by an armed forces investigative board from his last position in the army. PDIP in the 1990s was one of the principal victims of Suharto's repression and allegedly Prabowo's actions.

More to the point, perhaps, many PDIP leaders were not convinced that Megawati could defeat Yudhoyono. To save Megawati and the party from a second defeat at the hands of Yudhoyono, they proposed that Megawati not be nominated. They were also feeling the pain of having been in opposition for the past five years, which had significantly reduced the resources available to rebuild the party structure. One faction preferred the party to forge a coalition with Partai Demokrat and support the candidacy of Yudhoyono-Boediono, especially since Megawati was known to be close to Boediono.

Yudhoyono himself opened the door wide to PDIP and to Megawati herself. It soon became clear, however, that one of the members of Yudhoyono's coalition, PKS, had strong objections and that there was a high probability that PKS would withdraw in the event of a PDIP-Demokrat coalition. This objection reached Yudhoyono's ears. The president concluded, however, that even if PKS left the chances that he and Boediono would win were still very high. In Yudhoyono's view, PDIP and PKS voters shared a common characteristic: They were both very loyal to their organization and leaders. If PKS left, with its base of support of about 8 percent, it would be replaced by the support base of PDIP which was almost twice as large at 14 percent. So Yudhoyono felt safe if PKS left him.

In the end, Yudhoyono's attempt to form a coalition with PDIP failed. The most fundamental problem was Megawati's personal hostility. Megawati believes that Yudhoyono betrayed her when he withdrew from his position as Coordinating Minister for Politics and Security, then ran against and defeated her in the 2004 presidential election. In the middle of these difficulties and constrained choices, Megawati and PDIP embraced Prabowo and his Gerindra party.

Yudhoyono-Boediono won the election convincingly as had been predicted by most surveys. They won in the first round with 61 percent of the

vote, versus Megawati-Prabowo with 27 percent. Jusuf Kalla-Wiranto ran
a poor third with 12 percent.

A. The 2014 Presidential Election

Joko Widodo-Jusuf Kalla

In the 2014 election a new figure emerged: Joko Widodo, familiarly called
Jokowi. To most Indonesians, Jokowi is an average, ordinary citizen. He
was born and raised in modest circumstances on the outskirts of the city of
Solo, central Java, in a house considered shabby even by most Indonesians.
His greatest claim to elite status in his childhood was that his grandfather on
his mother's side was a village head.[15]

The family business was carpentry. As a youth, Jokowi worked for an
uncle who had a furniture business. In these circumstances, Jokowi's
parents and Jokowi himself thought that his best chance of success in
life was to remain in the business. Accordingly, at Gadjah Mada
University, a renowned state university located in Yogyakarta, he studied
forest engineering, graduating in 1985.

Back in Solo, Jokowi returned to the carpentry world, now at a higher
level as a furniture manufacturer, although he continued to present himself as a carpenter (*tukang kayu*), not as a businessman in the furniture
business (*pengusaha kayu*). At the same time, he showed some recognition
of the importance for business of government and military connections.
His business grew, to the point that he was able to export his products to
Europe.

During this period, Jokowi "became increasingly interested in trying to
improve the lives of ordinary citizens, who he believed were unjustly
trapped in bad public services managed by incompetent and corrupt officials" (Mietzner 2015, p. 25). In 2005, he was elected mayor of Solo, the
first popularly elected mayor since democratization. He was nominated by
PDIP, then the largest party in the city, with which he had not been
previously affiliated. He won reelection in 2010.

As mayor, Jokowi's many achievements and direct political style, in
sharp contrast to the stilted bureaucratic approach of most other officials,
brought him national attention as a role model for democratic leadership
at the local level. In 2012, he was nominated by PDIP for the governorship
of Jakarta, the country's most important office below the national level.

---

[15] Concerning Jokowi's family and childhood in the context of his political career see
Mietzner (2015).

Against the prediction of many, he defeated the well-funded and connected incumbent, and was elected to a five-year term.

His victory in the Jakarta gubernatorial election prompted a rapid rise in his national popularity. Close associates and potential political allies began to encourage him to run for the presidency as the candidate of the PDIP. This was not an easy decision for the PDIP itself, which had been expected to renominate former President Megawati. In the end, she and other party leaders were persuaded by the many opinion surveys, public and privately commissioned, indicating that Jokowi was by far the stronger candidate.

Jusuf Kalla, already vice president during President Yudhoyono's first term, and a presidential candidate himself in 2009, became his running mate. In addition to representing the outer islands and pious Islam against Jokowi's syncretism and Javanese base, Kalla was thought to add the weight of experienced governmental leadership at the national level, to which Jokowi was a newcomer. The partisan coalition supporting the ticket consisted of PDIP, PKB, Hanura, and Nasdem.

Prabowo Subianto-Hatta Rajasa
The Jokowi-Kalla team was opposed by only one other set of candidates, the presidential and vice presidential ticket of Prabowo Subianto and Hatta Rajasa. The social and historic contrast between the two presidential candidates was sharp.

Prabowo was born into an elite family.[16] His father, Sumitro Djojohadikusumo, was one of very few educated Indonesians before Indonesian independence in 1945 and his grandfather had been the founder of the Indonesian national bank. As a university student in the Netherlands, Sumitro joined the independence struggle, becoming an internationally prominent leader of the democratic socialist PSI (Partai Sosialis Indonesia, Indonesian Socialist Party). While it subsequently received less than 3 percent of the vote in the first democratic election in 1955, PSI was a powerful party during its early years, winning the support of many public intellectuals, especially non-Islamists, and wealthy indigenous business people. Sumitro himself was several times a government minister in the early to mid-1950s.

In the late 1950s, Sumitro joined the PRRI (Pemerintahan Revolusioner Rakyat Indonesia, Indonesian People's Revolutionary Government), an outer island based armed movement. The PRRI was soon defeated by the

---

[16] On Prabowo's background and career before entering politics, see Mietzner (2015).

central government's armed forces, and Sumitro went into exile abroad, not to return until the end of Sukarno's rule in 1967. Prabowo, born in 1951, followed his father into exile. On his return from exile, Sumitro was named minister of trade by the new Suharto government and also played a key role in building the renowned economics faculty at the University of Indonesia in Jakarta. At his death in 2001, he was widely regarded as the most important economic thinker in the history of the Republic.

Prabowo's family is not only highly educated, with deep roots in the revolution and a prominent place in the national leadership, but is also cosmopolitan. Sumitro, a Javanese Muslim, married a Christian girl from Minahasa who did not convert to Islam, a rarity in the national elite of the time. Compare with the polygamous then-President Sukarno, one of whose wives was a Japanese entertainer who bowed to convention by converting to Islam. That convention remains strong today.

But the Sumitro family behaved otherwise. Not only was Sumitro himself monogamous, and married to a Christian, but his children were given freedom to choose their own religions. Prabowo chose Islam, his older sister is Catholic, and his younger brother, prominent businessman and Gerindra financier, Hashim Djojohadikusumo, is Protestant. Few other Indonesian families, elite or mass, are so inclusive!

After returning to Indonesia at the beginning of Suharto's New Order, Prabowo chose a military career. He was accepted in the national military academy, from which he graduated in 1974, one class after Susilo Bambang Yudhoyono. He then joined the elite Kopassus (Komando Pasukan Khusus, Special Forces Command), eventually becoming its commander. In March 1998, he was named Commander of the Army Strategic Reserve Command (a position previously held by both Suharto and Wiranto), in control of troops guarding the national capital. His rank was lieutenant general, the highest he would achieve.

In 1983, Prabowo married one of President Suharto's daughters, after which his career advanced rapidly (they were divorced in 1998). From the early 1990s, he was widely projected to be Suharto's most likely successor as president, either through anointment by Suharto or by overthrowing him. Whatever his and Suharto's intentions, history was not on Prabowo's side. The 1997 Asian financial crisis shook the Indonesian economy, forcing Suharto to resign as president, ending thirty-two years of authoritarian rule.

Prabowo's military career ended with Suharto's resignation and replacement by Vice President B. J. Habibie. Prabowo was first demoted, then discharged from military service. The armed forces commander, General Wiranto, and an armed forces investigating board found him guilty of insubordination in the abduction of anti-Suharto activists in early 1998. After leaving the military, Prabowo moved to Jordan on the invitation of his friend King Abdullah II, where he pursued a business career.

Despite his disgrace, Prabowo was able to return to Indonesia and to politics before the 2004 election, when he ran unsuccessfully for Partai Golkar's presidential nomination. He then formed Gerindra, becoming Megawati's 2009 vice presidential candidate. In 2014, he finally became a presidential candidate, running with Hatta Rajasa. Hatta, then chair of PAN, had been a senior minister in the second cabinet of President Yudhoyono. Their supporting coalition included Gerindra, Golkar, PPP, PKS, PAN, and PBB.

The 2014 presidential election ended with the victory of Jokowi, an ordinary citizen from a humble background, over Prabowo, the scion of a privileged family but with a troubled personal past, by 53 percent to 47 percent, marking a significant break from the previous dominance of presidential politics by national level elites. Why did Jokowi defeat Prabowo? Why did Yudhoyono win over Megawati in 2004 and 2009, and also over Wiranto in 2004 and Jusuf Kalla in 2009? By observing the various combinations, together with the election strategies that were formulated by the respective campaign teams and party leaderships, we can construct a number of empirically testable hypotheses. Each strategy formulated by the candidates and their parties was based upon considerations and calculations about the probability of winning the parliamentary and presidential elections. The following chapters examine these possibilities empirically.

CONCLUSIONS

Indonesian national politics, in its first democratic decade plus, has been marked by substantial changes in voters' behavior. Turnout in parliamentary and presidential elections declined sharply, from about 85 percent in 1999 to about 70 percent in 2009, although it recovered somewhat to 75 percent in the 2014 parliamentary election. If turnout is an indicator of the quality of democracy, as many democratic theorists claim, we can conclude that Indonesian democracy today is of lower quality than it was ten years ago.

The pattern of political choice has also been transformed over this period. Four elections have produced three different parties receiving a plurality of the vote. Of these, one experienced a precipitous decline: PDIP, from 34 percent in 1999 to 14 percent in 2009, but improved considerably by 2014, to 19 percent. Another not yet born in 1999, Partai Demokrat, enjoyed a comparably steep rise and received 21 percent of the vote in 2009, but which dropped sharply to 10 percent in 2014.

Change is also visible in the presidential elections. Presidential candidates who have been supported by the largest party or by a coalition of parties with the most votes have not themselves always received the most votes. The decisions of party elites to form coalitions supporting particular candidates have frequently not been followed by those parties' voters.

What explains these characteristics of the Indonesian voter? We argue that the decline in voter turnout, the rapid change in relative party strengths, and the equally rapid vertical mobility that we have observed in the cases of Yudhoyono and Jokowi reflect the growth of a group of voters whom we have labeled critical democrats. Chapters 4–6 systematically explore the effects of the range of independent variables that have been proposed in both the comparative and Indonesian electoral literature on the formation of this group.

4

Sociological and Demographic Factors

In the sociological model, the prime movers of participation and political choice are differences in gender, age, ethnicity or regional residence, religion and level of piety, and social class as measured by urban versus rural residence, level of education, income, and type of employment. Indonesian scholars and politicians have paid most attention to religion, ethnicity, and social class, all of which have been considered prime movers (Samadhi and Warouw 2009; Aspinall and Mietzner 2010; Hadiz 2010; Winters 2011).

Examination of voters in these terms may also help us locate sociologically Norris' (1999, 2011) critical citizens in the Indonesian case. Of particular potential interest, perhaps, is the comparison between Indonesia and other Muslim-majority countries in an era in which there are few democracies in those countries. For these reasons, we open our analysis with consideration of these factors.

RELIGION AND RELIGIOSITY

Religion and Participation

Many studies show that religion, in older democracies such as the United States and newer ones in Asia and Latin America, influences citizens to become involved in their religious communities in ways that are not political, including societal organizations like churches, religious study groups, and charitable foundations. Further, citizens who are active in the socioreligious sphere tend to be active in the nonreligious sphere. They become volunteers in schools, orphanages, members of women's groups, farmers' groups, cooperatives, youth groups, and so on.

These active citizens subsequently find themselves in broader social networks that make them available for political mobilization. Political activists use these networks, leading to interaction between citizens who are religiously devout and active in socioreligious organizations and those who are active in nonreligious social organizations. These mobilized citizens in turn have more opportunities to be involved in politics, so they tend to be more motivated to participate in elections and election campaigns (Leege and Kellstedt 1993; Shin 1999; Tocqueville 2000).

Some argue that this pattern may only be relevant to the Christian world. Huntington famously (or notoriously) claimed that "political participation is a foreign concept in Muslim societies" (Huntington 1993, 284). If there is political participation in Muslim societies, he asserted, it is not likely to be secularly motivated, because in Islam there is no distinction between the religious and political communities (Huntington 1993, 307).

If Huntington is correct, Muslim Indonesian citizens are less likely to vote and also to participate in election campaigns. The Indonesian evidence, however, does not support Huntington's claim: Muslims are in fact more likely to participate in elections than Christians. The proportion of Christians and Muslims who vote for members of Parliament is about the same. In presidential elections, there is a substantial, though inconsistent difference, albeit in the opposite direction from Huntington's prediction! In the 2004 presidential election, for example, the proportion of Muslims who voted (85 percent to 69 percent in the first round, 77 percent to 65 percent in the second round) is greater than that for Christians.

These findings must be examined further to determine the independence of religious identity from other factors. It is possible that the difference is rooted in socioeconomic status (SES) components like level of education or type of employment, since Christians enjoy a higher SES status, and for that reason are more critical and act more often as freeriders, not participating in elections. We are getting ahead of our analysis, however, since free riding will be examined in detail in Chapter 5. Apart from that, the evidence shows at least that voting in national elections is not something that is foreign to Indonesian Muslims relative to Indonesian non-Muslims.

Another picture emerges in campaigns. There is a difference in level of campaign participation between Muslims and Christians, though the difference is inconsistent or statistically insignificant. In the first round of the 2004 presidential election and in the 2009 parliamentary election, Christians had a greater tendency to participate in campaigns, although this finding does not hold for other elections.[1] The lack of statistical significance is also apparent in the data on assisting in campaigns, donating, and persuading others to vote. There is no indication that proportionally fewer Muslims than Christians assist or donate to campaigns or try to influence others.[2]

Religion is not only a matter of identity but also of religiosity, or intensity of belief. This dimension may be more important in Indonesia because it measures a key concept in local religious life, the distinction between *santri*, pious orthodox Muslims, and *abangan*, less Islamically pious believers in a mix of animistic and Hindu-derived religious traditions that for a long time has captivated scholars' and politicians' understanding of Indonesian politics (Geertz 1960, 1965; Liddle 1970; Emmerson 1976; Gaffar 1992; Mallarangeng 1997; King 2003; Baswedan 2004).

This formulation has potentially greater value in explaining political participation in the Indonesian case. The connection between the two formulations, Islam versus Christianity and *santri* versus *abangan*, may be negative, as hypothesized by those who believe that political participation is a foreign concept for Muslims. In other words, the more religious a Muslim, or the more obedient in carrying out the obligations of his or her religion, the less likely he or she will be to participate in politics.

Before discussing the pattern of the relationship between Muslim religiosity and political participation, we should first look at descriptions of Muslim religiosity.[3] Most Muslim Indonesians seem to be pious, at least if we use the intensity of ritual practice as the basic measure of religiosity at the level of religious practice as did Geertz[4] (Geertz 1960; Hasan 2002; Mujani 2007).

[1] The levels of campaign participation between Muslims and Christians were 8 percent and 15 percent in the 2004 presidential election (first round), 14 percent and 26 percent in the 2009 parliamentary election, 8 percent and 7 percent in the 2009 presidential election, and 9 percent and 9 percent (the 2014 presidential election).
[2] The level of participation in those three types of activities were all below 10 percent and the proportional difference between Muslims and Christians was under 4 percent for the parliamentary elections of 2009 and 2014 and the presidential elections of 2009 and 2014.
[3] Scientific studies of religion or religiosity at the mass level through public opinion surveys focus on a number of measures connected to faith such as belief in God, the Last Judgment, and so on, and in religious rituals such as prayer or reading holy books (Leege and Kellstedt 1993; Inglehart and Norris 2006; Mujani 2007).
[4] Here we present only the behavioral component to describe religiosity. The belief component is not presented because of its lesser explanatory power due to the fact that there is so little variation among respondents. When asked in direct interviews, almost all Indonesians claim to believe in God, life after death, the existence of prophets sent from God, and so on. For these studies, see Mujani (2007) and Hasan (2002). In this study, religiosity in the form of ritual is only Muslim religiosity. This does not mean that the religiosity of others is not

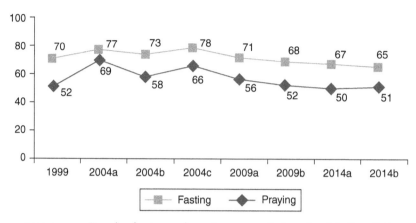

FIGURE 4.1 Regular fasting and praying among Indonesian Muslims (%)

A majority of Indonesian Muslims pray five times daily and fast annually during the month of Ramadhan, a religious requirement for all healthy adult Muslims[5] (Figure 4.1). On average, the proportions were around 57 percent praying and 71 percent fasting. A significant but atypical minority do not fast annually. The *abangan*, who are in a formal sense Muslims but do not or rarely carry out the obligations of their religion, like praying or fasting, are also a significant number. Finally, there are many Muslims who perform very frequently recommended but not required rituals such as salat sunnah or extra prayers (about 17 percent), collective prayers (about 16 percent), and participating in Islamic study groups (*kelompok pengajian*) (16 percent).[6]

---

important, but rather that it is very difficult to compare interfaith religiosity. For example, Muslim and Christian rituals are very different. In Islam there is an obligatory ritual, the five daily prayers, while in Christianity, especially Protestantism, this is not ritual but belief. Comparisons are easier at the level of belief but variation in levels of belief among Indonesian Muslims, as previously explained, is very small, and thus has little explanatory power.

[5] Other than prayer and fasting during Ramadhan, Muslims are required to pay alms and take the pilgrimage to Mecca. But both of these rituals have as a condition that the believer is economically able to perform them, which is not the case for prayers and fasting. For this reason, alms and fasting are not used in this study because they discriminate between more and less well-off Muslims. Moreover, the number is great, especially for those who are not prosperous enough to take the pilgrimage.

[6] Conceptually or theoretically, obligatory (*wajib*) and permissible (*sunnah*) rituals are different, and therefore must be treated differently. Factor analyses of the survey data

We find that those who carry out required prayers also perform recommended prayers, but not the reverse. If it is true that political participation is foreign to Muslim communities, we would expect that Muslims who perform these rituals, required or recommended, would not participate in politics. A correlation analysis indicates that this claim is incorrect. Pious Muslims who regularly carry out the obligations of their religion tend to be more active politically.[7] Or at least there is no indication of a significant and consistent negative relationship between Muslim religiosity and political participation such as voting in an election, participating in a campaign, supporting a candidate or party, or giving money to a candidate or party.[8]

In a previous, more comprehensive, study Mujani (2007) concluded that

There are no Islamic elements that correlate negatively and significantly with any dimension of political participation. Further, almost all of the elements of Islam correlate positively and significantly with almost all of the dimensions of political participation .... Islam does not correlate negatively and significantly with voting .... Recommended prayers, membership in a network of Islamic civic associations, Nahdlatul Ulama identity, Muhammadiyah identity, and Islamism correlate positively and significantly with campaign activities and cooperative social activities.

Huntington's further claim that political participation in Muslim societies is always connected to matters that are specifically Islamic is also not the

used in this study show that the two forms of ritual are in fact different. For elaboration, see Mujani (2007).

[7] As explained in the previous footnote, in the factor analysis these ritual items combine into two dimensions of Muslim religiosity – obligatory and recommended rituals. This demonstrates the validity and reliability of the measures of Muslim religiosity used in this study because the two forms of ritual do in fact differ conceptually and have a different meaning for Muslims. Nonetheless, to simplify the analysis and because the two dimensions correlate positively, we have combined them into a single index of Muslim religiosity scaled 1–4, where 1 means not at all religious and 4 means very religious. The coefficient of reliability of this index (Cronbach Alpha) is reasonably high, above .75.

[8] "Other participation" in this analysis for the 1999 and 2004 elections means ever participating in a campaign in the form of attending an open meeting or rally before an election with the code 1=ever, 0=never. For the 2009 and 2014 elections, other participation includes not only ever openly participating in a campaign but also supporting a party, campaign team or candidate, giving a donation, and persuading others to choose a candidate or party. Each item is coded 1 "forever" and 0 for "never." The score for these four items was combined to make an index scaled 0–4, where 0 means never and 4 very often. In the 1999 and 2004 elections other participation means participating in open campaign meetings or rallies. In the 2009 and 2014 elections, "other participation" refers not just to the campaign, but also to supporting and donating money to a party or candidate and persuading others to vote for a candidate or party.

case in Indonesia (Mujani 2007). Indonesian Muslims participate in all types of political activity without regard to Islamic or non-Islamic content. They attend citizens' meetings, organize society to resolve common problems, engage public officials, attend general meetings in campaign season, participate in campaign parades, support political parties, organize and sign petitions on public matters, participate in demonstrations, and other direct political actions. All these political activities are connected positively and significantly with their expressed piety.

To sum up the argument to this point: In Indonesia religion does not obstruct but instead drives participation. How does this happen? The "civic voluntarism" model asserts that socioeconomic status (SES) alone is not enough to ensure the political activity of a citizen (Verba, Schlozman, and Brady 1995). A person with a higher SES will not necessarily possess civic virtue or a higher level of civic-mindedness. It is entirely possible that a citizen with a lower SES will have a higher level of civic-mindedness because he or she has been more involved in social activities that do not require a higher SES.

These social activities often coincide with religious social activities that are motivated by religious belief. A religious person for example attends church on Sunday or participates as a volunteer in a church-sponsored activity, or he or she attends Qur'anic study groups in the evening. None of these activities requires much material outlay or level of education. During those religion-sponsored activities they can hear advice or have a discussion about matters of broader societal significance, including parliamentary and presidential elections. In these activities, they can also learn about the meaning of elections. In this way, it is not only citizens with high SES's who are involved in social activities who have a high probability of participating in elections and election campaigns. In the tradition of this civic voluntarism model, religion becomes an important factor promoting the spirit of societal involvement.

The positive connection between religion and political participation in the civic voluntarism tradition is connected to the involvement of citizens in the activities of religious communities, but not because of their religiosity. Many pious people carry out religious obligations such as prayers or fasting, but not necessarily or always in the religious context alone. Performing the five daily prayers, or engaging in Qur'anic study alone at home has little social content. There is a tendency, however, for citizens who are pious believers to be active in the community aspects of their religion as well, including collective Qur'anic studies, collective prayers for the deceased, collective ritual meals, membership in religious foundations, volunteering in church, and so on (Mujani 2007). Involvement in one's religious community opens a space for involvement in the larger nonreligious community.

Because of interaction in civic associations, an individual acquires information about various public activities and is inspired, influenced, and motivated to acquire additional information about public affairs. He or she becomes more active in discussing these affairs and subsequently forms attitudes toward those political institutions that are close at hand like political parties, and becomes more interested in politics. Finally, such a citizen participates directly in political activities.

There is thus a series of steps taken by citizens before participating in politics that helps explain the role of religion: first, they are religious, then they are involved in religion-based social organizations, then in nonreligion-based organizations (unions, *arisan* [rotating credit associations], village associations, farmers' groups, sports groups, and so on). Here they become psychologically involved and begin to follow political news, discuss politics, identify with parties, and finally participate in political activities.

In this model people participate in politics not simply because they have resources, such as a higher level of prosperity, but also because they become accustomed to participating in social networks, which prepares them for political mobilization. Nonetheless, the fact that individuals are more reachable is not in itself a sufficient condition for political participation. They must also have a desire or interest to do so. Even if they are wealthy, religious, active in social organizations, and know a lot about politics, but nonetheless are not interested in politics, they will not participate.

Verba, Schlozman, and Brady (1995, 15–16) formulated the problem clearly. Religious citizens tend to be active in religious social organizations, and citizens who are active in religious social organizations tend to be active in nonreligious ones as well. They care more about and are more interested in public issues, feel close to political parties, and are more active in politics, for example through voting, participating in campaigns, helping candidates or parties, persuading others, and so on. In this context, it is important to pay close attention to civic and political engagement.

The logic of the relationship between social involvement and political participation is found in the greater openness of the political network. Involvement in social activities via socioreligious organizations like Nahdlatul Ulama and Muhammadiyah and nonreligious organizations like neighborhood youth associations, rotating credit associations, neighborhood and ward associations, professional organizations, hobbyist groups, and so on, opens channels of information and communication concerning public affairs, encouraging citizens to become involved. In addition, people who are involved in social groups are very likely to be ready to be mobilized by that group (Parry, Moyser, and Day 1992, 85).

Involvement in citizens' associations and interest in politics also tend to have a direct influence on political participation, since involvement in citizens' associations and political involvement are closely interrelated (van Deth 1989, 12). The direct relationship is described by Olsen (1972, 317–318) as broadening one's sphere of concerns, exposure to others, and increasing acquisition of information. With this involvement, a citizen becomes more attracted to politics, discusses politics more, is better able to follow politics in the mass media, and not infrequently becomes attracted to a political party, leading to eventual partisanship. All of this reflects a psychological political model that can strengthen political participation, which we will discuss in Chapter 6.

What is the effect of involvement in social organizations on political participation? Bivariate analysis indicates that such involvement tends to increase the level of citizen participation in parliamentary and presidential elections, and also in other forms of participation such as participating in party and presidential campaigns, helping parties or candidates, and persuading others.[9] The gap between members and nonmembers is on average about 9 percent, meaning about 9 percent higher among members relative to nonmembers of the organizations who participate in political activities.

This confirms our previous finding that involvement in a Muslim religious organization tends to be inclusive, in the sense that Muslims

---

[9] In this analysis, membership in religious organizations is the total of the score for membership in NU, Muhammadiyah, and churches. Membership in nonreligious social organizations is the total of the scores of memberships in labor and farmers' groups and associations. Each item was coded 1 for "member" and 0 for "nonmember." For the crosstabs, this index was simplified into two categories: member if the score was 1 or more, and nonmember if the score was 0. "Other participation" in the 2009 data consisted of 4 items: participating in a campaign, supporting or donating to a party or candidate, and persuading others to vote for a candidate or party. Each item was coded into two categories: 1=ever participated; 0=never. The total scores for this participation formed an index from 0 to 4. For the crosstabs, the index was simplified into two categories: 0=never, 1 or more, ever participated or carried out the activity. In the 2004 data, "other participation" only consisted of one item, that is, participation in the campaign (code 1=ever participated, 0=never participated).

are also likely to be active in nonreligious organizations (Mujani 2007). Involvement in nonreligious organizations did not, however, contribute significantly to increased voting. Nonetheless it did help to increase participation in other political activities such as campaigns, helping and donating to parties and candidates, and persuading others to vote.[10]

Why are religious more important than nonreligious organizations in raising the turnout level? Those involved in religious organizations are far more likely to be political activists. As a result, citizens who are in this network are more likely to be mobilized than are those in nonreligious organizations. We can see this clearly in the higher level of contact by parties, politicians, and local notables with citizens who are members of religious compared to nonreligious organizations.[11] To be sure, there are large numbers of farmers, workers (and also citizens who engage in sports), but the data show that farmers and workers who become members of organizations are far fewer in number than religious believers who become members of the relevant religious organizations. "Bowling alone," Putnam's (2000) famous phrase coined for Americans, also applies to Indonesian workers, farmers, and people who engage in sports. They like sports, but engage in them alone. They farm, but farm alone. As a result, they are less well organized than they should be as a source of civic virtue.

In sum, the civic voluntarism model helps to explain why religion and religious organizations are important for political participation. Religion is important in the context of democratic participation in general, but its importance for partisan affiliation is perhaps even greater, because it divides the voters when they enter the polling place.

Religion and Elections

In the still embryonic Indonesian electoral research tradition, religion is the most talked-about factor, widely believed to be the most important in shaping citizens' political choices. This belief has deep scholarly roots in the early twentieth century, before Indonesia became a nation-state. At the beginning of the independence movement against Dutch colonial rule, many organizations emerged, some based on religion, others on secular

---

[10] It is always the case in all our surveys that the levels of participation in those activities among the members of nonreligious organizations have been higher than of those who were not members.

[11] In 2004a, 2004c, 2009a and 2009c, contacts made by parties and politicians with members of religious organizations were much higher than ones with members of nonreligious organizations.

nationalism. A famous debate between the early Muslim leader Mohammad Natsir and the secular nationalist Sukarno and the emergence of the secular Indonesian National Party (PNI) and religious Masjumi further reflected this division. The conflict between Muslim parties and the Communist party (PKI) also had a religious element.

In scholarship on religion and politics, especially relating to partisan polarization, religious differences were conceptualized in terms of *aliran*, current or stream, indicating both religious differences and social and political organizations based on them. Geertz argued that choice of, and support for, political parties in Java was connected to *aliran* affiliation. He identified three *aliran* among Javanese: *santri*, *priyayi*, and *abangan*. Citizens with a *santri* or pious Muslim orientation were affiliated with Muslim political parties of the 1950s like Masjumi and Nahdlatul Ulama. The *priyayi*, or traditional Javanese aristocrats, influenced by the Hindu religious tradition as it had been transmitted from India, were connected to PNI, and the more animistic *abangan* peasant class was connected to PKI. Geertz's finding was based on his anthropological interpretation of the relationship of politics and religion in Java.

Perhaps because the approach was anthropological rather than sociological, it does not contain ready-to-use systematic conceptualizations or operational measures that would enable us to test scientifically the connection between religion and politics. Nonetheless, Geertz's description lays a foundation for analytical measurement, comparable to the sociological model constructed by Lazarsfeld, Berelson, and Gaudet (1948) for voting behavior in America.

For Geertz, the *santri* are pious Muslims, that is, they regularly obey Islamic teachings. A *santri* regularly prays five times a day, fasts during the month of Ramadhan, pays alms and makes the pilgrimage to Mecca if he or she can afford to do so. An *abangan*, conversely, is a less- or non-pious Muslim, one who infrequently or never follows these religious dictates. Further, the *abangan* tend to follow ritual practices that are outside Islamic orthodoxy. The main ritual identified by Geertz was the *slametan* or ritual feast, including *ruwatan* (exorcism ceremonies), pilgrimages to the graves of ancestors, burning incense, keeping *keris* (sacred daggers) or other spiritually powerful talismans, and so on. The purpose of the *slametan* was to enable the individual to approach spiritual forces considered to guide man's life (Geertz 1960).

Since Geertz, there have been many critiques of the *aliran* concept, of which Suparlan's (1982) is most persuasive. To Suparlan, the concepts of *santri*, *priyayi*, and *abangan* do not describe the same phenomenon, that is religious orientation. *Santri* and *abangan* are comparable as religious categories, but not *priyayi*, which is better regarded as a class or social status category, the traditional Javanese aristocracy. Accordingly, we have adopted the dichotomous category of *santri* and *abangan* for the purpose of our analysis of voting behavior.

If these revised categories are valid differentiators within Indonesian Islam, we should find a relationship that is significant, positive, and consistent between voters who are less pious in their beliefs and practices and vote today for parties like PDIP (or historically PNI and PKI). Conversely, pious voters should choose Islamic parties or parties that have a connection to an Islamic social organization, such as PKS, PPP, PKB, or PAN (or historically Masjumi and Nahdlatul Ulama).

To test these arguments, we need measures and data concerning voters' *aliran*, in addition of course to their religious identity: Muslim, Catholic, Protestant, Hindu, Buddhist, or Confucian. Unfortunately, quantitative data concerning religious piety, or *santri*-ness, at the individual level are not available to reanalyze the 1955 election. Quantitative data are only available for the 1999, 2004, 2009, 2014 elections.

Religious Affiliation and Party

The most recent official census in 2010 (Badan Pusat Statistik 2010) shows that Muslims in Indonesia number almost 88 percent, while Protestants are 7 percent, Catholics almost 3 percent, Hindus almost 2 percent, Buddhists almost 1 percent and Confucians below 0.1 percent. These proportions were about the same in previous censuses in 1992 and 2000. A cautionary note: Because of the small variation among religious groups, we do not expect to find a statistically strong association between religious affiliation and the vote if we conduct our analysis with a representative national sample.

Our bivariate description and analysis do show nonetheless that religious affiliation correlates significantly with partisan choice.[12] Muslim

---

[12] We made cross tabulations between political parties and voters' religious affiliations for each election and found that they are correlated. Statistic: Chi-square: value/df/significance = 2014: 123.019/50/.000; 2009: 216.678/45/.000; 2004: 94.106/30/.000; 1999: 127.099/16/.000 (this analysis is limited to the five large parties in the 1999 election, the seven large parties in 2004, the nine large parties in 2009, and the ten large parties in 2014) because for the other parties the sample is too small, in accordance with the small percentage of votes they received, below 2 percent. Reading the cross tabulations for non-Muslim respondents it is necessary to be careful because the sample is small, especially for Hindus and Buddhists, so that the results are not stable.

voters, as predicted, have a tendency to choose Islamic parties, even though secular parties like PDIP, Golkar, and Demokrat also attract most of their voters from the Muslim population, who indeed number almost 90 percent. Conversely, non-Muslim voters, Protestants, Catholics, Hindus and Buddhists, have a strong tendency to choose secular parties, especially PDIP. Indeed, nearly all of the members of this latter group do not choose Islamic parties. In other words, the difference in identity or religious affiliation is important in determining the voter's partisan choice as predicted.

This finding implies that if the number of non-Muslims increases, the secular parties will become stronger, but not the reverse, because Muslim voters are polarized. In this respect, the non-Muslim voting pattern is more solid than that of Muslims. There are virtually no non-Muslim voters who choose Islamic parties. Conversely, Muslim voters more frequently choose secular or nationalist parties like Golkar, PDIP, Demokrat, Hanura, Gerindra, and Nasdem. We argue that members of minority religions are more cohesive and vote more solidly for non-Islamic parties because they are minorities and minorities tend to have stronger mechanical solidarity. If the population of non-Muslims in the country becomes larger, closer to the Muslim total, we believe that they will become more open and politically weaker in their solidarity like Muslims.

In the 1999 election, 57 percent of Muslim voters chose PDIP and Golkar, not to mention the Muslims who chose the smaller nationalist parties. In the 2004 parliamentary election, 45 percent of Muslims chose Golkar, PDIP, and Demokrat, while 18 percent chose the two largest Islamist parties, PPP and PKS, and 19 percent chose the two parties based on Islamic social organizations, PKB (based on Nahdlatul Ulama) and PAN (based on Muhammadiyah).

If these figures are added, the number of Muslims who chose the main nationalist parties is greater than the number who chose Islamist and Islamic organization-based parties combined. In the 2009 parliamentary election, almost 60 percent of Muslim voters chose the largest secular parties (PDIP, Golkar, Demokrat, Hanura, and Gerindra). At the same time, there is definitely a tendency for non-Muslims not to choose Islamist or Islamic organization-based parties. A similar pattern appears in the 2014 election, which is why the connection between religious identity and choice of party or candidate for Parliament is statistically significant.

Is the effect of religion consistent if we control for other factors like region, urban versus rural residence, education, social organization membership, plus psychological factors like campaign mobilization, leadership, and evaluations of the performance of the incumbent party? We examine all of these factors through multivariate analysis below, but first we conduct a bivariate analysis of the relationship between Muslim religiosity and votes for a party or a member of Parliament.

Analysis of Muslim religiosity may be more important than religious affiliation because it is connected closely to the debates about *santri* versus *abangan* and Islam versus secular nationalism. In addition, Muslim religiosity is likely to be more important than religious affiliation because of the large number of Muslim voters who choose secular parties. Most Indonesian Muslims are secular or *abangan* in the view of many social scientists from the 1950s until today.

Muslim Piety and Party

We operationalize Muslim piety, as defined above, as the performance of several rituals. Our data also show that there is a significant difference between voters for the secular parties (PDIP, Golkar, and Demokrat) and voters for Islamist parties (PKS and PPP) or parties based on Islamic social organizations (PKB and PAN) in terms of the proportion of Muslim voters in the *santri* category, that is, those who carry out both required and recommended obligations.[13]

In terms of voters for Islamist and Islamic social organization-based parties, the proportion of *santri* is larger than the proportion of *santri* voters for the nationalist or secular parties, particularly PDIP. This pattern is consistent across four elections. However, the relationship is not very significant in the 2014 parliamentary election at the 0.05 level.[14] We can conclude that, setting aside other factors, the *santri-abangan* dichotomy in general significantly explains partisan choice.

When Islamic religiosity is measured by the involvement of a Muslim in a religious organization such as Nahdlatul Ulama or Muhammadiyah, that is, self-identification as a member, that factor also has a significant relationship with partisan choice. This relationship is also consistent across the four elections. For PKB voters, for example, those who say

---

[13] For the cross tabulations, the index of Muslim piety, scaled 1–4, is divided into two categories: a score of 1–2.5=less pious or *abangan*, 2.6–4=more pious or *santri*.

[14] The analysis is limited to the sample of Muslims who answered the question of how often they carry out the five daily prayers, fast during Ramadhan, participate in religious study groups, and read the Qur'an (N 1999 = 1494; N 2004 = 804; N 2009 = 1268; N 2014 = 1401). Chi-square statistic: value/df/significance = (1999): 141,489/4/.000; (2004): 38.446/6/.000; (2009): 24.474/8/.002; (2014): 14.976/9/.092.

that they are members of an Islamic social organization are more than those who say they are not.[15] Conversely, for PDIP voters, those who claim to be members of an Islamic organization are fewer than the number who say they are not except in the 2014 election.[16]

This pattern confirms previous comparative studies about the relationship between religion and partisan choice (Lijphart 1979) and confirms the anthropological interpretation of Indonesianists concerning the importance of *aliran* in determining partisan choice. We must still ask, however, how consistent is this effect when controlled for other sociological factors such as ethnicity or social class? The apparent influence of Muslim religion or religiosity may be related to one of these factors or to evaluations of party leadership or the national economic condition.

In addition, the survey data show that most Indonesian Muslims are *santri* or pious (pious or very pious in our measure). Nonetheless, most of them do not choose Islamic parties. Those who claim to be members of Islamic social organizations still were more likely to choose PDIP in the 1999 election, Golkar in the 2004 election, Demokrat in the 2009 election, and PDIP in 2014 compared to those who chose Islamic parties like PKS, PPP, or PAN, with the exception of PKB. In the 2009 election, among those who claimed to be Islamic social organization members fewer voted for PKB than for Demokrat. Choice of party is therefore influenced by many factors. Religion has an influence, but a limited one. This issue will be discussed further below, where our multivariate analysis will include not only sociological but also psychological and political economy factors.

Religion and Choice of President

Is our finding repeated in the presidential elections? In 2004, Muslim voters were expected to disproportionately choose Amien Rais or Hamzah Haz because those leaders had strong social ties with the Muslim community. Amien is a former chair of Muhammadiyah, and at the time was chair of PAN, which had an informal relationship with Muhammadiyah. Hamzah Haz was the chair of PPP, one of the most important Islamist parties today.

[15] The proportions were 31 percent: 13 percent (1999), 24 percent: 6 percent (2004), 12 percent: 3 percent (2009), and 17 percent: 7 percent (2014).
[16] The proportions were 25 percent: 37 percent (1999), 9 percent: 20 percent (2004), 9 percent: 14 percent (2009), and 18 percent: 17 percent (2014).

In 2009, if the religious factor was important, the proportion of Muslim voters choosing the team of Jusuf Kalla-Wiranto should have been higher. Compared to either former President Megawati or the incumbent President Yudhoyono, Kalla was considered closer to the Muslim community. As a university student, he had been an Islamic organization activist, and had later been a Nahdlatul Ulama leader in South Sulawesi. In the 2014 presidential election, the religious difference was expected to have a significant effect because Prabowo was considered to more represent Islam and Jokowi to have more support from non-Muslims and *abangan*.

Our data show that, in the first round of the 2004 presidential election, the proportion of Muslims among Amien Rais (99 percent) or Hamzah Haz voters (100 percent) was indeed higher than the proportion of Muslims among Megawati (70 percent), Wiranto (95 percent), or Yudhoyono voters (95 percent). This tendency is also visible in the second round in 2004 and in the single round 2009 and 2014 presidential elections.[17]

In the 2004 second round, the proportion of Muslims among Megawati-Hasyim Muzadi voters was smaller than that among Yudhoyono-Kalla voters. Interestingly, though the leader of the country's largest Islamic social organization, NU, Hasyim did not help Megawati's candidacy much. In 2009, the proportion of Muslims among Megawati-Prabowo voters was also smaller than the proportion of Muslims among Yudhoyono-Boediono voters. The proportion of Muslims among Yudhoyono-Boediono voters was not much different from that of Kalla-Wiranto voters. As expected, in the 2014 presidential election, the proportion of Muslims among Jokowi-Kalla voters was smaller than that of Prabowo-Hatta voters.

Statistically, religion significantly influenced the presidential election, but only in a limited way. Religion does not help explain the competition between Amien Rais, Yudhoyono, and Wiranto in 2004 or the competition between Yudhoyono and Kalla in 2009. The reason is probably the small variation between Muslims and non-Muslims. The influence of religious difference in Indonesian elections is therefore not likely to be high unless the proportion of Muslims declines precipitously or the proportion of non-Muslims increases appreciably. The limited nature of the influence is also connected to the fact that all of the candidates for

---

[17] Our analysis shows there is an association between being a Muslim and political preference. Statistic: Chi-square (N/value/df/Significance): (2004a) 1133/147.1384/4/.000; (2004b) 69.692/1/.000; (2009) 1119/92,638/2/.000; (2014) 946/46,895/1/.000.

president were Muslim. Understood nominally (that is, just in the formal sense of being Muslim or not), religious affiliation has little effect on presidential choice.

Religiosity and Choice of President

How about the effect of Muslim religiosity? Muslim religiosity, the *santri-abangan* distinction, did have a significant but inconsistent influence on voting for president. In the first round of the 2004 and in the 2014 single round election, the association was significant, but not in the 2004 second round or the 2009 single round.[18] Interestingly, there were apparently many *santri* voters who chose Yudhoyono or Wiranto compared to Amien Rais or Hamzah Haz in the 2004 first round. The effect of Muslim religiosity is slightly different if the contestation had been limited to Amien Rais or Hamzah Haz versus Megawati. Megawati and Yudhoyono, regarded as similar in their religiosity, made it to the second round, where unsurprisingly religiosity did not matter. In 2009, the *santri-abangan* effect also lost significance even though Kalla claimed to represent santri voters. *Santri* and *abangan* were in fact distributed proportionately across the presidential/vice presidential candidates.

In the 2014 election, *santri-abangan* was significant even though both Prabowo and Jokowi are regarded as *abangan*. As mentioned earlier, the significance was probably associated with the incessant claim during the campaign that Prabowo-Hatta were more representative of *santri* interests. Kalla, Jokowi's running mate, does in fact have *santri* credentials. However, these credentials were underscored by the extensive campaign rhetoric. We conclude that the *santri-abangan* polarization in all presidential elections were impactful, but inconsistently so. Another reason why the *santri-abangan* distinction was less important than expected may be because *santri*-ness is measured by ritual behavior *a la* Geertz. If Islamicness is conceptualized in terms of involvement in a religious social organization like NU or Muhammadiyah, the outcome may be different. It is especially important to explore this dimension because of the tendency of presidential candidates to consider religious affiliation in their own choices and behavior.

In 2004, the nominations of Hasyim Muzadi and Salahuddin Wahid as vice presidential candidates were based primarily on the assumption that these two leaders were supported by vast networks of active Muslim

---

[18] Chi-square: N/value/df/P-value = (2004b) 979/36.167/4/.000; (2004c) 917/3.417/1/.065; (2009) 3.769/2/.152; (2014) 5.317/1/0.21.

organization members who would vote for them. Hasyim was picked by Megawati because he was chair of NU. Wiranto chose Salahuddin Wahid for a similar reason, since Salahuddin is a son of one of the most revered NU leaders, Wahid Hasyim, and the grandson of the founder of NU, Hasyim Asy'ari. It was hoped that Salahuddin would be capable of attracting a substantial number of NU voters, at the very least those who did not support Megawati-Hasyim.

The evidence shows, however, that neither the Megawati-Hasyim nor the Wiranto-Salahuddin pairing was able to attract substantial *santri* support. In 2009, Jusuf Kalla was the candidate who most self-identified as NU. During the campaign, Kalla also frequently visited traditional Muslim boarding schools, especially in voter-rich East Java, where the boarding school network is vast and dense. In this campaign, Hasyim, who was NU chair, provided much assistance to Kalla. The symbolic mobilization and the NU network were nonetheless not effective. Kalla won only 13 percent of the votes, in East Java only 9 percent, far below Yudhoyono (61 percent nationally, 60 percent in East Java) who was frequently attacked as the *abangan* presidential candidate.

Our statistical analysis demonstrates that the involvement of Muslim voters in Muslim social organizations did have a significant impact on the first round in the 2004 presidential election.[19] Muslim voters who claimed to be affiliated with NU voted in larger numbers for the Wiranto-Salahuddin pairing than for other candidates, with the exception of Yudhoyono-Kalla, than did the nonaffiliated. If NU affiliation did have an effect, that effect was apparently not for Hasyim or Hamzah Haz but for Salahuddin. Amien also was not helped very much by his organizational affiliation because of Muhammadiyah's relatively small size compared to NU.

No significant Muslim organization effect was seen in the second round of the 2004 election, the 2009 election, or the 2014 election. Muslims involved and not involved in religious social organizations were distributed among the presidential/vice presidential candidates proportionally. The effort of the Kalla-Wiranto team to identify itself as the most *santri* did not get a meaningful response from voters involved in Muslim organizations. These voters in general were apparently much more attracted to the *abangan* teams, Yudhoyono-Boediono or Megawati-Prabowo. In

---

[19] We include only Muslims in our analysis. The p-values for the first and second rounds of the 2004 presidential election and the 2009 and 2014 presidential elections respectively are .000 (2004b), .641 (2004c), .204 (2009), and .414 (2014).

sum, involvement in Muslim social organizations did not have a meaningful electoral effect.

Perhaps the reason for the lack of a strong and consistent effect of religion, religiosity, and Islamic social organizations is that we have not measured religious affiliation by ideology, specifically by Islamist political orientation. In our 2009 and 2014 surveys, a religiopolitical orientation was included.[20] In general, Indonesians, Muslim and non-Muslim, think of themselves as religious. Nonetheless, bivariate analysis shows that this orientation did not influence their voting behavior.

If the analysis is limited to Muslim voters, the religiopolitical variable does have an impact, although a sharply limited one. The influence was statistically significant when the competitors in 2009 were only Megawati versus Kalla. More Muslims with a religiopolitical orientation voted for Kalla and fewer voted for Megawati. For Yudhoyono's voters, the proportion of Muslims who had a religious or a secular political orientation was about the same.[21] In the 2014 election, the Islamic political orientations were also not significant even though Prabowo supporters claimed that their candidate was more strongly representative of Islamic interests.

Religion, Islamic religious affiliation (*santri* versus *abangan*), involvement in Islamic social organizations, and Islamist political orientation all exhibit very limited and inconsistent influence on presidential election voting behavior. This is an important finding for scholars as well as practitioners. Religion is apparently not as important a factor in Indonesian presidential politics as many studies have concluded.

---

[20] In our postpresidential election survey in 2009, two religious political orientation variables were included. The first was connected to attitudes toward two differing opinions in society about the relationship between religion and law on a scale of 1–10. A score approaching 1 showed an attitude of not agreeing with the opinion that all law in Indonesia must rest on religious teachings. Conversely a score approaching 10 showed agreement that all law must rest on religious teachings. The second variable was connected to attitudes concerning the importance of implanting religious values and traditions in society, or conversely leaving religious and traditional values entirely to the freedom of the individual. The closer the score to 1 the greater the secular orientation, while the closer the score to 10 the more religious. The scores on these two variables were combined to form a politicoreligious orientation variable. For the bivariate analysis, the 1–10 scale was simplified into two categories: 1–5 means a "secular political orientation," while 6–10 means a "religious political orientation." In the 2014 postpresidential survey, we used only one variable, that is, attitudes toward two differing opinions in society about the relationship between religion and law.

[21] This is shown in our Chi-square analysis (N/df/value/P-value): (2009) 748/2/8.039/.018; (2014) 706/1/.427/.514.

We will now offer some conclusions about the connection between religion, religious affiliation, involvement in Muslim social organizations, and Islamist political orientation on the one hand and the vote on the other. Religion in the form of level of Muslim religiosity is a source of involvement in volunteer activities in the religious community. A Muslim who is involved in those activities has a tendency also to be active outside his or her religious community. Such citizens are in a social network, appear on the radar, can be reached by political agents who influence or urge or mobilize them to participate in political activities like elections, campaigning, helping parties, and persuading others to vote for one's party or candidate.

Embracing a religion is also a source of political division. The Muslim voter tends to choose a party or legislative or presidential candidate with a stronger Muslim identity. Conversely, the non-Muslim tends not to choose an Islamic party or a presidential candidate whose Islamic identity is clear. Nonetheless, since nearly all voters are Muslims, the significance of the connection between religion and partisan choice is limited.

For that reason, most parties fight over Muslim voters. Even secular parties try to forge a connection with the Muslim community or at the very least avoid behavior that would offend Muslims. At the same time, we see that most Indonesian Muslims do not see Islam as their political identity. They are open to persuasion by various parties, including non-Muslim parties. The final product is a secular mainstream, in which a majority votes for the large secular parties PDIP, Golkar, Demokrat, and Gerindra.

This is also the case in presidential elections. Religious differences do influence presidential choice, but the influence is limited. The main reason is that non-Muslim voters are less inclusive, that is, they tend to vote for the candidate considered most nationalist or secular, Megawati in 2004 and 2009 and Jokowi in 2014. If they were more inclusive, this effect would not appear. At the same time, Muslim voters tend to spread their support broadly, almost proportionally. This characteristic makes the effect of religion weak in presidential elections.

The variation between *santri* and *abangan* apparently helps little to explain the partisan choices of Muslim Indonesians. *santri* voters are the majority component in the nationalist or secular parties, not only the Islamic parties, because a majority of Muslim Indonesians are *santri*. It is true that the proportion of *santri* voters which votes for Islamic parties is larger than the *santri* proportion for nationalist parties like PDIP, Golkar, Demokrat, and Gerindra, and more *abangan* vote for PDIP, but the difference is small. There are many more *santri* voters in PDIP than in

PKS, for example, because the total number of voters for PDIP is much bigger than for PKS.

In presidential elections, *santri* voters in general do not choose presidential candidates with a *santri* identity. In 2004, the total vote for *santri* presidential candidates like Amien Rais and Hamzah Haz was not more than 20 percent; in 2009, another *santri* candidate only received 12 percent of the vote in an electorate consisting mainly of *santri*. For that reason, voters for Yudhoyono-Kalla, Yudhoyono-Boediono, and for that matter Megawati-Prabowo were mostly *santri*. In 2014, the effect was weaker as the two presidential candidates were generally regarded as *abangan*, not *santri*.

Like Islam more generally, *santri* is apparently not a political identity for Indonesian Muslims. It is more an identity in the social, or social organizational sense, which Indonesian Muslims appear to differentiate from political identity. For that reason, religion and the *santri-abangan* distinction are not politically important, or at least not as important as has been believed up till now by both scholars and politicians.

When Islam is understood as involvement in a Muslim social organization, its influence on partisan choice is reasonably consistent. Those who say they are involved in Muslim social organizations tend to vote strongly for PKB and PPP, but not for other parties. Even so, this significance is limited because the number of Muslims who claim to be involved with a Muslim social organization is small, less than half of the population of voters. In addition, in every election so far there has been one large party, and that party is always secular: PDIP in 1999, Golkar in 2004, Demokrat in 2009, and Gerindra in 2014. Those large parties are highly capable of reducing the electoral effect of religious organizational membership.

The effect of Muslim social organizational involvement is even weaker in presidential elections. In the first-round presidential election in 2004, there was a positive effect that benefited Salahuddin Wahid. In subsequent elections, however, that effect has disappeared. Today, religion and religious affiliation are only important in politics that takes place outside the partisan arena, not in the choice of legislators or presidents. Religion operates more as a social force, on issues having to do with the public welfare, not for a specific group or party.

ETHNICITY

In addition to religion and religiosity, ethnicity and regionalism are potentially important to political participation. Their potential importance is connected not only to geographic but to demographic or developmental differences as well. Many analysts have concluded that there are developmental imbalances between Java and the islands outside Java, to both the east and west. These imbalances include sharp differences in levels of poverty, health, and education.

If it is true that there is a socioeconomic imbalance between regions, and also that level of education and economic prosperity are important for political participation, as we will claim below, it should be the case that regions at a higher socioeconomic level will have a higher level of participation. This is an easy hypothesis to test, because on Java the socioeconomic level is appreciably better than outside Java. It should therefore be the case that voters on Java are more active political participants.

Our bivariate analysis indicates that participation in parliamentary and presidential elections differs little between Java and outside Java. The most significant differences are in the parliamentary election of 1999, the first round of the 2004 presidential election, the presidential election of 2009, and the presidential election of 2014. A few more voters on Java used their right to vote than did voters outside Java. In the other elections there are no differences. This finding partially confirms the hypothesis, but we need further examination of the extent to which other factors are involved, for example the greater distances between polling places outside Java which may make it more difficult to vote.

After the first parliamentary election, participation in Java and non-Java was not significantly different. This indicates that in parliamentary elections the mobilization of voters is as strong, in Java and non-Java, as in presidential elections because of the greater number of candidates in parliamentary elections. Political participation should therefore be understood as a more complex phenomenon in which presence in social and political networks is a necessity in addition to having agents for mobilization.

The expectation that Javanese voters would be more active campaigners because their socioeconomic condition is better was not met. Just the reverse: Voters outside Java tend to be more active campaigners. The socioeconomic argument, as normally understood, obviously doesn't help us to understand this case. A different version of the argument may work better, that is, that campaigning is closely tied to mobilization, and mobilization is easier to carry out among populations at a lower socioeconomic level.

More evidence for this hypothesis can be seen in the differences in significance between campaigning in parliamentary and presidential elections. In parliamentary elections, the difference between the level of campaign participation between voters on Java and elsewhere is more significant and more consistent than in presidential elections. The probable reason is that the number of mobilizing actors and agents in the parliamentary is much greater than in the presidential election so that many more voters are mobilized to come to campaign locations. This mobilization is easier to carry out among a population at a lower socioeconomic level, which is in general truer outside Java.

It is common knowledge that in each election parliamentary member candidates and parties spend a significant amount of money for campaign attributes, food, and transport. The candidates and their teams often give money to citizens to come to campaign meetings and to the polls on election day. Mobilization, rather than voluntary participation, is quite common. This requires more agents, more easily provided in parliamentary than in presidential elections.

Claims for the importance of regional differences in Indonesian politics have mainly focused on political choice, not participation. In a comparative study, it was even found that the effect of ethnicity on partisan choice was greater than that of social class (Lijphart 1979). Liddle (1970) also found that ethnicity was important in explaining the distribution of support among Indonesian parties. King's more recent postdemocratization study (2003) found that party choice was connected to regionalism. He discovered that Golkar voters in 1999 came disproportionately from outside Java, while PDIP and PKB voters were predominantly from Java. PPP and PAN voters were mostly in West Java and outside Java.

Data from the General Election Commission show that voting patterns for parties have been shaped by regional origin. Partai Golkar, for example, tends to be stronger outside Java; PDIP is stronger in Central Java, East Java, Bali, East Nusa Tenggara, West and Central Kalimantan; and PKB is stronger in East and Central Java. The votes for other large parties are more evenly distributed. Partai Demokrat in its first election was strong in several areas, especially Jakarta, West Java, and East Java, but subsequently was more uniformly supported nationwide. However, in the 2014 election, Demokrat was weaker among Javanese. PAN's votes are also relatively widely distributed, with some concentration in Yogyakarta and Central Java. PKS and PPP display a similar pattern. A new party, Nasdem, also received ethnically proportional voters even though it was weak among the Sundanese, the second-largest ethnic group in the country.

When the distribution of voters is looked at by region, the regional influence is less. There is a tendency for large parties to become more national over time. PKB, previously strong only in East and Central Java, in 2009 had spread to Maluku and Papua. PKS, PAN, and PPP have become stronger in Yogyakarta and Central Java, not only in the areas of former Masjumi strength claimed by King (2003). So there have been changes in party strength by region for some parties while others have maintained their traditional strengths.

In 2004, Partai Demokrat voters were more concentrated on Java, especially Jakarta, East and West Java, but in 2009 the party's support spread, making the regional effect much less strong in the competition between Demokrat and the other parties that had previously been strong outside Java. In the outer islands, the proportion of Demokrat voters became larger, even larger than Golkar. In 2014, Demokrat was weaker in Java and stronger in the outer islands.

PDIP voters are concentrated on Java, especially Central and East Java, but PKB voters are even more so, especially in East Java. In 2009 and 2014, the PKB concentration declined, primarily because of the emergence of Demokrat in 2009, and the growth of Gerindra, and the emergence of Nasdem in 2014. As a result, region became less important for PKB and PDIP.

The regional factor coincides closely with ethnicity. Ethnic Javanese are concentrated in Central and East Java and Yogyakarta, Sundanese are mostly in West Java, and the same is true of the hundreds of smaller ethnic groups in Indonesia. Nonetheless, regional identity is not isomorphic with ethnicity. There are many Javanese in West Java, Jakarta, Sumatra, and other regions of Indonesia. Other ethnic groups like the Bugis from South Sulawesi, the Minangkabau from West Sumatra, and the Bataks from North Sumatra are famous for their tendency to migrate to regions outside their homeland. We must therefore separate analysis of the effects of ethnicity from that of region.

According to the last two national censuses, in 2000 and 2010 (Badan Pusat Statistik 2010), there have not been many changes in ethnic composition across the country. The Javanese remain the largest at about 40 percent, followed by the Sundanese of West Java at about 16 percent and the hundreds of other ethnic groups, none of which has more than 4 percent of the total population.

Our findings indicate that in terms of ethnic background, most post-New Order Golkar voters are not ethnic Javanese or Sundanese. Conversely, most PDIP and PKB voters are Javanese. For most other parties, the pattern of ethnic dispersion is more uniform. Partai Demokrat at the beginning was heavily Javanese, but in 2009 its voters were ethnically diverse, with particularly large support from the Sundanese. In 2004, only about 11 percent of Demokrat voters were Sundanese; in 2009 the number had risen to 22 percent, and in 2014 Javanese and Sundanese had proportionately declined among the party's voters. In 2014, Demokrats were disproportionally stronger among non-Javanese and non-Sundanese ethnic groups.

Also interesting is the ethnic composition of PKS voters. In 2004, when PKS, known as an Islamist party, nationally got about 7 percent, only about 25 percent of those voters were Javanese, well below the Javanese percentage in the population as a whole. PKS voters from the Sundanese ethnic group were about 20 percent, just ahead of the overall Sundanese percentage of the population, a pattern that held for other major ethnic groups as well. In 2009, when PKS got about 8 percent of the total vote, its Javanese voters increased to 42 percent, identical with the national ethnic distribution. A similar pattern occurred in 2014, so that it is now hard to claim that PKS is a non-Javanese party.

PPP, another Islamist party, is quite different from PKS. The party almost never receives support proportionally from Javanese. In 1999, Javanese voters were only 27 percent in the party. They significantly increased in 2004, becoming close to the Javanese proportion in the national electorate (42 percent). In 2009 and 2014, Javanese voters within the party significantly declined to 35 percent and 34 percent. Sundanese, on the other hand, were always overrepresented among the party's voters. PAN, based on the Islamic social organization Muhammadiyah, also tends to be weak among Javanese voters. Only in the first election in 1999 did the party voters mirror the proportion of Javanese voters. In subsequent elections the Javanese have always been underrepresented.

These patterns show both that ethnicity has a significant influence on Indonesian voting behavior and that that influence is not as strong as has sometimes been claimed. There is a general tendency over time for parties to become more national in both their regional and ethnic composition. This may in part be due to internal party socialization processes. The older a party, the more opportunity it has to spread its message nationwide.

At the same time, among those national parties, there are none that exhibit a strong preference for voters of a particular region. All parties tend to oppose discrimination on behalf of particular regions. To the extent there is imbalance between regions on Java and those outside of Java that issue impacts internally all of the parties in a similar fashion. Since it is not as strong as predicted, perhaps the significance of the regional and ethnic differences that we have found will become even less strong after we control this factor for others such as religion, social class, governmental performance, and psychological factors, especially party identification and leadership.

In the post-New Order, two major and old parties, Golkar and PPP, have tended to be weak among Javanese. We suspect that the source of this weakness is the fact that the party leadership no longer comes from the Javanese subculture. Golkar leaders Akbar Tandjung (1999 and 2004), Jusuf Kalla (2009), and Aburizal Bakrie (2014) are not Javanese. The PPP leaders, Hamzah Haz (1999 and 2004) and Suryadarma Ali (2009 and 2014), are also not Javanese. In our multivariate analysis below we will demonstrate the extent to which the leadership factor decreases the effect of ethnicity in voting.

What is the effect of regionalism and ethnicity on presidential elections? According to the conventional wisdom, ethnic Javanese voters support Javanese presidential candidates and non-Javanese support non-Javanese candidates. In 2004, the ethnic Javanese presidential candidates were Megawati, Yudhoyono, Wiranto, and Amien Rais, while the non-Javanese was Hamzah Haz, from Kalimantan.

Among the vice presidential candidates, the Javanese included Hasyim Muzadi (Megawati's choice), Salahuddin Wahid (Wiranto), and Siswono Yudohusodo (Amien Rais). In the case of Yudhoyono, his vice presidential candidate, Jusuf Kalla, came from the Bugis ethnic group of South Sulawesi, about 3 percent of the total Indonesian population. Hamzah Haz's vice presidential candidate, Agum Gumelar, is a Sundanese, who represent about 16 percent of the national population. In 2009, there were ethnic and regional differences in the backgrounds of the three presidential candidates. Yudhoyono and Megawati are Javanese, while Jusuf Kalla, as mentioned above, is Bugis. Yudhoyono's vice presidential candidate, Boediono, is not only ethnic Javanese but from the same province on Java and from the same historical culture, the ancient kingdom of Mataram. Megawati's vice presidential candidate, Prabowo Subianto, is also Javanese as is Wiranto, Kalla's running mate.

In the 2014 presidential election, the two presidential candidates, Joko Widodo (Jokowi) and Prabowo Subianto, were Javanese. Jokowi's running mate, Jusuf Kalla, is Bugis, while Prabowo's, Hatta Rajasa, is from South Sumatra. Seen from the ethnic background of the presidential candidates, ethnicity was supposed to be insignificant in the 2014 election because the candidates came from the same ethnic group.

If the ethnic or regional element is important for a presidential candidate, the non-Javanese Hamzah Haz (who makes much of his Kalimantan background) and Agum Gumelar should have gotten a substantial vote outside Java and Javanese. One might even predict they had a good chance to win the election, because the Javanese vote might have been divided among the other four presidential candidates, all of whom were from Java. Another possibility, if ethnicity is strong, would be for Kalla-Wiranto to win the 2009 election because Kalla was the one candidate who was perceived to represent the interests of ethnic groups outside Java while the other candidates, Yudhoyono-Boediono and Megawati-Prabowo, would be presumed to be competing for the Javanese vote. Kalla's strength should have been increased by the addition to his ticket of the Javanese Wiranto.

As has already been described, Yudhoyono's choice of Boediono as his running mate triggered controversy in the political elite. Amien Rais was among those who reacted sharply (*Tempo*, May 24, 2009, 33). According to Amien, Yudhoyono's choice violated a norm in which differences in religion or region should be an important part of a presidential candidate's calculation in choosing a running mate. Because Yudhoyono disregarded this norm, many were convinced that he would lose in 2009, or at least that there would be two rounds, as in 2004, and Yudhoyono would lose in the second round. As we know, the outcome was different. Yudhoyono-Boediono won in one round with an impressive percentage, 61 percent, while Kalla-Wiranto, who did follow the primordial conventional wisdom, only received 12 percent.

We can conclude that in 2009 regionalism and ethnicity were not important. At the very least, Kalla could not make good on his claim to represent the political interests of voters outside Java, who are in fact a very diverse group. Kalla did win among his own Bugis ethnic group, and in the provinces of South and Southeast Sulawesi and Gorontalo. But the Bugis ethnic group is in many ways not representative of other non-Javanese ethnic groups, and those provinces are also not representative of much of Indonesia outside Java.

To be sure, ethnicity did have a statistically significant impact on the 2009 election, but that influence was limited. Slightly more Javanese did vote for Yudhoyono or Megawati than for Kalla. Conversely, voters from other ethnic groups slightly favored Kalla. Nationally, Kalla received 12 percent; in regional terms, he won 7 percent of the total Javanese vote and 16 percent of the total non-Javanese vote. The statistical significance was perhaps connected to a campaign that frequently raised ethnic and regional issues. The Kalla-Wiranto team campaigned as a ticket that better represented the whole of the archipelago than other candidates, especially the Yudhoyono-Boediono team that was ridiculed as representing only the ancient kingdom of Mataram in Central and East Java.

The 2004 presidential election showed more strongly that ethnicity does not have a significant impact. Hamzah Haz was incapable of attracting substantial support based on non-Javanese ethnic sentiments. Ethnic Javanese and other ethnic groups distributed their votes proportionally to all candidates. Most importantly, the Hamzah-Agum team only won 6 percent. Like Kalla, Hamzah could not argue persuasively that his candidacy represented non-Java ethnic groups in general.

In the 2014 presidential election, ethnicity was slightly significant. The proportion of Javanese who voted for Jokowi was larger, while support from non-Javanese voters was almost the same for Jokowi and Prabowo. Jokowi was more associated with the Javanese than Prabowo even though both are Javanese. We expect that this significance is a stable control for other important factors. The voters may think that Jokowi is more Javanese since he was born, grew up, and started his political career in Central Java, while Prabowo is more cosmopolitan, did not grow up in and never had a public career in Central or East Java.

The lack of a consistent pattern of importance of regionalism and ethnicity in presidential elections is likely due to the specific composition of Indonesia's highly uneven ethnic structure. Even though the Javanese are not a majority (at about 40 percent), they are much larger than the second group, the Sundanese (16 percent), not to mention the typical midsize, and often regionally important, ethnic groups like the Bugis of South Sulawesi (3 percent). Because of this ethnic structure, most presidential candidates are Javanese and ethnic sentiment is relatively constant.

Hamzah in 2004 and Kalla in 2009 tried unsuccessfully to break through this ethnic structure, but they (and probably any other comparable candidates) were highly unlikely to represent the multiplicity and diversity of Indonesian ethnicity outside Java. Kalla could perhaps represent the Bugis ethnic group but could not claim plausibly to be the leader of other regionally significant ethnic groups in Indonesia, such as the Batak of Sumatra, the Toraja of Sulawesi, the Banjar of Kalimantan, the coastal Malays on several islands, the indigenous Betawi people of Jakarta, the Madurese on Madura off the coast of Java, the Balinese, and so on.

Kalla was in fact very conscious of this ethnic structure. Long before he nominated himself as a presidential candidate he admitted that he was reluctant to do so because he knew that his own ethnic group was very small indeed compared to the Javanese (Widyawati 2014, 200). The story might have been different if there were only one other major ethnic group, not a combination of many diverse ethnic groups of the sort that Kalla tried to represent in 2009. If the ethnic Bugis represented not 3 percent but 40 percent of Indonesia, and there were only two contestants, Yudhoyono versus Kalla, the possibility for Kalla to win would have been much greater. But this is only a supposition, offered to show that it is not so much that ethnicity is electorally unimportant but rather that Indonesia's specific composition of ethnic groups, very plural and unbalanced, is unsuitable for representation by a single candidate.

We may offer a few summary conclusions. First, regional and ethnic differences do have a slight influence on participation in both parliamentary and presidential elections. Slightly more voters on the island of Java come to the polling booth regularly compared to voters from outside Java. This phenomenon may be connected to socioeconomic differences between the two regions. But when participation is defined as campaign activity, voters outside Java are more involved in parliamentary but not in presidential elections. This is evidence that participation in campaigns is much influenced by mobilization, since in the parliamentary elections there are more candidates engaged in mobilization, in addition to which mobilization is more effective in lower-SES societies.

Second, regional and ethnic differences have an influence on political choice, but it is limited and not consistent. In addition, there are signs that the major parties are becoming more national in their support bases, so that the factors of ethnicity and regionalism are having less impact over time. In presidential elections, the effect of regionalism and ethnicity was not as strong as predicted because of the ethnic demographic structure that is both extremely unbalanced and contains multiple groups. There are many non-Javanese groups and they cannot be represented by a single presidential/vice presidential candidate team so that the influence of ethnicity on elections has no meaning.

SOCIAL CLASS

Social class is also thought worldwide to have an important impact on political behavior (Evans 1999). In Indonesian domestic politics, class has historically been a major issue. Its effects, including at the mass voter level, have long been of interest to foreign scholars (Geertz 1965; Liddle 1970; Wertheim 1980; McVey 2006; Mortimer 2006). Moreover, it is here that we are perhaps most likely to locate sociologically Norris' (1999, 2011) critical citizens as social class is defined in particular by level of education.

The nationalist PNI, the precursor to today's PDIP, had a strong element of class struggle in its ideology. Sukarno, one of the founders and the most charismatic figure within PNI, was a socialist and admirer of Marxism who developed his own Marxist-tinged nationalist ideology (Soekarno 1927). Even today there is a strong class element in PDIP's ideology, although the communist party has long since been rejected. Of all the major parties, PDIP, now led by Sukarno's daughter Megawati, is most identified as the protector of the *wong cilik*, (little people) in Javanese.

In Indonesian history, it was the Indonesian Communist Party (PKI) that most directly based itself on class politics. PKI has been banned since 1965, but its spirit is believed by many (friends and foes) to live on. After the fall of the New Order, several parties were founded implicitly to resume the struggle begun by PKI, most prominently Partai Rakyat Demokratik (PRD), which participated in the 1999 election, though it obtained only 0.06 percent of the total vote, fewer than 100,000 votes.

PRD does not appear in national surveys, including our own, because of its inability to attract voters. It is nonetheless possible that the spirit and tradition of PKI may still be found in PDIP (King 2003). Some data show that regions that were once a base for PKI, especially in East and Central Java, became bases for PDIP after democratization (King 2003). While it is true that all parties and candidates today claim to be committed to defending the *wong cilik*, PDIP would appear to have the strongest claim. We may accordingly predict that the lower class will vote disproportionately for PDIP.

Unfortunately, social class is not the easiest concept to measure. In the voting behavior tradition, the measures adopted have usually been socioeconomic indicators: education, type of employment (blue- versus white-collar), and level of income (Lazarsfeld, Berelson, and Gaudet 1948; Campbell, Converse, Miller, and Stokes 1960; Evans 1999). Of course, these indicators alone do not provide a convincing measure, and several studies have used self-identification with a given social class as an additional indicator. We used a self-identification question in our first post-election study in 1999, but the variation in responses was too low to make it a useful analytical variable. Most Indonesians identify as members of the middle class.[22]

---

[22] In the 1999 survey, few Indonesians identified themselves as members of the upper class (0.7 percent). Most called themselves lower class (43.6 percent) and middle class (50.7 percent). Because the variance was so small, we have not used the question in subsequent surveys.

For this reason, we approach social class via the indicators of education, type of employment, level of income, and involvement with labor unions or farmers' organizations.[23] Citizens with a higher level of education tend to be in the middle or upper class. Those who work as owners of capital or who have a higher level of skills or knowledge tend to be middle to upper class. A higher level of income is also associated with middle- to upper-class status. In Indonesia, citizens who live in urban rather than rural areas are also more likely to be middle or upper class. In general, farmers or sailors who live in the rural areas do not have access to large amounts of capital.

In this study, social class is limited to the objective indicators above. Our analysis is thus focused on the relationship between participation and political choice, on the one hand, and rural versus urban residence, high versus low education, employment as laborer, farmer, sailor and so on, versus businessperson or government official or professional, on the other.

Urban-Rural

The difference between rural and urban residence may be important for political participation because of the connection with political mobilization. Mass mobilization is more likely in cities because of the denser infrastructure and population. Participation and mobilization may also be connected to greater leisure time and level of education. The intensity of labor for rural citizens may be lower than for urbanites, especially in the lower classes. Lower-class villagers may have more time in general than lower-class urbanites and therefore have more time to be active in politics. These possibilities deserve closer empirical examination.

Our bivariate analysis indicates that rural citizens are more likely to show up on voting day than their city cousins. This refutes the claim that urbanites are more likely to vote because they are more reachable through mobilization or are more familiar with the meaning of elections because as urbanites they are more educated. Why is this the case? Before answering, we should look at the connection between place of residence and tendency to participate in campaigns and other election-related activities.

Political participation in the form of participating in campaigns shows a slightly different pattern. Rural voters tend to participate slightly less in

[23] In the psychological model, social class is also measured in terms of the voter's ideology. In democratic countries, this ideological orientation represents the voter's claim to be on the left or right politically (Campbell, Converse, Miller, and Stokes 1960).

presidential than in parliamentary campaigns. Two sources of this difference are the lower frequency of campaigning in presidential elections and the greater number of presidential campaigns in urban than in rural areas. Legislative campaigns tend to be more massive and more easily reach the villages, because there are more candidates and activities, so villagers have equal opportunities to participate in campaigns.

This difference appears unrelated to urban-rural differences in desire to participate in campaigns. The level of knowledge of urbanites about campaigns and politics may be higher because of their education, but this factor apparently does not push them to vote in greater numbers. The element of mobilization, rather than desire to attend campaign activities for legislative elections, seems stronger.

In related forms of participation, there is no significant difference between urban and rural citizens in activities that demand more desire, such as helping campaigns, contributing funds, and persuading others. Compared to campaigning, other forms are less related to mobilization. The highest levels were found in the 1999 parliamentary election at 24 percent (urban residents) and the 2004 parliamentary election at 25 percent (rural residents). Since then, the levels of participation have been much lower. In sum, differences in residence do not much help explain levels of participation. Urban citizens are not more active than their rural counterparts. On the contrary, rural citizens tend to participate more than urban citizens. Participation reflects mobilization more than knowledge or desire of citizens to participate in elections.

Does the rural-urban distinction have a similar effect on political choice? Villagers, in general have less education, on average are employed as blue-collar workers, and have a lower level of income. In terms of social class structure, voters from the villages tend to be more lower class than urban voters.

PDIP elites claim that the party belongs to *wong cilik* or lower-class voters, mostly from rural areas. To some extent this claim is realistic, but a significant change occurred in the 2014 election, when the proportion of urban voters within PDIP was larger. Does the party identification with the lower class remain stable despite this change? Might PDIP in 2014 have attracted more lower-class voters in urban areas, so that the party is still realistically identified with the *wong cilik*? Our 2014 data indicate that other social economic factors such as education and type of employment were not dominated by the rural voters. Therefore, PDIP in 2014 could not exclusively be identified with the lower class if rural voters are identical with class.

Partai Golkar and PKB more consistently represented rural voters. In four elections, the majority of Golkar voters were from rural areas, which are predominantly lower class. Golkar support is stronger outside Java where the majority of citizens live in villages. Why are there more Golkar voters outside Java or from non-Javanese ethnic groups? This question cannot be answered with a class argument. As we shall see in Chapter 6, the answer is connected to the presence of leadership after democratization, which has been dominated by non-Javanese such as B. J. Habibie and Akbar Tandjung in the elections of 1999 and 2004, Jusuf Kalla in 2009, and Aburizal Bakrie in 2014.

PKB was heavily dependent for support on Nahdlatul Ulama (NU), the largest Islamic organization in Indonesia, and its network. PKB was created by NU leaders, whose base is the village, from the time of its establishment in 1926 until now. PKB is therefore identified with villagers whose socioeconomic background is heavily lower-middle class. Their proportions were 77 percent in 1999, 67 percent in 2004, 58 percent in 2009, and 63 percent in 2014.

In contrast to PKB and Golkar, PKS, and PAN are believed to be more dominated by urban or middle-class voters. Four elections have shown the consistency of that claim for PKS; though changes have occurred, the party continues to be dominated by urban voters (75 percent in 2004, 55 percent in 2009, and 61 percent in 2014). Recall that PKS was built by Islamist activists with a base in the cities and on university campuses.

PAN also has an urban base because it has a link with the second-largest Muslim organization in Indonesia, Muhammadiyah, whose members are primarily urban. Moreover, PAN's founders were from the urban educated middle class which was against the authoritarian New Order regime. Amien Rais, founder and leader, was a primary symbol of opposition to that regime.

PAN's urban base is not, however, as consistent as PKS's. In the beginning (1999), 61 percent of PAN voters were urban. A significant change occurred in 2009 when this proportion dropped to 39 percent, after which PAN has no longer been an urban-based party. This change occurred because of an increase in the number of PKS voters in that election who were also pious Muslims and urban. In 2014, however, PAN regained strength in the cities as PKS lost it.

Demokrat, which first participated in the 2004 election, was then dominated by urban voters (71 percent), but the proportion declined in 2009 to 42 percent and further in 2014 to 34 percent. Unlike the parties already described, Demokrat is not rooted in a particular social base. It was established as a political vehicle for Yudhoyono, to enable him to become a presidential candidate in 2004.[24] Its mass support is closely tied to the specific leadership of Yudhoyono, which we will discuss in detail in Chapter 6.

Like Demokrat, Gerindra, Hanura, and Nasdem are tied not to particular social bases but to specific political leaders. Gerindra was created by Prabowo, Hanura by Wiranto, and Nasdem by Surya Paloh. The first two needed a party of their own to become viable presidential candidates. All three had originally been in Golkar, which is reflected in their support bases which are also similar to Golkar, that is, outside Java and rural, with the exception of Gerindra.

Gerindra is identified with Prabowo, and its economic policy platform is nationalist/populist, prolower middle class, like most other parties but especially like PDIP. Nonetheless, in the 2014 election its voters were disproportionately urban. This pattern fit the sharp increase in support for Gerindra in that election (12 percent) compared to 2009 (5 percent), a rise that was associated with the nomination of Prabowo as president in 2014, when he received many votes from the urban middle class. We will discuss these patterns further below and in Chapter 6.

The urban-rural division has another meaning beyond social class, that is, it distinguishes prostatus quo versus prochange, proincumbent versus anti-incumbent or opposition. Rural voters tend to be conservative and resistant to change, while more urban voters desire change. These distinctions are reflected in several ways in the dynamics of partisan strength. In 1999, the party in power was Golkar, and its main opposition was PDIP. In that election the Golkar vote plummeted from the 75 percent it had received in the last New Order authoritarian election in 1997 to 23 percent, 77 percent of which was from rural areas. The PDIP vote, on the other hand, mirrored the national distribution of rural and urban voters.

In 2004, PDIP was the ruling party and Demokrat the main opposition. Yudhoyono as the head of Demokrat was seen as Megawati's main presidential rival. The percentage of urban supporters for PDIP declined significantly, from 46 percent in 1999 to 34 percent. In 2009, Demokrat was the

---

[24] According to the Constitution, only a political party has the right to nominate a presidential candidate.

governing party and PDIP the main opposition; the proportion of urban voters for Demokrat declined significantly from 71 percent to 44 percent. In 2014 as well, when Demokrat was in power, it experienced a decline in urban support from 42 percent to 34 percent. PDIP as the main opposition saw its urban support shoot sharply upwards, from 38 percent to 56 percent.

We can conclude that there is a difference in partisan choice between urban and rural voters, and that this difference is statistically significant.[25] The likely reason, we have found, is that villagers favor the status quo while urbanites want change. However, rural-urban cleavage defined as a social class indicator did not consistently affect party choice. Golkar, historically identified with the state elite and with big business, apparently did not get support from the urban upper middle class. Instead, Golkar has been consistently popular in the villages. PDIP, on the other hand, though self-identifying with the lower class and with villagers, does not in fact receive as much support from those voters. This is also the case with Gerindra, which claims to be fighting for farmers, sailors, and other lower-class voters but in fact is stronger in the cities.

Urban voters who tend to be critical of the party in power are more consistent. They are in fact a principal component of our group of critical democrats or Norris' critical citizens. In presidential elections, the difference between the candidate of the status quo and the candidate of change is more obvious. A finding that rural voters favor the status quo and urban voters demand change should therefore be more clearly visible in the results of the presidential elections.

Our data also show only partial consistency with our hypothesis. In 2004, more rural (64 percent) than urban voters (36 percent) chose the status quo, President Megawati. But this pattern also characterizes voters for Wiranto, who was not the incumbent. For Yudhoyono and Hamzah Haz, the proportion of rural and urban voters was about the same. The most significant difference was for Amien Rais, whose voters from urban areas (61 percent) far outnumbered his rural voters (39 percent). At least in this instance, the claim that rural voters favor the status quo while urban voters favor change has some merit.

This argument does moderately explain the victory of Yudhoyono in the first round of the 2004 presidential election. Had Megawati and Amien been the only two contestants, it might have been stronger. In the

[25] The analysis includes all respondents from urban and rural areas. N 1999 = 1695; N 2004 = 897; N 2009 = 1730; N 2014 = 1556. Chi-square: value/df/significance = (1999): 80,717/4/.000; (2004): 102,038/6/.000; (2009): 34,274/9/.000; (2014): 77,727/9/.000.

second round the pattern is more visible. The voters for the status quo, that is, Megawati, were more numerous (63 percent) than the voters for Yudhoyono (57 percent), the candidate of change, in the rural areas.

The pattern did not appear in 2009. Incumbent President Yudhoyono should have received more votes from the rural areas than Megawati or Kalla, his principal opponents. But in fact the proportion of Yudhoyono voters from the villages was smaller (56 percent) than that for Megawati (73 percent) and Kalla (69 percent), while his proportion of urban voters was larger.[26] This evidence upends the argument that the incumbent will have more support from the rural areas, while the challenger will have stronger urban support because of the differences in attitudes toward change and the status quo.

However, urban voters are not necessarily antistatus quo. It depends on the performance of the incumbent and his or her challenger. If the incumbent is seen as performing well or badly he or she will be rewarded or punished by critical urban voters. Yudhoyono's performance as the incumbent was apparently evaluated positively by urban voters who then voted to reelect him, as we discuss in the following chapter. In addition, in 2009, Yudhoyono's principal challenger was Megawati, whom he had defeated five years earlier. Critical urban voters probably were less than satisfied with Yudhoyono's performance but nonetheless voted for him because they perceived him as the better alternative.

In the presidential election of 2014 there was no incumbent, and President Yudhoyono did not support any of the alternative candidates. His own Demokrat party did not officially endorse a candidate because it failed to find its own candidate and to negotiate successfully with one of the others. Analysis of rural-urban, pro- and antistatus quo, or critical versus traditionalist voters therefore becomes less relevant.

We can conclude that there really is an association between the rural/ urban divide and Norris' critical citizens. Rural voters are more conservative and urban ones more critical. Villagers tend to support the status quo and city dwellers desire change, if the contestants sufficiently embody those qualities. An opposition that does not credibly present itself as a force for change will not get support from Indonesia's critical democrats.

---

[26] Our statistical analysis shows that the association between rural-urban residence and choice of candidate is strong and significant. Chi-square (N/value/df/sig.): 1154/ 36,753/4/.000 (2004a), Chi-square (N/value/df/sig.): 1089/5.983/1/.011 (2004b), Chi-square: N/value/df/sig. = 1119/2/27.693/.000 (2009), and Chi-square: N/value/ df/sig. = 946/1/15.540/.000.

Establishing the connection between the rural-urban divide and partisan or presidential choice requires further analysis to determine the presence or absence of other factors. In the multivariate analysis below we will show the extent to which the connection is independent of other factors.

Education, Employment, and Income

The rural-urban distinction may represent an overly capacious concept, with too many internal dimensions, compared with education. Education is perhaps a simpler concept, and for that reason a clearer indicator of social class. In the electoral studies literature, education is an indicator considered important both for political participation and choice. Indeed, many studies show that education is the most important of the socioeconomic factors explaining political participation (Conway 2000, 25; Wolfinger and Rosenstone 1980, 9). The higher a citizen's level of education, the more likely he or she is to participate in politics.

There are several possible reasons for the strength of this connection (Conway 2000). Citizens who are more educated are more likely to follow events via the mass media and to become more conscious of the consequences of public policies that may impact their daily lives. They tend to live in a social environment that encourages them to be politically active. They tend to have a higher analytical capability, with relevant knowledge and skills, and typically discuss public affairs with others (Almond and Verba 1963).

The importance of education is also that it potentially spreads democratic values, like individual freedom and equality, and connects those values with elections. Several studies place greater emphasis on these democratic values in explaining the impact of education on participation in elections (Nie, Junn, and Stehlik-Barry 1996).

Norris (2011, 140) concludes that education is a strong foundation for encouraging a critical attitude toward politics on the part of citizens. "Democratic aspirations were positively associated with education. And the well educated were also less satisfied with the way that democracy works." More educated citizens recognize that the government does not always fulfill its promises, which makes them less trusting. They may believe that politics only serves the interests of an elite. In other words, education can encourage citizens to feel more alienated instead of more empowered.

This opinion is supported by data concerning conventional political participation in Western Europe, where more educated citizens tend not to trust political parties and abstain from voting in the current post-materialist era (Scarbrough 1995, 151; Topf 1995, 48–49; Inglehart 1997, 152–156).[27] Interestingly, Norris continues that in contrast to education, and "Contrary to theoretical expectations ... self-expression values, subjective well-being, social trust and associational activism were significantly linked with *more* democratic satisfaction, not less" [her emphasis].

What is the Indonesian pattern? Does education foster political aliena-tion, as in postmaterialist societies, or the opposite? Besides education, employment and income are believed to influence political participation. In other democracies, the relationship between income and participation is described as follows. Citizens with better income have more time to follow political issues, while citizens with lower income are under more pressure to fulfill their basic needs. Citizens with higher income also tend to have better access, at their place of employment, to information, some of which is directly relevant to government policies affecting them. They better understand the meaning of elections to them personally, and are thus more likely to participate (Conway 2000).

Several studies show further that employment (being employed versus unemployed) and social class (salaried versus hourly wage workers) are closely connected to political participation (Parry, Moyser, and Day 1992; Conway 2000). Unemployed citizens pay more attention to fulfilling their basic needs than to engaging in political activities (Rosenstone 1982, 33). Salaried employees have more resources (money, time, skill, and knowl-edge) than wage workers (Rosenstone and Hansen 1993). For Britain, Parry, Moyser, and Day (1992, 125–126) find that salaried employees tend strongly to participate in many forms of politics.

Place of work is also believed to influence political participation (Wolfinger and Rosenstone 1980). Public sector employees, for example, participate more. This connection varies from country to country. In the United States, public sector workers and farm owners participate more than others. Civil servants are directly influenced by state policies, while farm owners are dependent on government subsidies and import-export

---

[27] Inglehart emphases the importance of "formative security" tied to an individual's early socialization, and not to education itself, in shaping postmaterialist values. Here what is more important is the level of education by parents, where children with postmaterialist values have received a better education.

policies. They are more conscious of the impact of government policies on their lives, and more likely to participate in politics.

In Indonesia, land ownership is usually very small scale and there are few wealthy farmers. In terms of numbers of workers, however, the agricultural sector is huge. These workers mostly live in villages, have low levels of education, and pay less attention to farmers' organizations that might mobilize them politically. It is therefore likely that the participation levels of farmers are lower than that of private business employees or state officials.

In Indonesian society, according to the 2000 official census, 65 percent of eligible voters have an elementary school education or less. Tertiary students or graduates number only 5 percent. The remainder have a junior or senior high school education. In our bivariate analysis, we contrast the group with elementary or lower education with those who have a secondary or higher education to see the effect of social class on political participation and partisan choice.

Most Indonesian voters (65 percent) are blue-collar workers: agricultural laborers or sharecroppers, independent farmers with small plots, private company workers, informal sector workers, and so on. White-collar workers make up the remaining 35 percent. They include state officials, private sector employees, teachers, the formal business sector, including small shop and store owners as well as large businesspeople in the export and import sectors, plus professionals such as lawyers, accountants, academics, doctors, consultants, and so on. In our bivariate analysis, we deploy these two categories of blue- and white-collar workers to explore the effect of social class on political participation and partisan choice.[28]

There is substantial variation in the level of income per capita in Indonesia, from below the poverty line to well above it. For official census purposes, the poverty line is put at about USD 1 per day or lower. In this analysis, we contrast those whose incomes are in the bottom quartile versus those in the middle and upper ranges in order to assess the effect of social class on partisan choice.

[28] More precisely, the blue-collar category includes all occupations that do not require a high level of education or skill or large amounts of capital, including industrial workers, farm workers, farm owners who in general have small amounts of capital and land, household servants, street peddlers, drivers, and so on. White-collar workers have higher levels of education and skill and if they are independent businesspeople have relatively large amounts of capital and staff whom they employ. These include state officials, private business employees, managers, directors, owners of businesses with staff, professionals like journalists, consultants, doctors, lawyers, accountants and so on.

Level of education for the most part does not have a positive connection with participation in elections (Table 4.1). Although not very consistent, overall, fewer citizens with a higher education come to the polling stations on election day. A similar effect of education on participation in campaigns is also found. More educated voters do not participate in other types of political participation such as attending campaign (Table 4.1).

Why does the most educated group not participate in campaigns? Maybe they are free-riders, an argument that we pursue in Chapter 5. In addition, attending campaign rallies is likely to be the result of mobilization rather than individual desires. Those with higher education are not so easy to mobilize even though they are in mobilization networks and have the resources to participate.

Consistent with the pattern that participation in voting is associated with less educated voters, voting is also closely associated with voters whose income is less (Figure 4.2). In both parliamentary and presidential elections, higher-income citizens are more likely not to vote. Only in the 2014 presidential election were upper-income voters slightly more likely to participate, because there was such intense competition between supporters of the two candidates, Jokowi and Prabowo. One very divisive issue concerned Prabowo's history as a violator of human rights at the end of the Suharto era. Middle-class voters took strong positions on both sides of this issue. In addition, polls showed that the race was very close, tightening as polling day neared.

The more educated and those with higher income also tend to be free-riders. The outcome of an election, that is, an elected president or a member of Parliament, is a public good, the value of which is the same for all citizens, those who choose and those who abstain. That being the case, there is no point in voting if the result is the same.

As will be examined in Chapter 5, the free rider tendency displayed by individuals of higher education and income is connected to their perception of the meaning of an election itself as more instrumental than intrinsic. To the educated, elections are seen as a citizen's right, and accordingly they are not obligated to vote. To less educated and lower-income voters, elections are seen as an obligation, and therefore morally binding upon them as citizens. Alternatively, these voters tend to see elections as having value in their own right, making their behavior more ritualistic.

How about type of employment? Are white-collar voters more active participators in politics as the SES model predicts (Verba and Nie 1972; Wolfinger and Rosenstone 1980)? Our surveys show that white- versus

TABLE 4.1 *Logistic regression of voter turnout in parliamentary and presidential elections*

	1999	2004a	2004b	2004c	2009a	2009b	2014a	2014b
Constant	.486 (.456)	-.818 (.586)	.131 (.635)	-.100 (.546)	-.718* (.314)	-1.465** (.511)	-1.236** (.420)	-3.447*** (.508)
Religiosity	.517*** (.108)	.410** (.147)	-.328 (.184)	.419** (.416)	.225*** (.058)	.351*** (.096)	.536*** (.107)	.776*** (.125)
Religious Organization	.459* (.172)	.530** (.207)	.289 (.203)	.407* (.185)	.263 (.147)	.667** (.225)	.080 (.166)	.142 (.182)
Java Island	.282* (.134)	.072 (.168)	.178 (.197)	-.032 (.173)	-.170 (.127)	-.597*** (.159)	.086 (.137)	.625*** (.155)
Education	-.059* (.028)	.217** (.087)	-.060 (.097)	-.307*** (.080)	-.047 (.064)	.040 (.082)	-.048 (.032)	-.033 (.035)
Urban	-.216 (.142)	-.400* (.176)	-1.391*** (.216)	-.688*** (.174)	-.150 (.126)	-.086 (.169)	-.586*** (.144)	.033 (.006)
Age	-.004 (.005)	.018** (.007)	.058*** (.010)	.021** (.008)	.045*** (.005)	.029*** (.006)	.027*** (.005)	-.059*** (.157)
Male	.225 (.131)	-.239 (.166)	.040 (.199)	-.160 (.173)	-.242* (.117)	-.524** (.152)	-.145 (.130)	-3.447 (.508)
Pseudo-R²	.031	.070	.168	.111	.113	.137	.064	.123
N	2152	1056	981	1026	1650	1036	1501	871

***p = .001, **p = .01, *p = .05

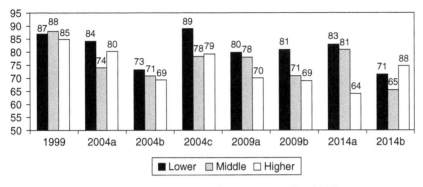

FIGURE 4.2 Voting according to income level (%)

blue-collar status does not have a significant effect on participation in either parliamentary or presidential elections.[29]

We may conclude that social class is not very important in determining political participation. Level of education, level of income, and type of employment have little influence in the Indonesian case. There is instead a tendency for citizens with less education and income to be more frequent voters and more active in attending campaign events. Only when participation is in the form of persuading others does level of education have a positive influence. There is clearly a strong mobilization component in political participation in the form of voting and attending campaign events.

The more educated are not easy to mobilize, and tend to be apathetic toward conventional forms of political participation as is also the case in older democracies (Inglehart 1997; Norris 1999). The fact that citizens from lower-class backgrounds participate more suggests that those participants have lower levels of information and understanding about politics than do the more educated. They are just followers. It may also be the case that the more educated and those from the upper middle class tend to free ride.

In voting for particular parties or candidates, social class is important. There is moreover a significant difference between voters in parliamentary and presidential elections. The social class effect is first visible in levels of education. Our data show the connection between level of education and

[29] The voting participation gap between blue and white-collar was either zero (2004a) or small (1999, 2004b, 2004c, 2009a, 2009b, 2014a, and 2014b). A similar pattern is found for other types of participation.

partisan choice. In our four national surveys after the 1999, 2004, 2009, and 2014 parliamentary elections, there were many more PDIP voters with an elementary school or lower education than PAN voters, and more than PKS and Demokrat voters in 2004 and 2009.[30] However, in the 2014 election, the dominant position of the less educated among PDIP voters was no longer the case. As has already been mentioned, PDIP voters now come proportionately from all levels of education.

It is Golkar and PKB that have consistently attracted voters from among the less educated.[31] Conversely, as has been the conventional wisdom, PAN and PKS win more support from educated voters. Many PAN voters come from Muhammadiyah, the largest Muslim organization that is primarily urban and also the home of many educated voters, and critical voters as well, at the time this party was founded at the end of the authoritarian New Order. For its part, PKS is the party that was founded by Islamist activists based on university campuses.

Change occurred within PPP in the 2014 election. Previously, PPP voters were mostly voters with less education, but in 2014 the proportion of those voters declined significantly, at the same time that the party was losing support in general to its main competitors, especially PKB. Apparently, the less-educated voter base was more attracted to PKB than PPP in that year's competition between the two parties for the support of the NU masses. Both parties have a connection to NU, although the links are much stronger with PKB.

Partai Demokrat also experienced the dynamic effect of education. In its first election in 2004, Demokrat had a stronger educated voter base. But in 2009, Demokrat, as the party in power, won a plurality of the vote (21 percent). Under the leadership of President Yudhoyono, Demokrat was apparently able to reach a broad spectrum of more and less educated voters across the nation, more than doubling its vote from five years

---

[30] The lower education proportions for PDIP were 58 percent (1999), 59 percent (2004), 67 percent (2009), and 41 percent (2014). For PAN, they were 26 percent (2004) and 43 percent (2009), PKS 18 percent (2004) and 35 percent (2009), Demokrat 21 percent (2004) and 51 percent (2009). Chi-square for partisan choice for the 1999 survey: N/value/df/sig. = 1794/124.168/12/.000 (1999); for the 2004 survey: N/value/df/sig. = 1794/124.168/12/.000; for the 2009: N/value/df/sig. = 1424/117.577/24/.000; and for the 2014 survey: N/value/df/sig. = 1556/62.623/27/.000.

[31] From the same surveys, the proportions of lower-educated Golkar voters were 54 percent (1999), 50 percent (2004), 46 percent (2009) and 56 percent (2014). For PKB, the percentages were 67 percent (1999), 48 percent (2004), 65 percent (2009), and 60 percent (2014). As for PPP, the proportions were 61 percent (1999), 58 percent (2004), 67 percent (2009), and 39 percent (2014).

earlier. Demokrat voters at that time were broadly representative of all levels of education.

In 2014, we again see a shift in the relationship between levels of education and Demokrat support as the number of Demokrat voters fell sharply, from 21 percent to 10 percent. In this election Demokrat weakened among voters with the least education. Many of these voters apparently shifted their support to PKB, especially in East Java, PKB's principal base, where many voters had chosen Demokrat in 2009. In other words, many PKB voters returned home after temporarily decamping to Demokrat.

Outside Java, where the least-educated voters are most numerous, some of Demokrat's voters joined a new party, Nasdem, especially in Sumatra. In addition, PDIP and Gerindra also played a role in shrinking support for Demokrat in 2014. These swings can happen easily because all these parties have similar ideological characteristics, that is they are all nationalist-religious and claim to represent the lower classes. Hanura and Gerindra in general were broadly representative of all levels of education in society. Their voters were comparable to Demokrat and especially Golkar voters.

Concerning the effect of education on partisan choice, while there is an impact there is no pattern that covers all. Only PKS and PAN are consistently supported by more educated voters, and Golkar and PKB are consistently backed by the less educated. The effect on others is inconsistent, a pattern that is itself a powerful determinant of which party wins a given election. In other words, Indonesian voters are open and can shift their partisan choice repeatedly, depending on party performance and the ability of parties to mobilize them. It is this quality that makes them critical democrats.

Does this pattern apply to presidential elections? In the four surveys connected with presidential elections the difference in levels of education significantly influences voters' choices. There is a general tendency for Megawati's voters, regardless of her choice of a running mate, to come from the less educated. In the first round in 2004 (2004b), 62 percent of Megawati's voters had an elementary education or less. The percentage was similar for Wiranto-Salahuddin Wahid voters, while only 45 percent of Yudhoyono's and 27 percent of the voters for Amien-Siswono had an elementary education or less.

This effect also occurred, though to a lesser extent, in the second round. The team of Megawati-Hasyim received more of the votes of the less educated than did Yudhoyono-Kalla. It was visible again in 2009, where

64 percent of Megawati-Prabowo's voters were in the less-educated category. Only 50 percent of Yudhoyono-Boediono's voters and 32 percent of Kalla-Wiranto's came from this category. Compared to voters for other candidates, more of Megawati's voters came from the least educated Indonesians. The evidence confirms the claim of Megawati's supporters that she has a stronger link with the lower class, at least as defined by education. In the 2014 presidential election, Jokowi was supported by Megawati, and the proportion of Jokowi voters from the least educated group was larger than that for Prabowo. In other words, education consistently matters in presidential elections.

Does this consistency also apply to social class as defined by occupation and income? Bivariate statistics indicate that many more PDIP, Golkar, PKB, and PPP voters are blue-collar workers compared to voters for PAN, PKS, and Demokrat. PAN, PKS, and Demokrat voters are disproportionately white collar. Social class, at least as measured by the white-collar/blue-collar distinction, does have an impact on partisan choice.

There is a tendency for this effect to weaken over time, however, so that by 2009 it was no longer significant. In the 2014 election it became significant again, but was not very strong. Blue-collar workers constituted a majority of the voters for each party. PAN and PKS, which used to be identified with white-collar workers, was no longer so identified in 2014. One source of the change was the ability of the white-collar parties like Demokrat, PAN, and PKS to gradually attract blue-collar workers. These parties have tended to lose any class distinctiveness and become catchall parties, as we argued in Chapter 3.

Type of employment also affected presidential elections. Megawati, compared to other candidates with the exception of Hamzah Haz, especially Yudhoyono and Amien Rais, regardless of running mate (Hasyim Muzadi or Prabowo Subianto) was disproportionately supported by blue-collar workers. The proportion of blue-collar voters who supported Yudhoyono was also high but smaller than for Megawati. Yudhoyono's supporters, through all three elections, spread more evenly across both categories.

The employment effect was strongest in comparing voters for Amien Rais with those for Hamzah Haz or Megawati in the first round of the 2004 presidential election. The proportion of white-collar voters for Amien was 38 percent, for Megawati 11 percent, and for Hamzah only 6 percent. The conventional wisdom that Megawati has strong support from lower-income groups like farmers, workers, and fishers turns out to have a solid empirical foundation, as does the belief that more of Amien Rais' voters come from the upper middle class and cities.

The findings hold when social class is seen through the lens of income. Voters from the lowest-income strata are found more often in PPP, PKB, PDIP, Hanura, and Golkar than in PKS, PAN, Demokrat, and Gerindra. This pattern is consistent across three parliamentary elections, spanning a decade, even though there are differences in each party's proportion of the vote. For example, 86 percent of PDIP voters were from the lowest-income strata in 1999, 66 percent in 2004, and 42 percent in 2009. Similar changes occurred in class voting for Golkar, PKB, and PPP. These changes parallel the overall decline in votes for these four parties.

Partai Demokrat, PKS, and PAN offer a different pattern in the three elections. They captured a smaller proportion of low-income voters. The proportion of PAN and PKS voters was stable in 2004 and 2009, while support for Demokrat from the lowest-income voters rose sharply. This change was accompanied by retention of the absolute number of voters with middle and higher levels of income, so that overall Demokrat surged from 7 percent in 2004 to 21 percent in 2009. A significant change occurred in 2014, when the proportion of lower-income voters by the same measure significantly declined. This decline is consistent with the increase of national income per capita.[32] The income effect is still statistically significant regarding choice of party.

There was another important change in the 2014 election. PDIP, usually identified with the *wong cilik*, blue-collar, or poorest voters, as we have seen during the three previous elections, was no longer so identified in 2014. Compared to Golkar voters, and even more so PKB and Nasdem voters, the proportion of PDIP voters who came from the lowest-income strata was smaller. Now the proportion is almost the same as other parties, with the exception of PAN, where it is a bit smaller. PDIP can no longer claim to be the party of the *wong cilik* according to this indicator. It is now Golkar and PKB that have more voters among the "little people." This change in voter base for PDIP is consistent with other social class measures, that is, rural-urban, type of employment, and level of education.

The income effect also occurred in the presidential elections. Lower-class voters for the PDIP chair, Megawati, were much more numerous than lower-class voters for other candidates, Hamzah Haz excepted. In

---

[32] Income per capita for 2000 was 6.2 million rupiah (about 900 USD at that time), and in 2013 had risen significantly to become 32.5 million rupiah (about 4000 USD). Badan Pusat Statistik (Central Statistical Body), https://bps.go.id/, accessed on December 4, 2015.

the first round of the 2004 presidential election, 70 percent of Megawati's supporters were from the lowest-income group, better than any competitor, with the exception of Hamzah Haz, who received 82 percent of his vote from this group. The comparable figures were 70 percent for Wiranto, Yudhoyono 62 percent, and Amien Rais 37 percent. In this election Megawati had about the same number of low-income voters as Wiranto and Hamzah Haz.

The most striking difference is in the comparison of low-income voters for Hamzah, Megawati, and Wiranto, on the one hand, and Amien Rais on the other. Amien's lower-class voters were only half as many, plus Yudhoyono's voters were consistently distributed more proportionally to population. Nonetheless, the evidence indicates that lower-income voters were not only in Megawati's camp. Yudhoyono, Hamzah Haz, and Wiranto were comparably strong.

Since Megawati supported Jokowi, the income effect can also be seen in the 2014 presidential election. Compared to Prabowo's voters, the proportion of voters for Jokowi who came from the lowest-income strata was larger, and conversely those from the highest strata was smaller. The income effect on the legislative and presidential elections in 2014 differed. PDIP was no longer identical with the lower class, but its presidential candidate Jokowi still had more lower-class support. This difference occurred because Jokowi was not only supported by PDIP but also by PKB, Nasdem, and Hanura, which have consistently had a strong base in the lower classes.

In sum, the four social class variables – rural-urban residence, level of education, type of employment, and level of income – have a significant, though uneven, impact on the political choices of Indonesian voters. The exclusive identification claimed by PDIP and Megawati with lower-class voters is not verified by our data. We find lower-class voters not only in PDIP but, and even more strongly, in PPP, PKB, and Golkar. Lower-class identification with Demokrat has also become stronger. In addition, a significant change occurred among PDIP voters in 2014. PDIP was no longer isomorphic with the "little people" as seen from the SES profile of its voters. The middle-class component has expanded. This is perhaps related to the hopes of critical voters toward the opposition after they had become disappointed with the incumbent party whose elites were tarred by corruption.

The social class effect on the presidential election was different. Megawati and her chosen candidate, Jokowi, have consistently been identified with the lower class. This consistency was maintained because Jokowi was supported not only by PDIP but also by a group of parties most heavily identified with the lower class, that is PKB, Nasdem, and Hanura. In addition, there was no incumbent in 2014. President Yudhoyono was limited by the constitution to two five-year terms, and neither he nor his party supported either of the two candidates who ran. In this contest, critical democrats or protest voters therefore became less relevant.

How independent is the social class effect on voting behavior? Is it independent of the influence of urban-rural regionalism, political mobilization, party leader evaluations, evaluations of the national economic condition and of government performance, and identification with political parties? These questions will be explored further in our multivariate analysis.

For a more comprehensive analysis, participation and political choice must also be seen in terms of other sociological factors in addition to religion, regionalism or ethnicity, and social class, the three factors that have until now been most prominent in Indonesian studies. Two other important components are gender and age.

GENDER

In the literature on electoral behavior, a number of studies have found that women participate less in politics, especially beyond voting, for example in campaigning, helping parties, and persuading others to choose their party or candidate. Our data show a relatively consistent pattern of little gender differentiation in voting turnout.[33] This balance is due in part to the basic requirements of voting; little is demanded of the voter in terms of level of education, exposure to political information, activity in social networks, and having political attitudes. To vote does not require much information, skill, experience, or profound political opinions, and so citizens in general, men and women, are equally able to participate in the electoral process if they desire.

Participating directly in election campaigns, for example in the form of attending rallies, imposes more conditions. Our surveys show a significant and consistent difference in the level of participation of men and women in both parliamentary and presidential campaigns.[34] Men participate more

---

[33] The highest gaps between the two groups were found in the two round presidential elections in 2004 at 6 percent and 4 percent. For all other elections, the gaps were 2 percent or less.

[34] The levels of campaign participation for men have been higher at 28 percent (1999), 32 percent (2004a), 12 percent (2004b), 6 percent (2004c), 21 percent (2009a), 10 percent (2009b), 17 percent (2014a), and 8 percent (2014b). For women, the percentages are 16

than women. When participation is measured as helping parties, candidates, or success teams during the campaign period, men also tend to be more politically active. The surveys also show that more men than women volunteer to help parties and candidates.[35] More men than women are active in persuading others to vote for their party or candidate, but there is no gender difference in donating money to parties or candidates.

The various forms of political participation described above and their association with gender differences confirm many previous studies that men are more politically active than women. Political participation other than voting tends to be a man's world (Parry, Moyser, and Day 1992; Verba, Schlozman, and Brady 1995).

Is it in fact gender that is driving these differences? A number of studies argue that it is not gender difference *per se* but related factors such as level of education, political information, opportunities to be socially active, exposure to public affairs, and so on (Burns, Schlozman, and Verba 2001). Women tend to have a lower level of education, fewer opportunities to be active in public affairs, less opportunity to be employed outside the home, and so on. We will examine this argument more comprehensively in Chapter 6.

In turnout, there is no evidence of a significant difference between male and female. How about political choice? Gender differences have the potential to influence choice of party, legislative or presidential candidate if there is variation in the electorate on issues of gender equality. Gender differences may also be influential if the competing candidates are men and women, and more specifically if those candidates offer different gender equality programs in their campaigns.

Gender differences also have the potential to influence voting behavior if voters are divided by liberal views that give greater priority to women's equality versus conservative views that see women as partners for their husbands or as subordinate to men more generally. The evidence shows that these differences do not, for the most part, influence voting in Indonesian parliamentary elections.[36] Men and women are spread evenly

---

percent (1999), 15 percent (2004a), 6 percent (2004b), 2 percent (2004c), 9 percent (2009a), 5 percent (2009b), 88 percent (2014a), and 4 percent (2014b).

[35] In four surveys (2009a, 2009b, 2014a, and 2014b), the level of men's participation has been higher in helping, donating, and persuading except for donating in 2009b where women's participation was slightly higher.

[36] The highest gap was 16 percent for Gerindra in the 2014 survey. However, our statistical analysis shows that there is no strong and significant association between gender and party choice. The analysis includes the whole sample of men and women (N 1999 = 1694; N 2004 = 895, N 2014 = 1556). Chi-square: value/df/significance = (1999): 10.574/4/.032; (2004): 7.307/6/.293; (2009): 8.214/9/.513; (2014): 12.795/9/.172.

across all political parties and parliamentary candidates. There are no parties that are more able to attract women than men, or vice versa, although one can see some small differences across parties.

It is possible that we do not see gender differences because of the lack of parties that have strongly defended gender equality. In election campaigns, all parties claim to be in favor of gender equality. The lack of polarization may also be because the issue is not strongly articulated in society, so that few people see it as pressing and parties see no reason to respond to it.

Several parties likely represent this conservative tendency whose source may be interpretations of religion or local customs, in which the leadership roles of men are taken for granted. We may suppose for example that the Islamist PPP and PKS are repositories for these more conservative aspirations from Muslims who oppose gender equality in public life.

In general, the gender difference is not statistically significant in the legislative election. Parties thought to be conservative on this issue like PKS and PPP in fact receive proportional support from women. Indeed, slightly more women than men tend to vote for PPP.

The gender difference effect may also be detected if there is a clear gender difference at the top of the party leadership. Men and women may be divided in their choice of party or legislative candidate if some parties are led by women and others by men. The issue will not necessarily surface in the statements of these leaders, but directly from the voting public which is sensitive to it. So PDIP, which is led by a woman, compared to the other parties, which are all led by men, might consistently attract more women voters. The evidence, however, is not consistent. PDIP female and male voters were roughly proportional to the general population. There is a significant difference between the elections of 1999 and 2014, when there were more women. But in other elections men are slightly more or the difference is not significant.

As in the parliamentary election, so in the presidential election gender has the potential to influence behavior. This would especially be the case if there were a relevant difference in agenda or program that was highlighted by the candidates, if the issue matters to voters, and if there are gender differences among candidates. In Indonesian presidential elections, the third condition has been met because Megawati has been a candidate in both rounds of the presidential election of 2004 and the one-round election in 2009. In this context, gender difference might influence behavior. More women voters might choose Megawati, the female candidate, in preference to the male candidates.

The survey data show that the connection is only slightly significant and tends not to be important in the two most recent elections. Indeed, in 2004 Megawati was chosen by more men (58 percent and 54 percent for the first and second rounds) than women (42 percent and 46 percent). The assumption that a female candidate will be more supported by women does not hold for Indonesian voters.

Gender is of course not just a matter of sexual difference, but an attitude and behavior that foregrounds the equality of males and females in various aspects of life, including politics. It is certainly possible for a man to support and a woman to oppose gender equality. We may therefore need a more sophisticated operationalization of gender equality to better observe its influence on voting behavior. Moreover, in future research we need to examine more closely differences in views on gender equality among presidential candidates, how that agenda is socialized to the public, and how able the public is to differentiate among candidate agendas.

AGE

After gender, age is the demographic factor believed to be most influential on both political participation and choice. Milbrath (1965, 66) found that "political participation increases by stages according to age, achieves its peak during the 40s, then decreases by stages after age 60." Below age 40 citizens are more mobile because they do not yet have a permanent occupation and place of residence. Moving frequently, they are less likely to vote. They are also more actively engaged in looking for employment or to advance their career opportunities. Voting and other political activities get less attention. Citizens over 40 have become more stable in employment and residence. It is easier for them to make time for public affairs. After 60, primarily for health reasons, citizens tend to participate less in politics.

Other studies emphasize not the aging process itself, but the tendency with greater age to engage in a wider range of activities, some of which are connected to or lead to political participation (Jennings and Markus 1989, 12). Older citizens are more active as volunteers in citizens' groups, church and school-related activities, that can lead to greater political activity. Another study finds that political participation is more tied to level of education (Nie, Verba, and Kim 1974). That is, it is not the age difference per se but its connection to greater age that leads to more participation.

In addition, political participation is more connected to nonpolitical social activities, called civic engagement, where individuals who are more engaged in civic affairs, regardless of age, will tend to be more politically active (Strate, Parish, Elder, and Ford 1989). A citizen who is involved in civic activities like religious study groups or neighborhood associations is more likely to feel called or inspired by participation in that group to participate in politics even though he or she is already retired.

Empirically, the persuasiveness of these various arguments will be explored in the multivariate analysis of subsequent chapters. In this chapter, we begin by describing the connection between age and political participation: how, setting aside other factors, age relates to participation in parliamentary and presidential elections in Indonesia.

The surveys show an inconclusive pattern. In the 1999 legislative election, age difference did not have a significant influence on participation. The likely cause is the powerful wave of euphoria that swept Indonesia when a genuinely democratic election was held for the first time in 44 years. In the 1999 election, the youth vote was slightly higher (86 percent) than that of older voters (80 percent). The pattern is different from the findings for other countries cited above, probably a result of that momentary euphoria. The citizens who took to the streets, even clashed with security forces, at the beginning of democratization, were the young, particularly university students.

The euphoria dissipated quickly. The influence of the age factor became significant in subsequent elections, which became the new normality, very different from the moment full of hope after decades of repression under Suharto. Since that time, citizens under 40 consistently participate less. In the legislative elections, their level of participation has continued to decline, from 86 percent in 1999 to 77 percent in 2004 to 64 percent in 2009, but rising to 71 percent in 2014. In the presidential elections, their level of participation has declined from 81 percent in 2004 (first round) to 73 percent (second round) to 67 percent in 2009, and finally to 60 percent in 2014. The findings of previous studies for other democracies that participation by under-40s is weaker than for the productive age group (41–55) is confirmed for Indonesia. The finding that retired people vote less, however, is not consistently found.

This pattern offers a warning for the future. According to the psychological model of voting behavior, the habit of political participation is formed at an early age. Citizens who vote when they are first eligible will tend to continue to vote as they get older. Conversely, those who do not begin voting at an early age tend to vote less frequently as they age (Campbell, Converse, Miller, and Stokes 1960).

In Indonesia, we find that the level of participation of the young is lower than that of older citizens. When the next parliamentary or presidential election is held, in five years' time, and if it is true that not voting is a habit formed early, the age group that is now entering its middle or productive years will tend not to vote, and this pattern will continue into the future. In the long term, we can project that the level of participation of both productive and retired citizens will decline. This tendency is already clearly visible, where turnout reached 93 percent in 1999 and declined to 71 percent ten years later before returning to 75 percent in 2014 as described in Chapter 3. The decline was sharper among youth.

Decline in participation by youth also characterizes participation in campaigns. From election to election fewer youth participate or can be mobilized to join campaigns. In the legislative and presidential elections, their campaign participation has decreased from 24 percent and 25 percent in 1999 and 2004 to 18 percent and 14 percent in 2009 and 2014 respectively. In the presidential elections, it has been even lower, from 9 percent in 2004 to 8 percent in 2009 and 6 percent in 2014. The young are apparently less and less attracted to politics, in the forms that are most common in democracies, voting and campaigning.

In sum, the effects of age on political participation show that parliamentary and presidential elections attract more senior citizens and fewer citizens who are still in their productive years. The tendency of younger voters shows a sharper decline. In the long run, if there is no intervention, Indonesian elections will continue to lose voters.

Does age also have an impact on partisan and candidate choice? Across the four elections, age does not correlate significantly with choosing parties or members of Parliament. Younger and older voters alike, first-timers and the retired, are spread reasonably equally across all parties. There is no party that tends to represent a particular age group, although PAN in 1999 and PKS in 2004 were slightly more attractive to first-time voters, garnering 17 percent and 16 percent respectively.[37]

The lack of importance of the age factor in determining voting behavior in Indonesia is likely due to the absence of a party that can claim to represent a particular age group. Moreover, no party has special programs for, for example, youth or senior citizens. Or, if they do have

---

[37] Even though the proportions of each age group among parties from election to election are different, as our surveys show, the differences are small. For example, the percentages of those who are above 55 in the 2014 legislative election are all around 30–38 percent for each political party except for Hanura (18 percent) and Nasdem (29 percent).

such programs, the voters are not able to distinguish which is better for them. Because of this lack of clarity, age group differentiation does not have a significant effect on the choice of parties or their legislative candidates.

An additional hypothesis is that younger voters aspire to change and are reluctant to choose the party in power. Conversely, older voters tend to be more conservative, to resist political change, and to choose parties that are currently in power. This hypothesis assumes the existence of an incumbent and an opposition party. In the 1999 election, it was not clear which party was in power and which was out of power because the country was undergoing a transition.

Golkar, the party of the New Order regime, was arguably the governing party at that time. Golkar did in fact control Parliament and the People's Consultative Assembly, the super-Parliament charged under the original 1945 Constitution with choosing the president and vice president, and the executive branch was controlled by Golkar as well. The Assembly chair was simultaneously the chair of Golkar, and President Habibie chaired the party's most senior advisory body, which meant that he was de facto more powerful than the Assembly chair.

Several parties may be considered to have been in opposition in 1999. PDIP in particular had led the struggle against Suharto and Golkar for the last decade of the New Order. If the comparative electoral literature is correct, younger voters should have voted for PDIP over Golkar and older voters the reverse.

Prior to the 2004 election, PDIP was the governing party. PDIP had more seats in Parliament than any other party and, more importantly, President Megawati was the PDIP chair. The opposition was less clear because most parties had joined in a governing coalition with PDIP. Perhaps the principal opposition parties at the time were the two new parties, Demokrat and PKS. If these assumptions are correct, PDIP in the 2004 parliamentary election should have received more votes from the young, while Demokrat and PKS should have received more votes from their elders.

Prior to the 2009 parliamentary election, Golkar had the largest number of seats in Parliament, but President Yudhoyono was from Partai Demokrat. Once again, the government was a coalition, this time with Golkar and Demokrat as principal members. PDIP had positioned itself as the opposition. For that reason, more young voters chose PDIP compared to Golkar and Demokrat, and more older voters chose the latter two parties. The proportion of voters from various age groups for PDIP and

Golkar was similar. This was also the pattern of the 2004 parliamentary election. The proportion of young voters was about the same for PDIP (in power) and Demokrat (in opposition).

The party that differed from this pattern, more in line with previous studies, was PKS. The proportion of PKS voters from the younger age group was larger than for PDIP or Golkar, parts of the governing coalition at that time. Why larger for PKS and smaller for Demokrat in the 2004 election? More research is called for, but we can suggest that the main reason may be that PKS's social base consists primarily of young people. PKS was born as a movement of Islamist activists, even though the core leadership group did not consist of students. It was not therefore because of opposition to the incumbent and youthful desire for change but specific circumstances applicable to PKS that made it more attractive to youth than Demokrat, which was also a party of change and the clear opponent to PDIP at that time.

The 2009 parliamentary election also showed that age group differences had no effect on political choice. The proportion of young voters who chose PDIP (in opposition) and Demokrat (in power) were about the same. This was also the case for other age groups. In 2009, Demokrat was the ruling party and PDIP the main opposition party. Other parties joined with Demokrat to support President Yudhoyono. Hanura and Gerindra inclined to be in the opposition but not as clearly as PDIP. In any case there was no significant difference in the preference of younger voters.

How does the effect of age on presidential elections compare with that on parliamentary elections? We hypothesize that younger voters want change, and therefore tend to pick the opposition, while seniors resist change and tend to choose the incumbent. If this finding is relevant to Indonesia, young voters in 2004 should have been more attracted to Yudhoyono and his running mate Jusuf Kalla, the main opposition to the incumbent President Megawati. Older voters should have preferred Megawati.

In the 2009 presidential election, the incumbent was Yudhoyono and his main opposition was Megawati. Confusing the issue, however, just before the election, incumbent Vice President Jusuf Kalla also became a presidential candidate. His running mate was former armed forces commander retired General Wiranto. The Kalla-Wiranto campaign was at least as confrontative as Megawati's in opposition to the incumbent President Yudhoyono. Kalla's campaign slogan was "faster will be better," implying that the quality of Yudhoyono's presidential leadership was diminished by his well-known slowness to act (*Tempo* June 7, 2009, 108–111). The public understood that Kalla's claim was based on his frustrating personal experience as Yudhoyono's vice president for the previous five years. We can accordingly consider both Kalla and Megawati as the opposition in 2009. In the 2014 election, however, there was no incumbent versus opposition and for that reason age was probably not significant.

Our data on the presidential elections confirm these hypotheses. In the 2004 first round, more young voters supported Yudhoyono-Kalla than Megawati-Hasyim. Conversely, more seniors chose the incumbent President Megawati over her main challenger Yudhoyono. In that election, the Yudhoyono-Kalla team was chosen by 34 percent of the voters. Among voters under 23, first-time voters, 38 percent chose Yudhoyono-Kalla, while only 25 percent of those over 55 did so. Conversely, the Megawati-Hasyim team, which had obtained 27 percent of the vote in the first round, was chosen by only 19 percent of first-time voters, and by 38 percent of older voters.

The second and first round results were consistent. More young voters voted for Yudhoyono-Kalla than for Megawati-Hasyim. Similarly, the proportion of older voters was greater for Megawati-Hasyim than for Yudhoyono-Kalla. In terms of the distribution of each group, 66 percent of younger voters chose Yudhoyono-Kalla compared to 34 percent for Megawati-Hasyim. Overall in this election Yudhoyono-Kalla won 60 percent and Megawati-Hasyim 40 percent, plus or minus 6 percent compared to the distribution based on age groups. Among seniors, those who chose Yudhoyono-Kalla and Megawati-Hasyim were about the same, each about 50 percent, with about a 20 percent gap in the total votes of the two candidates. This means that older voters preferred the incumbent over the opposition.

This pattern also describes 2009. The proportion of young voters who chose the incumbent Yudhoyono was smaller than the proportion who chose Kalla. In terms of the distribution, 52 percent of younger voters chose Yudhoyono, while 22 percent chose Kalla. Among all voters, 61 percent chose Yudhoyono, while Kalla won only 12 percent. In other words, the proportion of young Kalla voters was twice the proportion of his total vote. Yudhoyono was lower, that is, about 9 percent of this age group compared to his total vote of 60 percent. But this pattern does not explain the choice of Yudhoyono over Megawati. There was no significant difference in votes won by age group between these two candidates. In other words, Megawati, compared to Kalla, was less seen as a challenger to the incumbent Yudhoyono.

As we expected, in 2014 age was not important. Neither Jokowi nor Prabowo had an incumbent to oppose. Younger voters tend to choose the opposition, but in this election, they were not given that choice.

We may conclude that the difference in age groups was important in the presidential elections and in turnout, though not in the choice of members of Parliament. More seniors than juniors tended to come to the polling place. The desire to participate was more meaningful for the older generation. As we will explain later, the probable cause is a deeper understanding on the part of the older generation that participation in elections is a citizen's obligation.

The importance of age groups in the presidential elections is connected to the tendency of the young to want change and of the old to want to maintain the status quo. In the election of members of Parliament, distinguishing incumbents from opposition is apparently too complex a task for voters because of the large number of parties and the fact that for many parties it is not clear whether they are in the government or the opposition. In the presidential election, the opposition of challenger Kalla to incumbent President Yudhoyono was clearer than the opposition of Partai Golkar to Partai Demokrat.

The tendency of the young not to vote and to support the opposition or oppose the status quo shows that in future Indonesian voters are likely to become more critical. If the young are absent from voting now they will be absent in the future as well. In the long run, participation will decline even further. Voters will become more rational and free-riders.

THE INDEPENDENCE OF THE SOCIOLOGICAL EFFECT

Sociological factors have a range of effects on political participation and choice. Muslim religiosity impacts involvement in social activities and then political participation. Religiosity also influences political choice in both parliamentary and presidential elections. Is this influence independent of other sociological factors like ethnicity and regionalism, social class, gender, and age? In the comparative literature, sociological factors other than religion are known to have a range of influences on participation and choice.

The same question applies to the significant effect of regionalism, ethnicity, and social class. Do these factors have an influence independent of other sociological factors? In Table 4.1, multivariate analysis shows that several sociological factors have a significant, independent, and consistent effect, relatively independent of other factors, that is religiosity, involvement in religious organizations, and age groups.[38]

Muslim religiosity, including obligatory and recommended rituals, contains within it not only a commitment to faith but also a feeling of collectivity. Faith and obligatory ritual provide a positive evaluation of collective rituals, like collective prayer and Qur'anic study. Collective prayer and Qur'anic study are rooted in faith and obligatory ritual. Hierarchically, it is not possible to pray collectively or engage in Qur'anic study without an underlying faith and positive evaluation of obligatory ritual.

The product of obligatory and recommended rituals for a Muslim is a community that has social as well as personal value. Ritual plays a mediating role for citizens, enabling them to share problems facing the community. The religious community opens a way not only to talk about problems of religion but of the larger society as well. It is also a medium for the discussion of political affairs, such as parliamentary and presidential elections. Positive views of these elections are likely to emerge which will in turn motivate pious citizens to participate.

Related to this is the tendency of citizens who are active in performing religious rituals to become involved in large religious social organizations like Nahdlatul Ulama and Muhammadiyah. It is difficult to imagine someone who is active in NU but who does not believe that faith and ritual are important. The same is true for Muhammadiyah and other religious social organizations.

Religion and religiosity help to raise the level of participation in elections even though the citizen's level of education or socioeconomic level is low. This can be seen in the finding that education by itself does not motivate a citizen to vote. Indeed, there is a tendency, though not consistent, for citizens with higher education not to vote in either parliamentary or presidential elections. Similarly, urban citizens tend not to show up at the polling place on election day, while rural citizens do. Conversely,

---

[38] This multivariate analysis uses logistic regression (logit) because the dependent variable is nominal: voting or not voting. Linear regression cannot be used because the variable is not linear. Logit is a regression statistic that is suitable for dependent variables that are not continuous, ordinal, interval, or a ratio. The effect of each independent variable on the dependent variable (voting=1, not voting=0), is read as follows: The possibility of the influence of one independent variable on voting or not voting is ... controlled by other independent variables. Asterisks show the statistical probability of significant influence at a level of probability smaller than or the same as .001 (***), .01 (**), and with .05 (*). No asterisk means no statistically significant influence. Concerning logit see Long (1997).

age is positively associated with voting; the older the citizen, the more likely he or she is to vote.

This portrait shows that participation in Indonesian elections rests on conservative social forces: citizens who are religious, rural, and older. They are not a progressive force, which is much more present in cities, among younger and more educated populations. They do not vote for instrumental reasons, because they tend to have less information and knowledge concerning the purpose of elections. They vote in parliamentary and presidential elections without specific goals other than participating in those elections. Voting for them is the obligation of a citizen, with its own value, not an instrument to achieve other practical goals which they value. Voting is like a ritual, whose value is inherent in the ritual itself.

In the future, fewer citizens will vote as Indonesians become more urban and better educated and the generations change. As we wrote at the beginning of this chapter, first-time voters who do not use their right to vote will continue not to vote at subsequent elections. There are signs that younger voters use their right to vote less than older voters. With the passage of time, the number of citizens who vote will continue to shrink.

This tendency parallels developments in older and more developed democracies, especially in Western Europe. As described in Chapter 1, it is the question that drives Norris' *Democratic Deficit* (2011). Does it threaten democracy? If elections are the only form that democracy takes, the answer has to be yes. Fortunately, democracy is not only elections, but many other things as well, such as freedom of association and to have opinions, to demonstrate, protest, sign petitions, and so on.

The influence of religiosity and involvement with one's religious group on participation, defined as voting plus the other forms we have discussed – participating in campaigns, helping, donating, persuading – are also important, even though the associations are not consistent (Table 4.2).[39] Compared to other sociological factors, religiosity and involvement in religious social organizations are the most influential factors in explaining participation. Age is also important, while the influence of gender varies. In voting, male gender is not significant, and tends to be negative, but when participation is other than voting, gender influence

---

[39] In the 1999 and 2004 elections participation only consisted of two items: voting and participating in campaigns or general meetings. For the 2009 election, we added helping a party or candidate's success team, persuading others, and donating. Each item constituted a nominal scale: yes (1), no (0). From these items, we constructed an index of participation by summing the scores of all of the items to form an ordinal variable, from never (0) to more than one (2, 3, 4, and so on). For this reason, our multivariate analysis used linear regression.

TABLE 4.2 *Political participation regression*

	1999	2004a	2004b	2004c	2009a	2009b	2014a	2014b
Constant	.965 (.071)	.843*** (.112)	.824*** (.084)	.538*** (.078)	.919*** (.072)	.528 (.607)	1.144*** (.118)	.734*** (.143)
Religiosity	0.85*** (.020)	.063 (.034)	.005 (.026)	.078** (.025)	.076*** (.020)	.090** (.030)	.009 (.029)	.090** (.034)
Religious Organization	.009 (.033)	.187*** (.043)	.030 (.031)	.098*** (.028)	.084 (.049)	.269*** (.060)	.177*** (.044)	.133** (.051)
Java Island	.001 (.025)	-.036 (.038)	-.013 (.030)	.014 (.029)	-.087* (.043)	.066 (.598)	-.196*** (.038)	-.018 (.046)
Education	-.002 (.005)	-.002 (.019)	-.006 (.015)	-.032* (.014)	.032 (.022)	.019 (.025)	.007 (.009)	.005 (.010)
Urban	.024 (.026)	-.049 (.40)	-.101** (.031)	-.091** (.029)	.007 (.268)	-.009 (.052)	.034 (.039)	.074 (.047)
Age	-.096*** (.014)	-.003* (.002)	.055** (.019)	.055*** (.018)	-.005 (.029)	.057* (.029)	-.001 (.001)	-.002 (.002)
Male	.171*** (.024)	.176*** (.036)	.081** (.030)	-.013 (.029)	.148*** (.040)	.018 (.047)	.195*** (.036)	.108* (.045)
R²	.049	.054	.034	.061	.025	.057	.046	.030
N	2142	987	957	998	1619	1020	1446	846

is more significant, more consistent, and more positive. This indicates that men are more active in campaigning, helping parties and candidates, donating, and persuading others. In general, men are more active in politics than women, apart from class or religious social organization background.

It is important to underline here that religiosity and involvement in a religious group strongly support political participation apart from other sociological factors. Religiosity and group involvement counter the negative effect of education and age on voting. Indeed, it can be argued that it will be religion, not education, that saves the polling place from being abandoned by citizens.

How about the influence of these sociological factors on voting for parties and candidates? Does religion and religiosity have an impact? Even though much of the theoretical and practical debate about religion and politics is appropriately about variants of Islam, we need also to look at the impact of world religions present in Indonesia: Islam, Protestant and Catholic Christianity, Buddhism, Confucianism, and perhaps others. Even though the variation in religion understood in this way is small, and relatively consistent from election to election, we still need to examine its impact on political choice.

Table 4.3 displays the results of our multivariate analysis of the effect of religious difference and Muslim religiosity on political choice in the 1999–2014 elections. Without controlling for or considering the impact of other factors, religion in this sense is significant at $p<.05$ or better as we have already stated.[40] The direction of the influence, negative or positive, is also clear.

---

[40] In the multivariate analysis presented in all the tables in this section the dependent variable is nominal, that is party or parliamentary candidate from the relevant party and presidential/vice presidential pair of candidates. The characteristics of this nominally scaled dependent variable do not allow us to use linear regression analysis because the effect of the independent variable on the dependent variable is not linear, which forms a straight, but instead nonlinear, which forms an S curve. What is presented in the tables below are coefficients for the effect of every independent variable on the dependent variable in the form of the difference in predicted probability. This requires an additional statistic, the Monte Carlo simulation, to calculate the coefficient of difference in predicted probability from that logit. This coefficient is presented to help the reader to read more easily how significant (p value) and how large (coefficient) is the effect of each independent variable (religion, ethnicity, etc.) on each dependent variable. The way to read it is as follows: The effect of the difference in likelihood of choosing a party or presidential candidate that is calculated from the minimum to the maximum value of a given independent variable, significant at the level of probability of 0.05 or better is … (coefficient) percent when the other (control) independent variables are each made constant at their medians. Concerning logit, see Long (1997); Long and Freese (2005); Jann (2005); Jann (2007); Colton (2000).

TABLE 4.3 *Effect of religion on political choice in parliamentary elections, 1999–2014 (change in predicted probability)*

	PDIP	Golkar	PKB	PPP	PAN	PD	PKS	Gerindra	Hanura	NasDem
Religion										
1999[1]	-0.36***	0.01	0.15***	0.11***	0.09***					
1999[2]	-0.19**	NS	0.01*	0.04***	0.01*					
2004[1]	-0.30***	-.01	0.13***	0.10***	0.07***	-0.10	0.10***			
2004[2]	-0.09	NS	0.03	0.09**	0.05*	NS	0.02*			
2009[1]	-0.23***	-0.05	0.06***	0.07***	-0.01	0.04	0.10***	0.04*	-0.02	
2009[2]	-0.12**	NS	0.00	0.06**	NS	NS	0.03	0.02	NS	
2014[1]	-.21***	-0.02	0.05**	0.06***	0.07***	-0.02	0.06***	0.03	0.04**	-.06*
2014[2]	-.16**	NS	0.02	0.17***	0.07*	NS	0.14***	NS	0.03*	-0.02
Muslim Religiosity										
1999[1]	-0.70***	0.13**	0.28***	0.17***	0.11***					
1999[2]	-.32***	0.01	0.02**	0.07**	0.00					
2004[1]	-.38***	-0.10	0.21***	0.17***	0.04	-0.02	0.07			
2004[2]	-0.21	NS	0.03	0.08	0.00	NS	NS			
2009[1]	-0.35***	0.03	0.05	0.09**	0.05	0.00	0.11*	0.01	0.03	

(continued)

TABLE 4.3 (continued)

	PDIP	Golkar	PKB	PPP	PAN	PD	PKS	Gerindra	Hanura	NasDem
2009[2]	-0.07	NS	NS	0.02	NS	NS	0.01	NS	NS	
2014[1]	-.17**	-0.07	0.12***	0.03	0.06*	0.02	0.08**	0.05	-0.07	-0.04
2014[2]	-0.02	NS	0.08*	NS	0.05	NS	0.04	NS	NS	NS

[1] Analysis with only one variable (religion or Muslim religiosity).

[2] Analysis of the effect of religion or Muslim religiosity after being controlled for other sociological factors (ethnicity, education, rural-urban difference, age, and gender), political economy, and psychological factors (quality of leadership and identification with relevant party).

NS = if the analysis without control variables showed no significance the analysis was not continued.

*** p = 0.001, ** p = 0.01, and * p = 0.05

As many observers have argued, a lower proportion of Muslims compared to non-Muslims significantly and consistently picked PDIP across the four democratic elections. Non-Muslim voters mostly voted for PDIP at the national level but the non-Muslim population is only about 12 percent.[41] Conversely, within the PKB, PPP, PAN, and PKS, the proportion of Muslim is larger than that of non-Muslim voters. For the most part, there was no significant impact of religion on choice of Golkar, Demokrat, Gerindra, and Hanura during this period, and if there were significant relationships they were not consistent.

Before taking other factors into account, this pattern confirms the conclusion of many previous studies, but when religion is controlled for other theoretically relevant factors, its influence becomes less significant. If there are significant effects, they are not consistent. The influence of religious differences on PDIP drops sharply and even becomes insignificant in the 2004 election. The effect of religious difference on PDIP drops from 36 percent to 19 percent in 1999, and in 2009 23 percent becomes only 12 percent.

After considering other factors, PKB, PAN, and PKS experience still sharper drops in the relevance of religious differences. The effect of religious differences for PKB voters plummeted from 15 percent to 1 percent in the 1999 election, from 13 percent dropped to insignificant in the 2004 election, and from 6 percent to insignificant in the 2009 election (Table 4.4). PAN and PKS exhibit a similar pattern.

PPP is different. The effect of religious differences on PPP was significant across all elections after being controlled for other factors. Nonetheless, after considering those factors, the effect of religious difference was not great, on average below 10 percent. The likelihood that

---

[41] In this analysis, the dependent variables are the five main parties in the 1999 election, the seven main parties in the 2004 election, the nine main parties in the 2009 election plus all of the presidential/vice presidential pairs for each presidential election. The number of parties in the analysis is limited because all other parties received very small percentages of the votes (less than 3 percent), thus proportionally very few in our national survey samples (2500 in 1999, 1200 in all subsequent surveys). The dependent variables in this analysis were religion (Islam=1, others=0), ethnicity (Java=1, others=0), level of education scaled from 1 to 10: (1=never attended school, 10=graduated from a tertiary institution), social group, a combined score of active membership in religious (1), labor (1), farmer (1), sports organizations (1), and nonmembers in any organization received 0. In addition, place of residence (urban=1, rural=0), age (from 17 till the oldest), and gender (male=1, female=0).

TABLE 4.4 *Effect of religion on political choice in presidential elections,*
2004–2014 (change in predicted probability)

	Megawati-Hasyim (Prabowo) [Jokowi-Kalla]	Yudhoyono-Kalla (Boediono) [Prabowo-Hatta]	Wiranto-Salahuddin (Kalla-Wiranto)	Amien-Siswono	Hamzah-Agum
Religion					
2004a[1]	−0.47***	0.12***	0.16***	0.16***	0.03***
2004a[2]	−0.30***	0.04	0.07	0.05**	0.00
2004b[1]	−0.35***	0.35***			
2004b[2]	−0.06	0.06	0.03	0.09**	0.05*
2009[1]	(−0.38***)	(0.29***)	(0.09***)		
2009[2]	(0.15**)	(0.32***)	0.02		
2014[1]	[−0.32***]	[0.32***]			
2014[2]	[−0.21***]	[0.34***]			
Muslim Religiosity					
2004a[1]	−0.25**	−0.19*			
2004a[2]	−.07	0.17			
2004b[1]	−0.01	0.10			
2004b[2]	NS	NS			
2009[1]	(−0.19*)	(0.15)	(0.04)		
2009[2]	(0.00)	NS	NS		
2014[1]	[−0.31***]	[0.31***]			
2014[2]	[−0.25*]	[0.27*]			

[1]Analysis with only one independent variable (religion or Muslim religiosity)
[2]Analysis of the effect of religion or Muslim religiosity after being controlled for other socio-logical factors (ethnicity, education, rural-urban residence, age, and gender), political economy, and psychological factors (quality of leadership and identification with the relevant party).
NS = if the analysis without control variables showed no significance the analysis was not continued.
***$p = 0.001$, **$p = 0.01$, and *$p = 0.05$

Muslim compared to non-Muslim voters would choose PPP became only 4 percent more in the 1999 election, 9 percent in the 2004 election, 6 percent in 2009, and 5 percent in 2014.[42]

---

[42] According to some scholars, the effect of an independent variable on a dependent variable in logistic analysis may be considered large if it is above 10 percent (Colton 2000).

The maximum conclusion that can be drawn from these findings is that the influence of religious differences on political choice in Indonesian elections is small when considered together with other potentially important factors such as ethnicity, education, political economy, quality of leadership, party identity, and others. The effect of religion is restricted to PDIP and PPP. It is small on PPP, and inconsistent concerning PDIP. There is little effect on other parties.

The impact of religion on political choice becomes even less important if religion is understood as variation in the level of Muslim religiosity or the *santri-abangan* variant among Muslims and when the effect of this religiosity is controlled for other factors. The effect of Muslim religiosity, if we do not consider other factors, is significant, especially in the 1999 election. But this influence declines in the other elections.

Without considering other factors, the effect of Muslim religiosity is only significant for PDIP, PKB, and PPP in 2004, and only for PDIP, PPP, and PKS in 2009. This was also the case in 2014. The influence of religiosity, when other factors are set aside, is only relevant for PDIP, PKS, PKB, and to a small extent PAN. It does not explain the choice of other large parties such as Golkar, Demokrat, and Gerindra.

After considering other factors, in general the effect loses significance or at least weakens. Before considering other factors, the pious *santri* Muslims are 36 percent less likely to choose PDIP than the less-Islamically pious *abangan* in the 1999 election. But this effect declines to 19 percent after controlling for other factors. In that 1999 election, the significance and substance of the Muslim religiosity effect declines sharply for Islamist parties (PPP) and parties based on Islamic social organizations. For PPP the decline is from 17 percent to 7 percent, for PKB to 2 percent, and for PAN there is no longer statistical significance. The decline in effect is even greater in the 2004 election, especially for PDIP.

It is necessary to note here that the effect of Muslim religiosity is insignificant in the case of PKS, consensually considered the most Islamic party. This may be because what is meant by "most Islamic" for PKS is Islamist ideology rather than the intensity of carrying out of religious rituals. This possibility requires further research. The finding is the same for the 2009 and even weaker for the 2014 election. In 2014, religiosity was totally unimportant for all parties after considering other factors.

From all of the above findings, we can conclude that the effect of Muslim religiosity or the *santri-abangan* variant, measured by the intensity of ritual performance, is not important in shaping political choice in democratic Indonesia since 1999. Put differently, the *santri-abangan* effect has become increasingly unimportant in Indonesian elections. Muslim religiosity does not much help us to understand voters' partisan choices.

In the presidential election, the effect of religion is in general important, even after weighing other factors (Table 4.4). In 2004, the effect of religion was felt in the first round but not the second, where other factors like party ID and leadership were more important. This makes sense because in the second round the religion and religiosity profile of the two contestants, Yudhoyono and Megawati, was about the same. In the first round the religion effect was stronger because the additional candidates were Amien Rais and Hamzah Haz, well-known Muslim figures.

If we set aside other factors except religion or Muslim religiosity, Muslim voters were 47 percent less likely to choose Megawati compared to non-Muslim voters. Conversely, Muslim voters were more likely to choose Yudhoyono by 12 percent, Amien by 16 percent, Wiranto by 16 percent, and Hamzah Haz by 3 percent. After being controlled for nonreligious factors, the effect of religion on Megawati's vote declined from minus 47 percent to minus 30 percent, and for other candidates became insignificant.

The effect of Muslim religiosity, or the *santri-abangan* variant, was similar. Before being controlled for other factors, Muslim religiosity correlated significantly with choice of presidential/vice presidential candidates in the four elections surveyed. Nonetheless, this relationship became insignificant when Muslim religiosity was controlled by other factors. This was not because of religious homogeneity, because the candidates were in fact diverse. It was not only Yudhoyono and Megawati, both of whom might be called *abangan*, who contested, but also Amien Rais, Hamzah Haz, and Jusuf Kalla.

These three latter figures were known by the voting public to be closely connected to the *santri* community: Hamzah as the head of an Islamic party, Amien as a former head of Muhammadiyah, and Kalla as an alumnus of a major Muslim university student organization and an NU leader in his home region of South Sulawesi. Especially in the 2009 election, the *santri* background of Kalla was prominently displayed in his campaign to draw a contrast with the ostensibly *abangan* Yudhoyono and Megawati. But this effort did not have a substantial impact after voters weighed other factors, especially the political economy, quality of leadership, and party identity.

In 2014, however, the effects of religion and Muslim religiosity were important. Non-Muslim voters tended to choose Jokowi over Prabowo regardless of other factors. This was also the case when religion is understood as Muslim religiosity. Muslims who are religious tended to choose Prabowo over Jokowi. The effect had lessened compared to previous elections but was still significant at the p>.05 level.

The stronger effect of Muslim religiosity on the 2014 presidential election is actually not surprising as an empirical finding. Compared with previous presidential elections, the 2014 campaigns were full of religious charges and counter-charges. Prabowo was promoted by his supporters as an Islamic spokesperson, while Jokowi was portrayed as a non-Muslim, even antireligion or communist.

The reality was of course very different. Prabowo had no credentials as an Islamic leader. His family was cosmopolitan or pluralist. His mother was non-Muslim as were his siblings. His own father, while famous as an economist and public intellectual, was not a Muslim figure. So, it is more appropriate to regard Prabowo as a nationalist who is secular in his policy positions. Nonetheless, the mobilization of voters on the basis of religion was apparently successful enough to make religion and Muslim religiosity important in the election.

Of course, at the same time, the importance of this effect was limited compared to other factors so that Prabowo still was unable to use that issue alone to defeat Jokowi. This point will be elaborated in the following two chapters.

How about the influence of ethnicity? The difference in ethnic background had a significant impact on the choice of certain parties, especially Golkar, where it was negative, and PKB, where it was positive, with ethnic Javanese. After other factors are weighed, however, the influence of ethnicity for political choice weakens, and in general becomes not significant from one election to the next (Table 4.5). The difference between ethnic Javanese and other voters becomes unimportant for all parties except PKB and PPP in the 1999 election, Golkar in 2004, and PKB in 2009. Even where there is some effect it is small, typically below 10 percent. In 2014 the effect disappeared.

The evidence for this proposition is even stronger in the case of presidential elections except in 2014. After controlling for other factors, it is apparent that ethnicity is not important in shaping the citizen's vote for president and vice president. This is not because of a lack of diversity in the ethnic backgrounds of the presidential candidates, but rather because of the power of other factors. Hamzah Haz and Jusuf Kalla, prominent non-Javanese, were contestants in these elections, it will be recalled, but their backgrounds did not have a significant effect on the vote.

TABLE 4.5 *Effect of ethnic background on political choice in parliamentary and presidential elections, 1999–2014* (change in predicted probability)

	PDIP	Golkar	PKB	PPP	PAN	PD	PKS	Gerindra	Hanura	NasDem
Parliamentary Election										
1999[1]	0.14**	−0.17***	0.14***	−0.10***	−0.01					
1999[2]	0.03	−0.01	0.02*	−0.03***	NS					
2004[1]	0.07*	−.14***	0.03	0.00	−0.03	0.03				−0.09***
2004[2]	−0.03	−0.13***	NS	−0.01	NS	NS	−0.01			
2009[1]	0.05	−0.06*	0.06***	−0.02	−0.02	0.00	0.01	0.00	−0.02	
2009[2]	0.03	−0.01	0.07***	NS	NS	NS	0.03	0.02	TS	
2014[1]	0.08***	−.05**	0.06***	−0.02	−0.02	−.04*	0.01	−0.03	−0.01	0.00
2014[2]	0.06	−0.02	0.03	NS	NS	−0.03	NS	NS	NS	NS
Presidential Election	Megawati-Hasyim (Prabowo) [Jokowi-Kalla]	Yudhoyono-Kalla (Boediono) [Prabowo-Hatta]	Wiranto-Salahuddin (Kalla-Wiranto)	Amien-Siswono	Hamzah-Agum					
2004a[1]	−0.01	0.05	−0.05	0.01	0.00					

(continued)

142

2004a²	NS	NS	NS	NS	NS
2004b²	0.06	-0.06			
2004b²	NS	NS			
2009¹	(0.03)	(0.07*)	(-0.10***)		
2009²	NS	(0.02)	(-0.01)		
2014¹	[0.07*]	[-0.07*]			
2014²	[0.12**]	[-0.09*]			

[1] Analysis with only one independent variable (ethnicity: Java=1, other=0).

[2] Analysis of the effect of ethnicity after being controlled for other factors (Muslim religiosity, education, rural-urban residence, age, and gender), political economy, and psychological factors (quality of leadership and identification with relevant party).

NS = if the analysis without control variables showed no significance the analysis was not continued.

***p = 0.001, **p = 0.01, and *p = 0.05

However, as in the case of religion and religiosity, the effect of ethnicity was important in the 2014 presidential election. After controlling for other factors, Javanese voters tended to prefer Jokowi and outer island voters Prabowo. Both are in fact Javanese, although Jokowi may have been perceived as more Javanese because Prabowo is more cosmopolitan. Jokowi was raised in Java and his political career began in the heart of traditional Javanese culture, in Surakarta, Central Java. Prabowo, on the other hand, as the son of a national political figure was raised outside that culture, indeed spent many of his formative years outside the country. After finishing his military education, he also had a career at the national level in the army.

What was the effect of social class? We limit ourselves here to the role of education. Across the parliamentary elections, education in general did not have a significant effect controlling for other factors (Table 4.6). Even PAN and PKS, previously thought to be supported by the more highly educated, turn out not to be. The effect of education has declined from election to election.

A different picture appears in 2014. As in the case of religion and ethnicity, the effect of education also continues to be important after controlling for several other factors. Education had a positive effect for Prabowo but not Jokowi. In other words, the more educated tended to choose Prabowo.

This is an interesting finding because of several issues relevant to more educated voters, particularly human rights and opposition to racial, ethnic, and religious discrimination, which seem, in the end, not to have been important for many educated voters. Prabowo was attacked as a person not fit to become president because of his alleged human rights violations, including the murder of dissidents and fomenting racial disturbances in 1998. Prabowo had in fact been discharged from the army for these violations, even though he was one of the highest-ranking officers at the time. This fact was apparently not important for educated voters who supported Prabowo anyway.

It is also likely that for educated voters Prabowo's presumed competence as a leader was more important than his integrity. In the debates, Prabowo certainly appeared to be more intelligent and more familiar with national and international politics than Jokowi. His rhetorical style was also perhaps more convincing than Jokowi's, to the point that educated voters were willing to overlook his seemingly disqualifying military service record.

TABLE 4.6 *Effect of education on political choice in parliamentary and presidential elections, 1999–2014 (change in predicted probability)*

	PDIP	Golkar	PKB	PPP	PAN	PD	PKS	Gerindra	Hanura	NasDem
Parliamentary Election										
1999[1]	-0.17***	-0.04	-0.11***	-0.09***	0.41***					
1999[2]	0.03	TS	-0.01	-0.04*	0.06					
2004[1]	-0.24***	-.17***	-0.07	-0.11***	0.05	0.01	0.27***			
2004[2]	-0.07	-0.13***	NS	-0.12*	0.10	0.01	0.07*			
2009[1]	0.05*	-0.06*	-0.06*	-0.06*	-0.02	0.00	0.14***	0.08	0.00	
2009[2]	0.03	0.04	-0.01	-0.03	NS	NS	0.01	NS	NS	
2014[1]	0.03	-.09***	-.11***	0.02	0.08**	0.02	0.07**	0.04	0	-.07***
2014[2]	NS	-0.01	-0.02	NS	0.08	NS	0.04	NS	NS	-0.06
Presidential Election	Megawati-Hasyim (Prabowo) [Jokowi-Kalla]	Yudhoyono-Kalla (Boediono) [Prabowo-Hatta]	Wiranto-Salahuddin (Kalla-Wiranto)	Amien-Siswono	Hamzah-Agum					
2004a[1]	-0.22***	0.09	-0.16***	0.32***	-0.03					
2004a[2]	-0.17**	NS	-0.22***	0.15***	NS					
2004b[1]	-.11	-0.11								

(continued)

145

TABLE 4.6 (continued)

	PDIP	Golkar	PKB	PPP	PAN	PD	PKS	Gerindra	Hanura	NasDem
Parliamentary Election										
2004b[2]	NS	NS								
2009[1]	(−0.28***)	(0.07)	(0.21***)							
2009[2]	−0.01	NS	(0.08*)							
2014[1]	[−0.23***]	[0.23***]								
2014[2]	[−0.12]	[0.22]***								

[1] Analysis only with one independent variable (level of education).
[2] Analysis of the effect of education after being controlled for other sociological factors (religion, ethnicity, rural-urban residence, age, and gender) political economy, and psychological factors (the quality of leadership and identification with the relevant party).
NS = if the analysis without control variables indicates no significance the analysis was not continued.
$***p = 0.001$, $**p = 0.01$, and $*p = 0.05$

146

CONCLUSIONS

The effect of sociological and demographic variables on political participation and choice may be summarized as follows. Muslim religiosity helps shape social solidarity through the formation of a religious community. The involvement of citizens in this community is not exclusive. This finding is contrary to the claims of scholars like Huntington, who believe that Islam as political ideology is inimical to interreligious cooperation and indeed to democracy in Muslim-majority countries.

In the Indonesian case, Muslim religiosity tends to be inclusive, to encourage involvement in nonreligious social groups. Religious Muslims are more active in social networks which makes them open to various sources of information, motivation, and mobilization to participate in politics, including parliamentary and presidential elections.

At the bottom of society, Muslim religiosity helps citizens whose socioeconomic status is low, who have little education or income, work in blue-collar jobs, and live in villages to participate in elections. Because they are less educated and live in villages, these citizens most likely do not vote for instrumental or rational reasons. They are not critical democrats. Their participation is more ritualistic, done on its own terms and for its own sake. For these voters, parliamentary and presidential elections tend to take the form of quinquennial celebrations, giving thanks (*syukuran*), or family or village ritual feasts (*selamatan*), not instruments to achieve other goals.

In the cities, however, we observe the emergence of urban Muslims who do take a critical posture in their relationship to political participation, both voting and campaigning. We have seen that urban voters, especially those who are younger and with higher education, most of them of course Muslim because of Indonesia's huge Muslim majority, tend not to vote. If Indonesians become more prosperous, more educated, and more urban, it is likely that more and more of them will not vote. This social change almost certainly cannot be altered, and the negative effect on political participation therefore cannot be avoided. These are Norris' critical citizens and they are the group of voters that is most likely to expand.

At the same time, partisan choice has become increasingly unstable in the selection of members of Parliament. During each of the four elections there have been significant changes. Nearly every election produces a new party and a shift in the relative strengths of parties even though sociologically the patterns of support are stable. Secular parties have dominated throughout the period, while Islamist parties and parties based on Islamic social organizations have been in the minority. But there is little evidence of loyalty to particular parties. Parties once triumphant have often collapsed in the following election, as we have seen in the cases of the PDIP in 2004, Golkar in 2009, and Demokrat in 2014.

The emergence of critical democrats and their effect on the polity must be seen in the context of the institutions and supply of leaders and policies offered by the political elite. Voters tend to be critical of the incumbent and to desire change. If they perceive an option for a better choice they will tend to make that choice, in the process abandoning the incumbent. If that option does not exist, and if the incumbent doesn't participate in the election, their critical attitude will not be accommodated. In that situation, sociological factors like religion and regionalism play a bigger role in influencing their choices. Nonetheless, so far at least, both of the successful presidential candidates in the era of direct elections have been secular and Javanese.

The tendency toward the emergence of critical democrats and its effect on voting and political choice will be examined in more detail in Chapter 5. We next ask how rational and critical Indonesian voters have become.

5

Rational Voters

Chapter 4 has shown that sociological factors are not a sufficient explanation for Indonesian voters' behavior. Religious, ethnic, and social class differences have not much changed in recent years, in contrast to the rapid changes experienced in support for parties and candidates in parliamentary and presidential elections. This chapter explores the extent to which voter rationality helps us explain these changes. Does the decline in participation that we have observed reflect the increasing rationality of the Indonesian voter? In other words, is it true that if elections represent collective goods and do not provide personal incentives citizens will tend not to vote? Further, do the changes in relative party strengths in Parliament and also in the presidency reflect voters' rational decisions to reward and punish the parties and candidates?

POLITICAL PARTICIPATION

In Chapter 3, we discovered that the level of participation in voting in parliamentary elections declined significantly, from 93 percent (1999) to 84 percent (2004) and 71 percent (2009), although it slightly increased to 75 percent in 2014. In the direct presidential elections, it declined from 80 percent in the 2004 first round to 76.5 percent in the second round, 73 percent in the 2009 single round, and 71 percent in the 2014 single round. These declines are significant. Do they indicate that the voters are increasingly rational as expected by rational voter theorists?

In rational voter theory, human beings are actors who calculate the costs and benefits of their personal or individual actions (Downs 1957;

Olson 1965; Riker and Ordeshook 1968). Every action must benefit the individual himself or herself, not any collective to which the individual belongs. However, elections produce public goods, elected officials or public policies, and therefore any contribution of citizens to elections, small or large, does not provide personal or selective incentives.

The concept of a collective good in this literature has broad meaning. For our purposes, it may be applied to a publicly documented decision such as an election result. Candidate A is elected to Parliament, party B receives a million votes, presidential candidate C wins an absolute majority, and so on. These events are documented in the form of decisions made by an authoritative election body, in Indonesia the National Election Commission or the Constitutional Court.

"Cost" or "capital" may include physical activity or time as well as material capital. One spends money to buy a meal, but spends time to exercise the right to vote. The personal benefit of voting to most individuals is less clear. There are voters who do receive direct benefits: the actual candidates for Parliament, regional legislatures, or the presidency, but they are a very small percentage of the total number of voters.

Election results are, however, a "public good," that is, a good that benefits all the members of the public regardless of their individual contributions. An elected member of Parliament is a member for all of the people, not just for a group or a specific individual. The same is true for an elected president. If the result will be enjoyed by all relatively equally, why should any given individual take the trouble to vote because those who do not vote will equally still have the benefit of having a member in Parliament or a president who leads the country?

Some studies of rational voting argue that voters do in fact have a direct interest in participating in elections. They feel a loss if the victorious parliamentary or presidential candidate does not represent their interests. They take the trouble to vote because they want to fight for their interests through their representatives or national leaders (Downs 1957). Norris takes the argument a step further, connecting the rational voter to her critical citizen, our critical democrat. In her words (2011, 210), "if citizens feel that the party they prefer consistently loses, over successive elections they are more likely to feel that their voice is excluded from the decision-making process, producing generalized dissatisfaction with the regime."

Is it true that citizens do not vote because they are rational actors who calculate personal benefits and losses (that is, voting does not give them a selective or personal incentive)? Alternatively, perhaps citizens are not convinced that their candidate or party will win, or do not have enough

TABLE 5.1 *Reasons for not voting in parliamentary and presidential elections (%)*

	2004b	2004c	2009a	2009b	2014a	2014b
Less important or unimportant	46	46	38	50	64	50
Not registered or ill	46	37	56	49	23	20
No answer	8	17	6	1	13	30
Total	100	100	100	100	100	100

information to differentiate between candidates, and therefore don't know which to choose?

Table 5.1 provides a general picture of why Indonesian citizens who have the right to vote do not exercise that right. There are many reasons, but when simplified we can see that about half regard elections as unimportant and accordingly choose to engage in another activity. This view tended to increase over time in the elections that we studied. In 2014, among those who said they did not vote in the legislative election that year, 64 percent said it was because they thought the election was personally unimportant.

For the presidential election, among those who did not vote, 50 percent said it was not important to vote. Among those who said they did not vote because they were not registered or ill (which may imply that for them elections remain important), the proportion declined significantly. This indicates that the percentage of citizens who feel a personal and direct benefit has been declining. Possible explanations for this are that they feel alienated or have chosen to become free-riders.[1]

If level of education is used as an indicator of voter rationality, we argue that it is the more educated voters who are the more rational, and therefore the more educated a voter is the more likely he or she is not to vote. The data show that there are consistently more college graduates

---

[1] The reason for not voting was only asked in these six national surveys. The answers were very diverse, including being out of town or out of the region, not at home, needed to work, confused as to which party to choose because of the number of parties, lack of differentiation between presidential candidates, and no influence on the voter's life, giving the impression that elections are not important events but can easily be avoided. Other reasons were technical, that is, the citizen wanted to vote but couldn't because he or she was not registered or was ill.

relative to citizens with elementary education who did not vote. In the 2004 presidential election the difference was 22 percent, in the 2009 legislative and presidential elections it was 23 percent and 50 percent, and in 2014 it was 37 percent in the legislative and 22 percent in the presidential election. Since there is a tendency for the more educated population to grow over time, we can predict that the number of rational voters will grow and participation in elections will decline.

Decline in voting turnout is a problem in many democracies, as Norris (1999, 2011) and many others have argued. Nonetheless, in the Indonesian case, more than half of Indonesian voters still avail themselves of their right to vote. Why?

In the rational voter perspective, this question is answered by testing various concepts that are asserted to have a connection with rationality, like a feeling of embarrassment or shame toward other members of society if one does not vote, internalized guilt for not being a good citizen, or even a religion-derived feeling that one has sinned by not voting (Blais 2000, 93). Riker and Ordeshook refer to it as a feeling of civic duty that persuades citizens to vote even though they must pay a cost, for example in time spent going to the polling place (Riker and Ordeshook 1968).

There are various ways to measure the concept of civic duty in the context of electoral participation, for example, by asking voters if they feel guilty if they do not vote (Blais 2000). In our several surveys, we asked voters directly why they vote.[2] Their answers varied. The greatest number, but less than a majority, said they felt an obligation to vote. All of the other answers – they believed it to be their right as citizens, or they wanted better leadership, they wanted to live better, or they were following someone else, and so on – taken together were a larger percentage.

The meaning of voting as an obligation is in fact obscure. It could be expressive or instrumental. It is expressive or symbolic if the meaning is internal to the voter himself or herself, in other words a ritual act. An example is an expression of happiness or pride with democratic elections because "democracy" or "freedom" has positive value, or it demonstrates a higher level of political culture to the individual.

"Obligation" can have an instrumental meaning if it is meant to avoid a feeling of guilt or embarrassment if others do not vote, or to be afraid that

---

[2] The wording was: "In the election for members of Parliament (president) that is just past, there were citizens who did not vote, with a range of reasons. How about you, did you vote?" 1. Yes 2. No. Those who said yes were told that everyone has a reason for voting, then given a list of possible reasons from which to choose.

one's candidate will lose. Other reasons, like one's right as a citizen, or wanting to have better leadership, or following others, are more instrumental than expressive. And these numbers are greater. This is what makes a majority of voters continue to show up on election day even though seen through a rational lens voting remains a paradoxical act.

Our tentative conclusion is that the level of participation of Indonesian voters has been declining. This is happening at the same time as the voters' economic condition has been improving, meaning that the middle class has been growing. They are more educated and more open and exposed to a range of political news. This indicates that the number of rational versus the number of expressive or symbolic voters has been growing, which in turn raises an alarm concerning future elections because it is this group that tends not to vote.

How about choosing particular candidates or parties? How rational are they in their choices?

POLITICAL CHOICE

Does rationality explain why a voter chooses candidate A or B, party C or D? The model of the rational voter is based on the conviction that human beings have material interests that are important to them. Voters calculate profits and losses when they make choices in the polling booth. They will vote for a candidate or party if they feel that that candidate or party is responsive to their material concerns (Downs 1957).

In this model, profit and loss are understood in terms of the voter's economic life, not other aspects of life such as security and order or morality. If security and order are important and influential, it is in so far as they have an effect on the economy. This model therefore specifies that the voter's evaluation of economic condition is connected to the choice of candidate and party.

For some scholars, rational voting is connected to issues that are believed to be most urgent or important for the voter, especially symbolic or identity issues versus technical issues. Symbolic issues are anchored in social group identities that are intrinsic or inherited, not instrumental, and have meaning only for the relevant group. Debate and competition are exclusive to specific groups, most prominently religious, ethnic, and regional groups, which are unable to accommodate the interests of other identity groups.

Muslim voters choose Muslim candidates because they intrinsically value being Muslim. Questions of competency or leadership ability do not arise, or are of lesser importance. Another example is putting a high value on Muslim dress for women and supporting government regulation of Muslim dress codes. This issue is of course only relevant to Muslim voters.

A similar argument applies to voting for candidates and parties on the basis of regional or racial affiliation. An ethnic Javanese voter chooses an ethnic Javanese candidate for that reason alone, not because the candidate is perceived to have more integrity or competence as a leader.

At the same time, many policy issues are technical issues with relevance to the whole society, not just particular ethnic or regional groups, and are transactional in nature. An example is the issue of the nine basic commodities (*sembilan bahan pokok* or *sembako*) that are a frequent and major subject of public discussion and policymaking in Indonesia. Everyone must consume these commodities, whatever his or her social or cultural identity. Muslims and Christians, Javanese and Buginese, West Javanese and West Sumatrans, NU members and Muhammadiyah members, all need to eat, drink, be clothed, have housing, and so on.

These technical issues are rational in the sense that their presence or absence, their quantity and quality, how necessary or important they are, are evaluated in terms of rational considerations regardless of identity. They are transactional in the sense that they can be exchanged for other commodities based on rational calculations of gain and loss.

If there are two parties that offer subsidies on basic commodities for the very young and the very old, for example, whether one party or the other wins will be determined by voter evaluations of how the policy is formulated and implemented and whether it conflicts with other policies, for example financing education. Let us say that Party A promises that if it comes to power the state budget will devote 20 percent of its resources to education, while Party B counters with a promise of 40 percent. Voters who care most about education will tend to vote for Party B, regardless of whether that party is Islamic or secular.

Symbolic issues, having to do with religion, race, ethnicity, and regionalism are prominent in every Indonesian election, even though not all voters consider them relevant. Some parties position themselves as more Islamic than others. Because the party leaders consider these symbols to be important in influencing voters, leaders of other parties also claim to have a commitment to religious values. One way to delegitimize a candidate or party's use of religious symbolism is by claiming that its program is in conflict with the Constitution or Pancasila, the national ideology. For example, it is alleged that if a particular Islamic party wins, the country will become an Islamic state, or Pancasila and the Constitution will be replaced with Islamic law.

In point of fact, through the 1999–2014 elections, there were no parties that explicitly proposed to make these fundamental changes in the political order. No parties even promised to end prostitution, the sale of alcoholic beverages, or to ban bank interest on the ground that these activities contravene Islamic law. Symbolic issues usually emerge implicitly during the campaign, and frequently in a negative form, to attract voters without promising to change public policies.

For example, when a party spokesman during a campaign bemoaned the decline of religious observance among youth, his statement of concern was not followed by a promise that if his party came to power it would formulate and implement policies to regulate religious observance. Symbolic issues of this sort typically only emerge during campaigns with no postelection follow-up.[3]

PKS and PPP, usually perceived as Islamic parties, have never explicitly promised to implement Islamic criminal law if they win a majority of seats in Parliament or elect a president. They have never directly proposed to ban bank interest, regardless of whether they consider it prohibited by religion or not.

The absence of explicitly raised symbolic issues during campaigns is probably due to party elites' assessment that voters do not assign high priority to this issue. According to our surveys, this perception is accurate. Before the 2009 legislative election, for example, potential voters were asked what national issues were most important and urgent for the government to address. Almost all the answers had to do with material or technical, not symbolic or identity issues. Many more voters highlighted the economic crisis, unemployment, poverty, governmental corruption, and similar issues, not symbolic issues like the decline in religious observance or regional issues.[4]

---

[3] It should also be stated that from the beginning of the authoritarian New Order until today there have been legal prohibitions on raising sensitive issues of religion, class, race, or ethnicity in election campaigns.

[4] The question was: "In your opinion, is there one problem that is most urgent that must be dealt with by the government in the next five years?" The question was open and the answers were spontaneous. In other surveys conducted by the Indonesian Survey Institute there have been closed questions, with responses that can be categorized into two issue categories, symbolic issues (moral problems, religion, regionalism, ethnicity, etc.) and material or technical issues (that is, employment opportunities, unemployment, poverty, health, education, corruption, etc.). The answers to the two types of questions are very similar. Most voters choose the material or technical issues, not the symbolic ones.

Awareness of this fact apparently persuades party leaders and candidates not to directly address identity issues as a way of attracting voters. It indicates that the behavior of the political elite and the parties is rational, conforming to the desires of the voters so that they can attract as many of those voters as possible.

The mechanism by which material issues, in particular economic condition, connect with rational voting behavior is relatively simple. The voters are happy with or feel that they benefit from an economy that they evaluate positively. Conversely, they feel angry or disadvantaged if they regard the condition of the economy as poor. Economic condition is then connected to government policies and actions. In other words, the government is regarded as being at least partially responsible for the condition of the economy. If the economic condition is good the government is praised, and if it is poor the government is blamed. In elections, this praise took the form of voting for the incumbent party or its parliamentary member or reelecting the incumbent president. Conversely, if the economic condition was poor, voters expressed their anger by voting for the opposition.

The rational voter model assumes the existence of a governing and an opposition party. In countries with simple party systems, particularly two party systems like the US, the difference between governing and opposition party is usually clear (Downs 1957; Fiorina 1981; Kiewiet 1984). In a multiparty system, on the other hand, especially if it is extremely fragmented as in the case of Indonesia since 1999, it is not easy for common citizens to judge which party is in and which is out of power.

Among the forty-eight parties contesting the 1999 election, it is not easy to determine which was in power and which in opposition, although Golkar at the time did have the most seats in Parliament and incumbent President Habibie was affiliated with Golkar. We can therefore assert that Golkar was the incumbent, even though its erstwhile New Order supporters were now spread among many competing parties.

Which party was the main opposition party? This was also difficult to determine, although PDIP perhaps most represented the spirit of opposition at the time because it had emerged at the end of the New Order as Golkar's principal antagonist. Other new parties also stood out as New Order opponents, however, and should also be considered, for example the Marxist PRD (Partai Rakyat Demokratik, Democratic People's Party), even though it too in the end did not win many votes. PKB was led by Abdurrahman Wahid, known from the 1980s as an opponent of the New Order, and PAN was created by Amien Rais, who had questioned Suharto's leadership starting in the mid-1990s.

With these players, one would expect that the effect of an objectively poor economy would be negative on Golkar, at least in contrast with PDIP, PKB, and PAN. Conversely, greater prosperity would have a positive impact on Golkar compared to these same opponents. In the 1999 election, PDIP won the most votes and the most seats. Nonetheless, the People's Consultative Assembly (at that time still the body with the constitutional authority to elect the president) did not choose Megawati, who was chair of PDIP, to become president. She was defeated by Abdurrahman Wahid but then elected vice president. Other large and medium size parties supported these choices, forming a coalition without parliamentary opposition.

The Assembly subsequently impeached and convicted President Wahid, so that his government fell and Megawati automatically replaced him as president. Wahid and PKB of course rejected the impeachment, forming an embryonic opposition. Prior to the 2004 election, however, Wahid was denied nomination for the presidency on physical fitness grounds by the National Election Commission. PKB was split on the issue, and both Wahid and the party became too weak to function as a proper opposition.

Prior to the 2004 elections, opposition to Megawati and her party came mainly from retired army general and former cabinet minister Susilo Bambang Yudhoyono, who established his own party, Partai Demokrat, just before the 2004 election. Competition between these two camps became intense as the parliamentary and presidential elections approached. It is here that we can see the first true pattern of contestation between an incumbent and an opposition. Other parties that had won seats in the previous 1999 election were in coalition with Megawati, including a faction from PKB.

The rational voter model is perhaps better equipped to explain this contestation, especially that between Megawati and PDIP on one side versus Yudhoyono and Partai Demokrat on the other. If, at that time, most voters had felt positive about the economy, they should have strongly supported Megawati and PDIP; if they felt negative, they should have supported Yudhoyono and Demokrat. In the 2004 parliamentary election PDIP declined sharply, after which Megawati was defeated by Yudhoyono in the presidential election. The number one position was taken over by Golkar; Partai Demokrat, even though a newcomer, won 7 percent, defeating Amien Rais' PAN.

The 2004 parliamentary and presidential elections made Yudhoyono and Demokrat the governing party, PDIP and Megawati the opposition.

Yudhoyono formed a coalition government in which Golkar become its main parliamentary support. The Golkar leadership was taken over by Jusuf Kalla, now vice president. Other parties joined their coalition.

In this context, prior to the 2009 elections, the rational voter concept was applicable to the relationship between Yudhoyono and Demokrat, in power, and Megawati and PDIP, out of power. If the economy was perceived positively, voters would tend to choose Yudhoyono and Demokrat, while if it was perceived negatively they would more likely vote for Megawati and PDIP.

The effect on other parties in the coalition would arguably be similar to that on Demokrat, but possibly there would be no effect because their position as coalition members was unclear. Golkar, for example, was in the coalition in 2004 but before the 2009 parliamentary and presidential elections it became an opposition party. To the degree to which the public found it difficult to understand Golkar's position, the rational voter logic becomes difficult to apply.

Prior to the 2014 elections, the pattern changed significantly. The main governing party in the Yudhoyono administration was Demokrat. The main opposition was PDIP. However, in the presidential election the difference was obscured for many voters, making a political economy argument less relevant. The Constitution limits presidents to two terms. This is what happened to President Yudhoyono in 2014. Yudhoyono's vice president in his second term, Boediono, a leading economist but nonpartisan, was also not nominated.

In the end, Yudhoyono and his party did not officially nominate anyone. The reason was that Demokrat's support in the parliamentary election in April of that year had plunged precipitously from 21 percent in 2009 to 10 percent. Demokrat was therefore unable to nominate its own candidate and subsequently failed to form a coalition with others.[5] The difference between incumbent and opposition had disappeared, so that the political economy model became irrelevant to this election.

The effect of the rational voter model also depends to a considerable extent on how the concept of economic condition is operationalized. Several studies rely on aggregate data on the national economic condition

---

[5] According to the Constitution, only a party or a coalition of parties with at least 20 percent of the seats in Parliament may nominate a president. The Demokrat Party and President Yudhoyono tried to find a candidate by holding a party convention, but the candidate produced by this process did not succeed in attracting support from other parties, so in the end Demokrat had no candidate of its own and was not part of any coalition.

from one time period to another, or on regional economic conditions within a country. Economic condition in this operationalization is mainly measured in economic growth, level of inflation, and level of unemployment (van der Brug, van der Eijk, and Franklin 2007, 69).

At the individual level, the economic condition is the voters' evaluation of their household's economy or the national economic condition in general. At the time of an election, voters who feel that their family's or nation's economic condition is better than a year previously will tend to vote for the incumbent candidate or party; conversely, if the economic condition is worse than the previous year, voters will tend to choose the opposition (Downs 1957; Kiewiet 1984). Kiewiet found that perceptions of the national economic condition are better predictors of the vote than perceptions of the family's economic condition because the former is more connected to the collectivity or nation (sociotropic) than to the individual (egotropic).[6]

Before assessing the importance of voters' evaluations of the national or family economic condition, we need to describe voters' assessments of those conditions at the time of the elections. Figure 5.1 shows variation in evaluations of national economic condition during parliamentary and presidential elections. In the first post-New Order election in 1999, most voters perceived that the national economic condition was worse than before the East Asian economic crisis, which started in 1997.[7]

That perception was supported by the facts on the ground. According to Central Statistical Body data, the condition of the economy in 1996, one year before the 1997 crisis, the economic growth rate was 7.8 percent, inflation 6.63 percent, and the level of unemployment 4.89 percent (Table 5.2).

The peak effect of the crisis was felt in 1998, when the growth rate plummeted to minus 13.1 percent, inflation surged to 77.63 percent, and the level of unemployment rose to 5.46 percent compared with 4.89 percent in 1996, prior to the crisis. In the 1999 election year, the economy began to recover, with a growth rate of .08 percent and a decline in the rate

---

[6] In the survey, the voter was asked to evaluate whether the present national economic condition, at the time of the election, was better, the same, or worse than the condition one year ago.

[7] In the postparliamentary election survey in 1999, the question used differs from that which we have used subsequently. In the 1999 survey, the question asked respondents to evaluate the economy before the 1997 crisis, not one year previously.

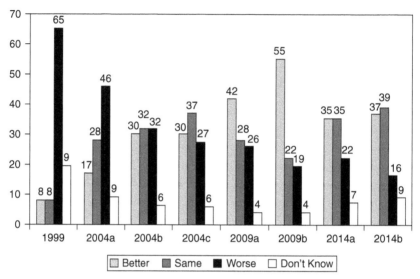

FIGURE 5.1 Perception of present national economic condition compared with last year, 1999–2014 (%)

of inflation to 2.01 percent, although unemployment continued to climb. According to the rational voter logic, the incumbent was almost certain to be hated by the voters.

The national economic condition in 1999 was better than 1998, to be sure, but still too weak to be made a useful argument by the incumbent. Economic growth was very low compared to the high expectations of the public after the powerful negative effect of the crisis. Inflation was low but that was not perceived as a positive sign. People were not able to buy goods because they had no money.

In the 2004 parliamentary election, there were more voters who said the national economic condition was better this year than the previous year, but the number was still smaller than those who said the opposite. The economy had in fact almost recovered. Growth in 2004 was 5 percent and inflation was relatively low (6.4 percent), although unemployment continued to rise (9.86 percent), indeed was at its highest level since 1997. The effect of the crisis on unemployment had continued even though the growth rate improved.

The situation at the time of the 2009 parliamentary election was very different. The context was a global economic crisis, during which some economists calculated that the effects could be worse than 1997–8,

TABLE 5.2 *Economic growth, inflation, and unemployment, 1996–2014 (%)*

	Growth	Inflation	Unemployment
1996	7.8	6.6	4.9
1997	4.7	10.3	4.7
1998	−13.1	77.6	5.5
1999	0.8	2.0	6.4
2000	4.9	9.3	6.1
2001	3.6	12.6	8.1
2002	4.5	10.0	9.1
2003	4.8	5.1	9.7
2004	5.0	6.4	9.8
2005	5.7	17.1	11.2
2006	5.5	6.6	10.3
2007	6.3	6.6	9.1
2008	6	11.1	8.4
2009	4.5	2.8	7.9
2010	6.1	7.0	7.1
2011	6.5	3.8	6.6
2012	6.2	4.3	6.1
2013	5.8	8.4	6.3
2014	5.0	8.4	5.9

Source: Badan Pusat Statistik (https://bps.go.id/)

because the new crisis was affecting advanced economies like the United States and Europe. Precrisis, the advanced economies were a source of recovery for the East Asian nations. If they were themselves in crisis in 2008–2009, it would be difficult for them to assist the recovery of other countries like Indonesia.

As it happened, the Indonesian economy in 2009 still grew satisfactorily at 4.5 percent, much better than during the 1997–8 crisis. Now the economists argued that the lack of an effect was due to the lesser integration of Indonesia into the global economy, compared to neighboring Singapore and Malaysia which experienced the effects much more severely. Like China and India, also less affected by the global crisis, the Indonesian economy was still based mainly on domestic consumption (Hill 2012).

Inflation in 2009 was low at 2.78 percent, markedly lower than the previous year, when it had been driven to 11.06 percent by the global crisis. The level of unemployment was also lower, indeed at its lowest point since the impact of the first increase in fuel oil prices by President Yudhoyono at the end of 2004. In 2005, the level of unemployment rose to 11.24 percent as a result of the rise in fuel oil prices, the highest level of unemployment since 1998. Unemployment then declined steadily until 2009.

These events sparked an increase in positive sentiments among voters, so that many more said that the national economy was better than said it was worse. Indeed, after the 2009 presidential campaign, a majority of voters said that the national economic condition was better even though at that time the country was shadowed by the global crisis. Descriptively, we can conclude that voters' sentiments toward the national economy were strongly negative in 1999, and still on average negative at the time of the 2004 elections. The voters' attitudes became more positive in 2009, a tendency that was in line with the objective improvement of the Indonesian economy at this time, ten years after the democratic transition.

What are the implications for political choice of these evaluative shifts? Did they also influence shifts in support for national political actors across the four parliamentary and three presidential elections? At the aggregate level, the differences do correlate with changes in the election victors. Before 1999, the political situation had changed dramatically, in part as a consequence of the 1997 monetary crisis. After two negative years, economic growth had barely begun to recover. Anti-New Order sentiment was rife. Forty-eight parties (compared to the three permitted parties during the New Order) emerged to compete. Partai Golkar, as the party most associated with the New Order, faced the hardest test. Indeed, many predicted that it would disappear from the national political map.

Many changes had occurred in Golkar posttransition, but there were also many continuities in personnel and program. Golkar was not prohibited from participating in the election (despite attempts to ban it by prodemocracy activists). The second most prominent Golkar leader after Suharto before his fall was Vice President B. J. Habibie, who had now succeeded constitutionally to the presidency. Since Golkar was still in power, we may label it the incumbent party even though it was in crisis as a result of the collapse of popular support for the New Order.

In the 1999 election, in accordance with the evaluations of the national economic condition that were so negative, support for Golkar as the incumbent party under President Habibie experienced a drastic decline, from on average above 60 percent of the national vote in New Order elections to 23 percent in 1999. Conversely, PDIP, widely identified as the main opposition party to the New Order and Golkar, received the most votes (34 percent). If it is reasonable to compare PDIP's totals with 1997, when Megawati had left the party, PDIP experienced a more than ten-fold increase. In the last nondemocratic Suharto-era election in 1992, PDI had obtained only 3 percent. Moreover, PDIP's 1999 vote represented a more than 100 percent increase compared to the 1992 election, when Megawati was still a leader.

At the aggregate level, therefore, we observe the expected relationship between economy evaluations and votes for the incumbent versus the opposition party in the 1999 election. Because of the monetary crisis, still deeply felt in 1999, many voters blamed the incumbent party, Golkar, and did not vote for it again. Conversely, support for the main opposition party, PDIP, increased greatly as a protest. PDIP was more widely supported because it had symbolically stood out the most in opposition to the New Order, especially compared to PPP, the other nongovernment party from the New Order era. The vote for PPP (12 percent) was not much different, indeed slightly lower, than it had typically received during the New Order.

The anti-New Order protest vote also produced a number of new parties that were relatively successful, such as PKB (13 percent) and PAN (7 percent). Admittedly, it is difficult to compare the 1999 results with New Order elections because the basis for competition had altered dramatically. If the New Order elections had been democratic, it is likely that no single party would have been able to win a large majority such as Golkar obtained in every election it contested from 1971 to 1997.

It will be difficult to understand the 1999 parties' strength if we attempt to relate it to the previous nondemocratic elections. For the same reason, it is difficult to test the rational voter model or the effect of evaluations of the national economy on voters in 1999 at the aggregate level. More problematic, as we have already pointed out, the rational voter model emerged in the context of a two-party democratic system, like the US, where the distinction between incumbent and opposition is more straightforward.

Prior to the 1999 election, it was difficult to distinguish between the governing and opposition parties. Golkar was of course the best candidate for incumbent party, but the reformed Golkar created by a wing of the old national leadership under Akbar Tandjung made a major effort to distance itself from the party's past. In addition, President Habibie's control over the reformed Golkar, under the independent-minded Tandjung, was no longer as strong as it had been throughout the New Order.

The difficulty in distinguishing incumbent from opposition can be seen in the relationship between evaluations of national economic condition and choices of political parties at the level of the individual voter.[8] Even though there is a significant difference between positive and negative evaluators in their choice of a political party, the difference is not great, especially if we compare it with subsequent elections, as we do below for 2004.

In the 1999 election, the rational voter effect is most consistently displayed only in the case of Golkar. For PDIP it is inconsistent, and for other parties it does not exist. Twenty-five percent of Partai Golkar voters say that the national economic condition is much better than the previous year and 18 percent say the opposite. Among those voters who say that the national economic condition is much better, 25 percent chose PDIP, while 36 percent said the opposite.

For the median categories better and worse, there is not much difference among PDIP voters. There is also no significant effect with regard to voters for other parties, PKB for example. Among those who perceive that the economic condition is better compared to those who think it is worse, more chose PKB, even though at that time PKB was not a government party. PKB could indeed be said to have been in opposition to Golkar.

For the 2004 elections, we see a very different picture in which incumbent and opposition are much clearer. PDIP is the governing party and its chair, Megawati, is the incumbent president, while the principal opposition is Partai Demokrat with its central figure Yudhoyono. Entering the 2004 parliamentary election, the position of PDIP was clear, that is, it was the governing party, even though other parties were in coalition with it. This clear position helped the voters to evaluate the government and its party in accordance with their evaluation of the national economic condition at that time.

In 2004, because the number of voters who said that the economic condition was better were fewer than those who said it was worse, support

---

[8] In a crosstab analysis, about 25 percent of the people who said that the national economy was better this year than last voted for the incumbent party (Golkar), but the same proportion also voted for the main opposition (PDIP). Only 18 percent of the people who stated that the economy had become worse voted for the incumbent (Golkar), while 36 percent voted for the main opposition (PDIP). The difference is statistically significant.

for PDIP declined at the aggregate level, from 34 percent to 18.5 percent. The voters punished PDIP because they judged it incapable of improving the economic situation as they had previously hoped. Conversely, the new Partai Demokrat, led by Yudhoyono, perceived as Megawati's main opponent prior to the 2004 parliamentary election, was rewarded with 7 percent of the vote.

The impact of economic evaluations can also be seen in the 2004 presidential election. Voters who said that the economic condition was better tended to vote for the combination of Megawati and Hasyim Muzadi instead of the other contestants, especially Yudhoyono-Kalla. The juxtaposition of an incumbent and an opposition was even stronger in the 2009 elections, though with positions reversed. In 2004, Demokrat and Yudhoyono were the opposition, while in 2009 they were the incumbents.

In the 2009 parliamentary election the economic evaluation of voters was once again different and the implications were also different. This time, there were more voters who said that the nation's economic condition was better than there were who said it was worse. Demokrat as the governing party was accordingly rewarded by the voters with a convincing increase from 7 percent to 21 percent. Conversely, PDIP, strongly opposed to the Yudhoyono/Demokrat government, was again punished with a drop from 18.5 percent to 14 percent.

If we compare these results with economic growth statistics from the Central Statistical Body, we get the opposite finding, that is, that economic growth for 2009 was lower than for 2008, mainly as fallout from the global financial crisis. For the voters, it was apparently not only the rate of growth that they considered but also the effect of inflation and of the rapidly implemented emergency programs of the government for health and education, in addition to the direct cash transfers that softened the blow for the poor from the increase in fuel oil prices. Inflation in 2009 was lower than in 2008, 2.78 percent compared to 11.06 percent.

In 2008 fuel oil prices had risen, causing inflation to soar and poverty to rise. In 2009, even though there was a global economic crisis, the government lowered the price of fuel oils and increased its funds for the emergency programs. In addition, campaign spending in 2009 apparently had a downward redistributive effect in the form of goods distributed by campaigns and the disbursement of cash and basic commodities directly to the poor by the government (Resosudarmo and Yusuf 2009). All of these moves seem to have had a direct positive effect on voters' evaluations of the national economic condition.

TABLE 5.3 *Association between assessment of national economic condition and voting for party (%)*

Economic Condition	Better	Same	Worse
Incumbent 1999 (Golkar)	25	31	18
Opposition 1999 (PDIP)	25	33	36
Incumbent 2004 (PDIP)	38	21	12
Opposition 2004 (Demokrat)	4	10	10
Incumbent 2009 (Demokrat)	24	19	19
Opposition 2009 (PDIP)	12	15	17
Incumbent 2014 (Demokrat)	10	11	9
Opposition 2014 (PDIP)	19	17	22

At the individual level, the effect was significant (Table 5.3). Voters who perceived the economy to be worse tended to vote for the opposition while voters who perceived it to be getting better tended to vote for the incumbent. In the 2004 parliamentary election, the voters who said that the national economic condition was better than the preceding year tended to vote for PDIP, and those who said the opposite tended to vote for Partai Demokrat.[9] If all voters had thought that the economy was better compared to last year, PDIP would have been chosen by as many as 38 percent of the voters; conversely, if all voters had said that the current economic condition was worse, PDIP would only have won the votes of 12 percent. For Demokrat, if all voters in the 2004 parliamentary election had thought that the national economic condition was better than the previous year, that party would have won only around 4 percent, and if the reverse were the case it would have won about 10 percent.

In 2009, the governing party was Partai Demokrat. While the most obvious opposition party was PDIP, the new Partai Gerindra could also be considered to have been in opposition throughout the previous year. The political economy effect is most marked for these three parties and not for the others, whose position as opposition or incumbent was obscure. Golkar, PKS, PAN, PKB, PPP, and others were in ostensible coalition with Demokrat in Yudhoyono's government but their behavior was

---

[9] The effect of evaluations of the national economic condition on other parties is not presented because it is unclear whether they are incumbent or opposition parties. In any event the effect was not significant.

inconsistent. Sometimes they supported government policy, but at other times opposed it, even threatening to leave the coalition. This ambivalence cannot be explained by the political economy model, which is limited to just two forces, indeed two parties. It also simultaneously demonstrates the limitations of the political economy model in a multiparty system when the parties behave inconsistently.

If in the 2009 election all voters had evaluated the national economic condition as better than the previous year, Demokrat would have obtained about 24 percent of the vote, PDIP 10 percent, and Gerindra 2 percent. If conversely all of the voters that year had evaluated the national economic condition as poorer than the year before, Demokrat would have obtained only about 19 percent, PDIP 17 percent, and Gerindra 8 percent.[10]

In 2014, the political economy effect was not so strong for Demokrat, PDIP, or Gerindra. This is an anomaly and is most probably connected to the facts that incumbent President Yudhoyono was not eligible for reelection and that Demokrat did not have its own presidential candidate. The door of opportunity for Demokrat to lead the government had closed and the incumbent versus opposition factor became irrelevant. The sharp drop in votes for Demokrat in that election was probably due to political factors, in particular the pervasive understanding that Demokrat was a corrupt party after a number of its top leaders were arrested. News coverage of Demokrat corruption was massive and continuous throughout the last years of the Yudhoyono presidency.

In sum, perceptions of the national economic condition are certainly an important influence on Indonesian voters' behavior. A condition that is perceived as better than at a previous time will benefit the party in power; conversely, a condition that is perceived as worse than at a previous time will benefit the opposition.

Nonetheless, as stated above, this model clearly has limitations. Even if all citizens had evaluated the national economic condition as worse than last year, PDIP in the 2004 parliamentary election would still have won 12 percent; Demokrat in the 2009 election would still have won 19 percent. Conversely, if all voters had given positive evaluations to the economy in 2004, Demokrat would still have won about 4 percent; in the 2009 election PDIP would still have won 10 percent. This means that other factors also influence voters' behavior.

---

[10] The effect of the evaluation of national economic condition on the choice of other parties is not displayed in the graph. It was not significant because their position as incumbent or opposition was not clear in the minds of the voters.

In the 2004 presidential election, as we have already shown, those who evaluated the economy positively and negatively were about equal, with those who said there had been no change slightly greater in number. Put differently, the number who said the economy was better in that year was not large, or not large enough to be persuasive. In the 2009 presidential election, however, the voters who said that the national economic condition was better were far greater in number than those who said it was worse.

This pattern is consistent with the results of the presidential elections. In the first round, President Megawati was able to obtain about 27 percent of the vote because the number of voters who evaluated the economy negatively was not too large, while the number of candidates was large. In the second round, where there were only two contestants, the fact that only about 30 percent of the voters evaluated the economy positively was too few to enable her to overcome Yudhoyono's challenge. The situation was reversed in the 2009 presidential election, when Yudhoyono was the incumbent. Many more voters perceived the condition of the economy to be good compared to those who perceived it to be poor. This aggregate-level evaluation is consistent with the fact that Yudhoyono won in just one round, and with a very convincing 61 percent.

The consistency is also evident and strong at the level of the individual voter. Table 5.4 shows a pattern of association between evaluations of the national economic condition and choice of incumbent versus challenger. In 2004, Megawati was the incumbent and Yudhoyono the principal challenger. In 2009, Yudhoyono was the incumbent and Megawati the challenger. The pattern is clear: Positive evaluations help the incumbent,

TABLE 5.4 *Association between national economic condition and voting for president (%)*

Economic Condition	Better	Same	Worse
Incumbent 2004–1 (Megawati)	30	26	20
Opposition 2004–1 (Yudhoyono)	30	33	39
Incumbent 2004–2 (Megawati)	46	39	34
Opposition 2004–2 (Yudhoyono)	54	61	66
Incumbent 2009 (Yudhoyono)	66	62	48
Opposition 2009 (Megawati)	21	24	45

while negative evaluations boost support for the main challenger while reducing incumbent support.

At the same time, as in the parliamentary election, the effect of economic evaluations does not explain all of the variation in the presidential vote. In 2004, Megawati was still supported by many voters disappointed with the performance of the economy. The same was true for Yudhoyono in 2009. Even among voters who evaluated the economy more negatively, many still voted for Yudhoyono (48 percent) even though the effect might have been to force a second round. This demonstrates that there are many factors influencing voting behavior in addition to perceptions of economic condition.

In the 2014 presidential election, the institutional requirement of incumbent versus opposition was not fulfilled. In that election, as already described, there was no incumbent. The PDIP candidate, Jokowi, was hard to perceive as the opposition candidate versus Prabowo because Prabowo and his party were also in opposition to the governing Demokrat coalition at the time. Both presented themselves in opposition to President Yudhoyono. We therefore expected no effect from our political economy variable.

We may conclude that the economy, according to the voters, represented a factor more important than the symbolic ones we have previously discussed. The impact in both parliamentary and presidential elections was significant and consistent when the empirical reality was in accord with the requirements of the model, that is, the presence of an incumbent and a challenger.

The effect was not so apparent if the positions of the contesting parties or candidates were more obscure or ambiguous. This model has therefore only limited application when the electoral contestants are members of a governing coalition who behave inconsistently, sometimes supporting and sometimes rejecting key government policies. In addition, the model becomes irrelevant if the concept of an incumbent versus an opposition is not fulfilled, as we clearly see in the 2014 presidential election.

EVALUATION OF GOVERNMENT PERFORMANCE

The hypothesized relationship between perceptions of the national political economy and political choice assumes considerable overlap between governmental performance and economic condition. There is an alternative view that the economy is less under the control of the government and should be seen more as part of the larger society. Perhaps we can agree, however, that at the very least the government plays a role in creating a supportive climate for economic activities of individuals.

This is especially true in the context of the Indonesian state where the direct role of the government in the economy still looms large. The Constitution explicitly states, in a much-referenced article, that the state has the responsibility to provide for the greater good through control over all land, water, and air resources. The dominance of state enterprises, national and local, in many sectors is evidence of the continuing power of this commitment. Other aspects of state power are also critical for the economy, such as the rule of law, eradicating corruption, and the provision of political stability and security. Important events affecting these institutions and services occur frequently and are capable of changing public opinion from election to election.

In 1999, the critical issue was the condition of the economy following the 1997 monetary crisis, so it is necessary to examine voters' evaluations of the Habibie government's performance in overcoming the crisis. Another hot issue at the time was Suharto's alleged violation of human rights, in particular whether the Habibie government would be accountable for those violations or would take action against Suharto. Doubts were also raised about whether the Habibie government was capable of fighting corruption. Beyond these issues, we asked the voters to more generally evaluate the capabilities of the Habibie government.

The key finding is that very few citizens were confident in that government. Their evaluation correlated strongly with their choice of political party. Many more citizens who evaluated Habibie's governmental performance positively, or felt sure that Habibie's government was capable of dealing with the issues of the day, especially the issues that were important in 1999, like the economic crisis, eradicating corruption, and Suharto's human rights violations, chose Golkar over the other parties.

If all voters had evaluated Habibie's government performance positively, Golkar would have won about 50 percent of the vote, that is, it would have won the election. So, the connection between evaluations of government performance with support for the governing party, Golkar, was very positive and very strong.

The 2004 survey did not examine directly the Megawati government's performance. The issues we addressed were limited to evaluation of the political situation in general, employment opportunities, and household expenditures. The effect on partisan choice was significant though not strong. We suspect that the weakness of the effect is more likely connected to problems of measurement than to the performance of Megawati's government. Nonetheless, it is clear that, at least for the economic indicators, citizens who evaluated them positively were more likely to vote for PDIP.

In the 2009 elections, Yudhoyono's government's performance was measured by several indicators: satisfaction with his work as president and evaluations of his performance in eradicating corruption, keeping prices on basic commodities low, reducing poverty, and reducing unemployment. Voters' evaluations were in general positive. As many as 79 percent were satisfied with his performance as president, 89 percent evaluated positively his anticorruption efforts, 66 percent liked his policies to keep prices low, 54 percent approved his efforts to reduce poverty, but only 46 percent rated him successful in reducing unemployment.

Though corruption is still a huge problem in Indonesia, there has been modest recent improvement. Most scholarly observers believe that between 2004 and 2009 the Yudhoyono government engaged in intensive anticorruption activities. Many state officials were indicted and convicted, including the father of President Yudhoyono's daughter-in-law. The latter case carried a powerful symbolic meaning, that even a close relative of the president is not above the law. For the voters, it prompted a positive evaluation of the government as corruption fighter.

Voters' evaluations of several economic issues are consistent with indicators from the Central Statistical Body and evaluations by expert observers. In the year before the 2009 election, the prices of basic goods were under control and the inflation rate was relatively low. These objective factors, we believe, shaped voters' opinions about government performance in these areas.

Reduction in the number of Indonesians unemployed and living in poverty has been more challenging for the government. Unemployment and poverty figures a year prior to the 2009 elections were still high. According to the Central Statistical Body, 7.87 percent of Indonesians were unemployed, a number only marginally lower than the previous year. Public opinion, as expected, was not favorable on this issue.

The effect on partisan choice in 2009 was also significant, especially when voters for PDIP as the main opposition party and Partai Demokrat as the main governing party are compared. Voters who positively evaluated government performance also tended to choose Demokrat in greater numbers than did voters who were less satisfied with government performance. Conversely, fewer voters who approved the performance of the Yudhoyono government chose PDIP. The effect on other parties was not significant.

Consistent with the lack of clarity between governing and opposition party due to the absence of Yudhoyono or another Demokrat candidate in the 2014 election, voters' evaluations of various government policies in relation to partisan choice were in general not significant. While there was a significant influence of satisfaction with the performance of the president on partisan choice, more specific evaluations of government performance did not have significant influence.

Prior to the 2009 elections, after the spike in fuel prices, the Yudhoyono government created several special antipoverty programs. Both Partai Demokrat and the president campaigned hard on the claimed success of those programs. The government offered subsidies to needy citizens in the form of direct cash transfers, funds to equalize educational opportunities, health insurance, small business and microcredit, people's empowerment programs, and other innovative programs.

No political parties opposed these subsidies or criticized the budgetary sources from which they were taken.[11] Most of the people were aware of the programs and supported them. They had indeed been the subject of a massive promotional campaign by the government and Partai Demokrat. Almost 60 percent of respondents believed that these programs made it easier for citizens to fulfill their basic needs.

The effect of the programs on partisan choice was also striking. Among those who said that the programs made the people's burden lighter, 23 percent chose Demokrat and only 12 percent chose PDIP. Conversely, among those who said that life was still difficult even though there were subsidies, more chose PDIP (21 percent) compared to Demokrat (12 percent). In other words, if the subsidies were not important and effective, PDIP, not Demokrat, would have won.

There were no significant electoral effects on other parties. Among those who said that the assistance made life easier or said that it made no difference, the proportion of voters was about the same for Golkar, PKB, PPP, PAN, PKS, Gerindra, and Hanura. The position of these parties on the subsidies was therefore unclear in the minds of voters, that is, whether these parties were a part of the governing coalition or the opposition.

This ambiguity especially characterized Golkar voters. Their party was initially on the side of the government, but prior to the election its chair, incumbent Vice President Jusuf Kalla, spoke critically of President

---

[11] Megawati once criticized these policies at the beginning of the 2009 campaign, but not thereafter.

Yudhoyono as though he were in the opposition, no different from Megawati and Prabowo. There was therefore no rational voter effect.

In the presidential election, Megawati's voters were divided in their evaluations of her approach to solving economic problems and eradicating corruption. At the same time, a majority of voters labeled "good" or "very good" Yudhoyono's approach in protecting the price of commodities, in reducing unemployment and poverty, and in eradicating corruption. While these economic variables cannot be compared directly because the measures are different, the positive evaluation by many voters of the Yudhoyono government's performance in the three socioeconomic arenas compared to the lower support for Megawati is consistent with the voters' evaluation of the national economic situation under President Megawati's and President Yudhoyono's governments, where the latter received twice the approval rating of the former.

The voters' evaluation of corruption was similar. Under Megawati, voters were divided, while under Yudhoyono, voters labeled "good" or "very good" Yudhoyono's performance in eradicating corruption. At the aggregate level, there is consistency between these evaluations of voters' socioeconomic situations and eradication of corruption with votes in the 2004 and 2009 presidential elections. In general, voters were less than enthusiastic about Megawati's approach to governance, causing her to lose the parliamentary and presidential elections in 2004. Conversely, voters in general gave good marks to the Yudhoyono government's performance concerning certain popular issues (poverty, unemployment, eradication of corruption) and thus reelected him in 2009.

This consistency is also apparent at the individual level. Our bivariate statistics indicate a strong relationship between evaluations of governmental performance or governance approach and votes for president in 2004 and 2009. Voters who liked President Megawati's conduct of her government and her efforts at eradicating corruption tended to reelect her, while those who evaluated her negatively tended to choose other candidates, especially Yudhoyono.

The same happened in 2009. Voters who evaluated positively the socioeconomic performance and corruption-fighting of the Yudhoyono administration tended to vote for him, and those who evaluated him negatively tended to vote for other candidates, especially Megawati. If it had been the case that a majority of voters had evaluated negatively Yudhoyono's performance, it is likely that there would have been a second round. This did not happen because most voters in fact evaluated the Yudhoyono government positively on these matters.

All the bivariate analyses between economic variables and presidential choice show a significant association. This indicates that voter rationality operated in both presidential elections. An incumbent tended to be reelected if his or her performance in office was evaluated positively across a number of socioeconomic or politicoeconomic issues. Conversely, if the voters evaluated negatively the performance of the incumbent they tended to punish him or her by voting for the opposition.

INDEPENDENCE OF THE POLITICAL ECONOMY

How independent is the effect of these political economy factors on choosing a presidential candidate or a party if the analysis is controlled for sociological factors, especially religion, regionalism, and social class? Is the effect still significant or not? If not, perhaps voter rationality is linked to a sociological bias.

Our multivariate analysis shows the extent of significance and consistency of the effect of voter rationality or political economy on choice of party, member of Parliament, and presidential candidate.[12] In general, evaluations of the condition of the national political economy have a significant and consistent influence on political choice in democratic Indonesian elections, controlling for other factors that are considered potentially relevant in shaping citizens' political choices (Table 5.5).

---

[12] In this analysis, we used logistic regression as described in Chapter 4. The political economy variable in 1999 was an index constructed of a number of items: the national economic condition now compared to last year (1=better, 0=worse or no change), the Habibie government's performance in resolving several national issues (1=good, 0=bad), in uncovering Suharto's misdeeds (1=good, 0=bad), and in eradicating corruption (1=good, 0=bad). The index is the total score of these evaluations. In the 2004 parliamentary election, the political economy variable was an index constructed of evaluations of the national economic condition today compared to last year (1=better, 0=worse), family expenditures (1=low, 0=high), employment (1=enough, 0=less than enough). In the 2004 first- and second-round presidential elections the indices were constructed from several items evaluating the national economic condition today compared to last year (1=better, 0=worse), President Megawati's performance in eradicating corruption (1=good, 0=bad), and in resolving the problem of the economy (1=good, 0=bad). In the 2009 and 2014 parliamentary and presidential elections, the political economy variable was an index constructed of several items: evaluation of the national economic condition now compared to last year (1=better, 0=worse), the Yudhoyono government's performance in controlling the prices of basic commodities (1=good, 0=bad), in reducing poverty (1=good, 0=bad), in reducing unemployment (1=good, 0=bad), in eradicating corruption (1=good, 0=bad), and satisfaction with President Yudhoyono's performance (1=satisfied, 0=unsatisfied).

TABLE 5.5 *Political economy effect on partisan and presidential choice, 2009 & 2014 (difference in predicted probability)*

	PDIP	Golkar	PKB	PPP	PAN	PD	PKS	Gerindra	Hanura	NasDem
Parliamentary Election										
1999[1]	-0.31***	0.48***	-0.05*	-0.18***	-0.05***					
1999[2]	-0.16***	0.05	0.00	-0.05**	0.00					
2004[1]	0.37***	-0.13	0.04	-0.06	-0.05	-0.09	-0.09			
2004[2]	0.18	NS	NS	NS	NS	NS	NS			
2009[1]	-0.19***	0.02	0.00	-0.01	0.01	0.23***	-0.02	-0.06*	0.01	
2009[2]	-0.06*	NS	NS	NS	NS	0.15***	NS	-0.04	TS	
2014[1]	-0.08**	0.02	0.03	0.01	-0.04*	0.08**	0.02	-0.04	0.02	-0.02
2014[2]	-0.06*	NS	NS	NS	-0.06	0.03	NS	NS	NS	NS
Presidential Election	Megawati-Hasyim (Prabowo) [Jokowi-Kalla]	Yudhoyono-Kalla (Boediono) [Prabowo-Hatta]	Wiranto-Salahuddin (JK-Wiranto)	Amien-Siswono	Hamzah-Agum					
2004a[1]	0.74***	-0.40***	-0.14**	-0.23***	0.04					
2004a[2]	0.32***	-0.46***	-0.13*	-0.08**	NS					
2004b[1]	0.67***	-0.67***								
2004b[2]	0.57**	-0.57***								

(continued)

TABLE 5.5 *(continued)*

	PDIP	Golkar	PKB	PPP	PAN	PD	PKS	Gerindra	Hanura	NasDem
2009[1]	(−0.54***)	(0.50***)	(0.04)							
2009[2]	(−0.27**)	(0.20*)	NS							
2014[1]	[−0.07]	[0.07]								
2014[2]	NS	NS								

[1] Analysis with only one independent variable (political economy).
[2] Analysis of the effect of political economy after being controlled for sociological factors (religion, ethnicity, education, urban-rural, age, and gender) and psychological factors (quality of leadership and party ID for the relevant party).
NS = if in the analysis without control variables there was no significance we did not continue the analysis further.
*** $p = 0.001$, ** $p = 0.01$, and * $p = 0.05$

In the 1999 parliamentary election, political economy had a significant and positive influence on votes for Golkar, but this influence disappears after being controlled for other factors, especially the quality of Habibie's leadership and Golkar party ID. At the same time, the negative political economy effect of the Habibie government with regard to PDIP still had a strong influence, apart from other factors, including the quality of Megawati's leadership and PDIP party ID.

After being controlled for a number of other factors, voters who evaluated positively the national economic condition and Habibie's governmental performance were 16 percent less likely to vote for PDIP compared to voters with a negative evaluation. The significant negative association between political economy and choice of PDIP indicates that PDIP, compared to the other parties contesting at that time, represented the strongest opposition to the Golkar Habibie government. This pattern also fits with the historical fact that PDI and PDIP under Megawati's leadership did act as the principal opposition toward the New Order and Golkar. At the same time, the lack of significance of the political economy effect toward other new and old parties, that is PKB, PAN, and PPP, demonstrates that the position of these parties was less strong either in support of or opposition to the government of Habibie.

In the 2004 legislative election, the political economy factor was not significant controlling for other factors, especially leadership quality and party ID. In other words, evaluations of the condition of the political economy in this parliamentary election were associated mainly with the quality of leadership and party identity. In addition, under President Megawati's administration, incumbent and opposition were not very clear. All parties were in Megawati's governing coalition. Partai Demokrat had just been formed and only participated for the first time in 2004. As an opposition party, apart from its main figure, Yudhoyono, it was little known to the voters.

In the 2009 parliamentary election, the political economy effect was stronger and more consistent even though controlled for the quality of leadership and party identity. Citizens with a more positive evaluation of the political economy and the performance of President Yudhoyono were 15 percent more likely to choose Demokrat than those with a negative evaluation. At the same time, citizens who evaluated the Yudhoyono government more positively were 6 percent less likely to vote for PDIP compared to those who evaluated the Yudhoyono government negatively. In this election, the main governing party and the main opposition party were much clearer than in the 2004 legislative election.

The political economy effect is stronger and more consistent in the presidential elections in 2004 and 2009. Controlling for several other factors, the positive evaluation of the national economic condition, the political condition, strengthening the rule of law and evaluations of governmental performance increased the probability of choosing the incumbent and reduced the probability of choosing the opposition. Voters who evaluated more positively the condition of the political economy during the Megawati government were 30 percent more likely to choose Megawati-Hasyim Muzadi compared to those who evaluated the political economy negatively. Voters who evaluated more positively the condition of the political economy were 46 percent less likely to choose Yudhoyono-Kalla compared to those who evaluated it negatively.

A significant effect is also seen in the choice of the Wiranto-Salahuddin and Amien Rais-Siswono Yudhohusudo tickets. Voters who evaluated the political economy more positively at that time were 13 percent less likely to choose Wiranto-Salahuddin and 8 percent less likely to choose Amien-Siswono relative to voters who were more negative about the economy. This pattern indicates that not only Yudhoyono but also Wiranto and Amien Rais were perceived by the voters to be Megawati's challengers. The political economy effect on Hamzah Haz was not significant, evidence of Hamzah's ambiguous position at that time. He was nominated for the presidency while serving as President Megawati's vice president.

In the 2004 presidential election, round two (2004b), the political economy effect was clearer because the competition itself was clearer and more straightforward: Megawati as the incumbent faced Yudhoyono the sole challenger. Voters who evaluated the condition of the economy positively under Megawati were 57 percent more likely to choose her in comparison with those who evaluated the political economy negatively; they were also 57 percent less likely to choose Yudhoyono.

The political economy effect was significant as well in the 2009 presidential election. Voters who evaluated positively the political economy under President Yudhoyono were 20 percent more likely to reelect him than voters who evaluated it negatively, and 27 percent less likely to choose Megawati.

The pattern of association between the political economy factor, on the one hand, and Megawati versus Yudhoyono on the other, shows that Megawati was a genuine opposition force during the first Yudhoyono government. The political economy effect on Jusuf Kalla, as on Hamzah Haz, was not significant. The position of Kalla, like Haz in the 2004 presidential election, was confusing to the voters. He put himself forward in opposition to incumbent President Yudhoyono, and was quite open and sharp in his criticisms of the president, while at the same time continuing to serve as Yudhoyono's vice president. At the very least, he put himself in an awkward position with regard to the voters' perception of his candidacy.

It was Yudhoyono, not Kalla, who took greater advantage of the voters' positive evaluations of the economy, so that in the end most of those voters chose Yudhoyono. In other words, governmental success was identified with the administration and political campaign of incumbent President Yudhoyono, not incumbent vice president and presidential challenger Kalla.

This pattern is not surprising. Even if Kalla as vice president had been an important policy implementer, in a political sense he did not have the main responsibility for governmental success or failure. Kalla tried to change this reality as the parliamentary and presidential elections approached. He and his campaign team claimed that whatever the Yudhoyono government had achieved, especially in economic policy, was in fact Kalla's contribution. He did not hesitate to criticize whatever was felt to be lacking in the Yudhoyono administration, pointing out that if he became president he would be a more effective leader (*Tempo* June 7, 2009, 108–111).

From the perspective of rational voter theory, these claims had no effect. Kalla certainly tried to position himself during the campaign as the opposition, including in his choice of retired army General Wiranto as his running mate.[13] Wiranto, unlike Kalla, had been criticizing Yudhoyono's leadership for the previous two years. Despite their efforts, their campaign had no influence in terms of voter rationality. When Wiranto ran with Kalla, the effect was not to offer a credible opposition but rather a confusing pairing whose policy positions were unclear. In the end, the voters did not reward this ticket, but punished it with a vote percentage far below their hopes at around 12 percent. Kalla's defeat recapitulated the defeat of Vice President Hamzah Haz who had also tried to challenge his president, Megawati, in the 2004 presidential election. Their positions were also ambiguous, perhaps even odd or strange in the eyes of the voters.

In sum, four parliamentary and presidential elections in democratic Indonesia display a similar pattern in which voters' evaluations of the

---

[13] Kalla's choice of Wiranto as his running mate cannot be separated from the fact that Golkar was not able to nominate a president on its own. It had to form a coalition in order to meet the legal nomination threshold of 20 percent of parliamentary seats. The only party that enabled Kalla to meet this condition was Wiranto's Hanura.

national economy have a significant influence on their voting behavior. This pattern is especially pronounced when there are two parties and two candidates whose positions are clear: the governing party or presidential candidate and the challenging party and presidential candidate. If their positions are ambiguous the effect of the political economy model is not significant as we see in 2014 when there was no division between incumbent and opposition. This pattern is comparable to the findings of political economy studies in other democratic countries.

CONCLUSIONS

This chapter has shown the extent to which the rational choice or political economy model explains voting behavior in Indonesia's four democratic elections since the transition. On the question of turnout in either parliamentary or presidential elections, the model helps explain our findings even though it does not do so consistently. At the very least there are indications of an explanation for the secular trend of turnout decline, that is, there has been a growth in the number of voters who do not vote because they see no value in the elections for their personal interests or selective incentives. This opinion is stronger among more educated voters, an indicator of rational voting. With continued economic growth, this group will certainly grow larger. In the end, voter turnout will decline as has also happened in many other democracies.

The rational voter perspective also helps explain political choice. In a competitive context, where there is a distinctive incumbent and opposition, a contextual precondition for rational voting, political choice in both parliamentary and presidential elections is strongly influenced by evaluations of the condition of the national political economy, which we have used as a measure of the rational voter. In general, controlling for sociological factors, voters who evaluate more positively the condition of the economy tend to vote for the incumbent party, legislative or presidential candidate. Conversely, voters who evaluate the condition of the economy more negatively tend to vote for the opposition. In addition, in the Indonesian case, government performance in various sectors, not only the condition of the economy, is a better predictor of partisan choice.

As turnout declines, as an indicator of the increase of rational voting, the more dependent the results of the legislative and presidential elections are on the condition of the economy and the performance of the government in various sectors that are sensitive to the needs of the voters. In other words, Indonesian voters are open and rational. Economic growth, specifically the improvement of education and the transformation of information technology, including the internet and social media, has encouraged this trend. It is these factors that have produced Indonesia's critical democrats.

Do these critical democrats discard their party identity as they react to the dynamic flow of issues and government policies? This question, together with the effect of leadership, will be discussed in Chapter 6.

6

Party Identity and Political Leaders

In previous chapters we have learned that Indonesian voters are at base critical, open to many political choices, including deciding not to vote. Choosing not to vote has indeed become increasingly popular. In addition, every election has produced a new party with a sizeable number of seats in Parliament, plus a different party with the most seats. In the 1999 election PDIP won the most votes. In 2004 it was Golkar, followed by Partai Demokrat in 2009. In 2014, PDIP once again won the most seats. The pattern is one of increasing instability and fragmentation. In 1999, five parties won a significant number of seats. In 2004 there were seven, in 2009 nine, and finally, in 2014, ten. All of this indicates that Indonesian voters are open to alternatives, and critical toward the existing parties.

Much voting behavior literature argues that psychological factors increase participation and stabilize partisan choice. Does the decline in participation and the instability of partisan choice mean that psychological factors are not important in the Indonesian case?

Psychological factors have been taken seriously in voting behavior research at least since the publication of *The American Voter* by scholars at the University of Michigan (Campbell, Converse, Miller, and Stokes 1960). Even though the psychological model was introduced long ago, and has continued to develop as an important approach ever since, it is relatively new in Indonesia. During Indonesia's first democratic period, in the 1950s, the model was too new and Indonesian political science still embryonic. In the late 1950s Indonesia ceased to be a democracy.[1]

---

[1] During the nondemocratic New Order period, the model was tested in seminal studies of electoral behavior in doctoral theses by Afan Gaffar, "The Javanese Voter" (1992) and Andi Alfian Mallarangeng, "The Indonesian Voter" (1997).

Psychological models could only be properly tested after the 1998 transition. Liddle and Mujani (2007) and Mujani and Liddle (2010) published the first scientific studies testing the psychological approach, finding it an important component in explaining modern Indonesian voting behavior. In particular, we discovered that two psychological factors, identification by voters with particular political parties plus support for individual leaders, were the most important shapers of partisan choice in Indonesia's first two democratic elections in 1999 and 2004. We also suspected that the former was powerfully driven by the latter, that is, that voters were "strongly attached to national party leaders, an attachment that appears to be a principal reason for voting for political party or for president" (Liddle and Mujani 2007, 839).

This chapter develops and extends our early findings with the much more extensive data that we have collected for the four post-New Order elections. Liddle and Mujani's analysis was limited to political choice, paying less attention to how psychological factors were shaped, while Mujani (2007) was more attuned to democratic culture and political participation without discussing political choice. This chapter discusses both but without further elaboration concerning democratic culture and without measuring participation more extensively. We limit analysis of participation to parliamentary and presidential election turnout and campaign behavior.

Despite the lack of scholarship on the subject, Indonesian politicians are familiar with the view that party is an important influence on presidential candidate choice. They believe that the larger the party or party coalition that supports a candidate, the greater the probability that candidate will win. Many politicians therefore try to build the largest possible partisan coalition to support their candidate.

What politicians mean by party size is mainly electoral strength. When we relate party strength to the results of presidential elections, however, we have to pay close attention to the ways in which psychological factors operate in practice. It has already happened, and may happen frequently in the future, that a presidential candidate who is supported by a party or coalition of parties with a larger total of votes in the preceding parliamentary election nonetheless does not win the election. This was the experience of Megawati and Wiranto in 2004 and Prabowo Subianto in 2014.[2] Accordingly, it is

---

[2] In the 2004 presidential election, Megawati was nominated by the party with the second-highest vote in the immediately prior parliamentary election, PDIP, plus some other

critical, both intellectually and practically, to examine the psychological mechanisms behind the choice of party and presidential candidate.

PARTY IDENTITY

The unique contribution of the psychological approach is the concept of self-identification with a political party, often shortened to "party ID." Typically, most individuals have multiple social identities such as religion, race, or ethnicity. Partisanship is the comparable identity in politics, according to the Michigan school, which found that most American voters identify with a particular political party. "Identification" is defined as an "affective orientation of the individual toward important groups in society" (Campbell, Converse, Miller, and Stokes 1960, 121–122). "Self-identification with a party" is "an orientation of affect, attitude or feeling of an individual toward a political party in a given society." It may be either positive or negative.

A positive attitude is defined as one in which an individual identifies with a particular party, while a negative attitude means not identifying with any party or expressing a negative attitude toward a party. Positive party identification is comparable to identification with a specific religion, in the sense that that religion becomes one's religious identity. Individuals who possess a religious identity will respond "Muslim," "Christian," "Buddhist," and so on of if asked by surveyors to name their religion; alternatively, they may respond negatively, that they do not have a religion. It is the same with politics: When asked to name their party, Indonesians will answer "PDIP," "Partai Golkar," "Partai Demokrat," and so on, or they will say, "no party, I do not belong to a party."

Party identity may exert a strong influence as an independent factor on various political attitudes (toward public policies, evaluations of government performance, and of parties and candidates), and toward political behavior (political participation, choice of party or legislative candidates, choice of presidential candidates, or choices of specific public policies).

---

parties. Wiranto was nominated by the largest party, Partai Golkar, and Yudhoyono was nominated by the fifth largest, Partai Demokrat. In the 2009 parliamentary election, Yudhoyono's Demokrat won the most votes, and was nominated by this party plus others. In 2014, PDIP won the most votes. Joko Widodo (Jokowi) was nominated by PDIP plus some other parties, whose total vote share was less than that of the parties nominating Prabowo. Jokowi of course won that election. See Chapter 3. Regional executive elections display similar characteristics where a candidate who is chosen by a large party or coalition of parties nonetheless frequently fails to win election.

Party ID theorists are convinced that political attitudes and behavior, though tightly connected, are separate entities. Party identity exists at the level of attitude or orientation, not action or behavior. Possession of an attitude does not guarantee action on behalf of that attitude (Campbell, Converse, Miller, and Stokes 1960, 122). Americans who identify with the Democratic Party, for example, do not necessarily support the policies of a Democratic government, and individuals who identify as Republican do not necessarily vote for a Republican candidate. In the 2009 presidential election in Indonesia, PDIP identifiers did not necessarily choose Megawati, nor did Demokrats necessarily choose Yudhoyono or Golkar identifiers choose Jusuf Kalla.

Several recent experimental studies have demonstrated that party identity represents an independent factor relative to political attitudes and behavior such as political participation and choice (Gerber, Huber, and Washington 2010; Zucco and Samuels 2010). In American presidential elections, for example, voters choose a candidate because of a feeling of closeness to the candidate's party, not the reverse, choosing a party because of that party's identification with a candidate (Campbell, Converse, Miller, and Stokes 1960; Miller and Shanks 1996; Lewis-Beck, Norpoth, Jacoby, and Weisberg 2008).

An Indonesian example is a citizen who claims to be a PDIP member and then votes for Megawati, the PDIP's presidential candidate. In this instance, it is the identification with PDIP that causes the voter to select Megawati, not the other way around. Not all voters who identify with PDIP choose Megawati, however, and not all voters who choose Megawati identify with PDIP, evidence that party ID is an attitudinal factor independent of behavior.

A survey respondent described the complexity of the choice: "I feel like a member of Golkar because my father is a party activist and official. But in the most recent election I did not vote for Golkar because my wife was a Partai Demokrat candidate. So, I voted for Demokrat." Party identity is not the same as voting for a party, but can be overcome by a more personal connection, such as the spousal relationship in this example.

The concept of party ID arose in the United States to explain why support for political parties is relatively stable. Only a few voters who had previously chosen a candidate of the Republican Party subsequently shifted their vote to a Democratic candidate or vice versa. Party identity explained this phenomenon.

In the US, the stability and continuity of partisan support is undergirded by party identity. If there is a vote swing, it is not large, and in the end, it adds to the stability of the party system. If enough voters have strong party ID, it is difficult for a new party to gain much support. Britain is another good example of this phenomenon. In both countries, there are many parties which compete in every election. But in general, and over a long time period, only two parties have won a significant number of votes, Republicans and Democrats in the US and Labour and Conservatives in the UK.

Norris (2011) excludes party ID from her analysis of the formation of critical citizens. She accepts the finding of many scholars, comparable to our evidence for Indonesia, that "Dealignment has progressively weakened the social psychological attachments binding loyalists to the same party over successive elections, contributing to aggregate electoral volatility and more individual vote switching, facilitating the sudden breakthrough of new parties and restructuring party competition, as well as more generally weakening linkages between citizens and the state."

At the same time, she remains unconvinced that "these trends should be interpreted as a sign of psychological disengagement from regime institutions or from political authorities. The idea of institutional confidence concerns generalized orientations toward the party system rather than attitudes such as identification with particular parties" (34–35). What can our Indonesian survey data contribute to this discussion?

MEASURING PARTY IDENTITY

How is party ID measured? The first measure employed was unidimensional, ascertaining whether voters considered themselves Republican or Democrat (Campbell, Converse, Miller, and Stokes 1960). The follow-up question dealt with the degree of support for the relevant party. The combined score constituted a party ID scale of 1–7. This measure was subsequently modified to become a thermometer with a scale of 1–100, where 0 represented strong identification with Republicans, 100 strong identification with Democrats, and 50 an independent position.

These measurements presumed a simple party system with only two major parties. For comparative analysis, modifications have to be made for more complex multiparty systems such as those found in countries like Germany, Italy, the Netherlands, and Indonesia. Several studies have proposed modifications. For Barnes, Jennings, Inglehart, and Farah (1988), party ID was understood as "feeling closer to a party." "The party closeness question asked respondents, 'Which political party do you feel closer to?' Those who name a party are then asked, 'Would you say you feel very close, fairly close, or not very close to that party?'" (217). This operationalization was subsequently used in the American National Electoral Studies in 1996 (Weisberg 1999, 706).

In this study, we use these modified measures because they are most appropriate in the multiparty Indonesian context. To test the validity of our measure, we also use a slightly different one. We directly ask voters to score their level of closeness to the major political parties, as discussed below.[3]

THE DYNAMICS OF PARTY IDENTITY

The response of Indonesian voters to the basic question if there is a party to which a citizen feels closer or with which he or she identifies has varied considerably from election to election, indeed from month to month (Figure 6.1). The overall trend, however, has been sharply downward.

In the beginning, during the 1999 parliamentary election, the level of voter identification with political parties was very high at 86 percent. This was probably connected to intense partisan mobilization plus the euphoric feelings associated with the new democratic freedoms. Citizens were optimistic about parties and welcomed their freedom to establish new parties or support old ones free of fear of government repression. Antiauthoritarian sentiment was at a fever pitch.

Freedom had only been enjoyed for about a year, after Suharto stepped down and new President Habibie promised democratic elections. There was great optimism and hope directed toward the new party system, which contrasted sharply with the artificial Suharto-era construction. Many were convinced that this strength from below would bring the parties closer to their voters, more able to channel popular aspirations to the top party and governmental leadership. For all these reasons, most people claimed to be close to a particular political party.

The optimism soon declined, however, perhaps because for many voters their party did not accomplish as much as they had hoped. The

---

[3] In the 1999, 2004, 2009, and 2014 parliamentary elections, also in the 2004 presidential election, we used a series of three questions. In the 2009 and 2014 surveys, we added a direct question about the nine and ten major parties: Do you feel very much closer, much closer, less close, or not close at all to a party? From these responses, we constructed a four-point scale of party ID.

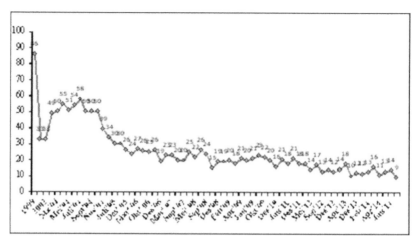

FIGURE 6.1 Party ID trends (feeling close to a particular party) among Indonesian voters, 1999–2014 (%)

number of Indonesians identifying with a party declined sharply. In the two years after the 1999 election, party ID dropped to 33 percent. It continued to drop in 2002, but one year before the 2004 election it rose significantly, reaching a peak of 55 percent. This reversal may be due to the inherent appeal of the 2004 election, the first direct presidential election, combined with powerful partisan mobilization in that year. The increase, however, was still well below the 1999 high.

Party identity dropped to 30 percent in 2005 and continued to fall to 18 percent in March 2009, surprisingly during the parliamentary legislative campaign of that year. It remained low at 20 percent through the campaign period and indeed through the presidential election later in the year. This time, the campaign and its accompanying mass mobilization did nothing to increase the level of party identification.

Five years later, in the 2014 legislative election, it fell again. In that election, voters who felt close to a particular party numbered only 14 percent; three months later the number dropped again to 9 percent. If we compare the four parliamentary elections from 1999 to 2014, the decline in party ID among Indonesian voters is abundantly clear. Fewer and fewer voters liked or felt close to a particular party despite extensive party mobilization efforts.

If our analysis is limited just to the election periods, the decline at the aggregate level is particularly sharp, from 86 percent in April 1999, the first parliamentary election, to 55 percent in April 2004, 20 percent in

April 2009, and 14 percent in April 2014. The pattern is similar for the four presidential elections. At the time of the two-round 2004 election the level was about 50 percent, declining to 21 percent in 2009 and to 9 percent in 2014.

This decline is consistent with the level of trust in political parties, which has also dropped continuously, suggesting that the decline in identification with particular parties is associated with a broader decline in trust in the party system as a whole. More and more people do not believe that political parties in general fight for the interests of the voters. In 2001, 79 percent of voters believed that the parties fought for their interests. This level dropped to 57 percent in 2005, 39 percent in 2008, and 31 percent in 2013.[4] In the beginning most voters were optimistic about the parties' ability to reflect their interests but over time the parties have apparently become less trustworthy.

PARTY IDENTITY AND POLITICAL PARTICIPATION

At the aggregate level, what is the meaning of the decline in party ID for participation and choice? In Chapter 3 we described a sharp decline in turnout in both parliamentary and presidential elections. The 1999 level of turnout, 93 percent, dropped to 84 percent in the 2004 parliamentary election and even further to 71 percent in 2009, and slightly increased to 75 percent in the 2014 parliamentary election. In the presidential elections, there was also decline: in 2004, from 80 percent to 76.5 percent in the two rounds; in 2009, to 73 percent; and in 2014, to 71 percent. Was the decline in turnout caused by the decline in party ID? What caused party ID to decline?

Many studies have concluded that levels of turnout and party ID are closely related (Campbell, Converse, Miller, and Stokes 1960; Verba, Schlozman, and Brady 1995). The feeling of closeness or identification

---

[4] In several surveys in nonelection years we asked about levels of trust in parties. In 2001 and 2002 the form of the question was: To what extent do you trust that political parties can struggle for the interests of their voters? The answers were: strongly trust, trust enough, trust less, and do not trust at all. In subsequent surveys the form of the question was: There are those who have the opinion that political parties only struggle for their own interests, not those of their voters. To what extent do you agree or disagree with this statement? The responses included: strongly disagree, disagree, agree, and strongly agree. These two forms of the question differed considerably and therefore cannot be compared directly. We use them here to roughly approximate the views of voters about party. In the table, the responses displayed are from the answers trust greatly, trust, disagree, and strongly disagree.

with a particular party psychologically connects that person to politics
or public affairs via partisan affiliation. Political parties provide sentiments and feelings about what is true and false and about who constitutes "we" and "they" in political life.

Parry, Moyser, and Day (1992, 190–191) argue that parties contribute to the formation of long-lasting political opinions for most citizens.
This represents a potentially powerful psychological force for political
participation. Partisanship encourages citizens to participate in politics,
to support their party and take political actions such as voting in elections. It follows that when the level of party ID declines, turnout will also
decline.

Bivariate analysis indicates that most citizens who feel close to a
particular party tend to participate in elections. The difference between
those who feel close and those who do not was 14 percent in 1999, 12
percent in 2004, 14 percent in 2009, but only 1 percent in 2014. Citizens
also tend to participate more in direct campaigning, to assist or financially support a party or candidate, and to persuade others to vote for
their preferred candidate or party.

The 2009 legislative election was the first time that party identity did
not significantly influence voting. This pattern was repeated even more
clearly in 2014, both in the parliamentary and presidential elections. Party
ID was significantly related to other forms of participation, such as
campaigning, helping candidates, providing financial support, and persuading others. For directly attending campaigns, the difference was 11
percent in 1999, 12 percent in 2004, 13 percent in 2009, and 16 percent in
2014. In persuading other people and helping a political party, the differences are also significant. For helping a party, it was 15 percent in the 2009
legislative and 23 percent and 17 percent in the 2014 legislative and
presidential elections respectively. However, the populations participating in these activities were relatively very small, as described in Chapter 3.

The case of participation in parliamentary and presidential elections in
Indonesia appears to confirm, but without much confidence, those previous comparative studies which concluded that party identity encourages
citizens to be more active politically. At least in the case of Indonesia, the
influence is not consistent.

The relationship between party identity and turnout is also not consistent when sociological factors and voter rationality are included in the
analysis (Table 6.1). In the first two legislative elections, party ID inde-
pendently affected turnout. But in 2009 and 2014 the effect disappears,
both in the legislative and presidential elections.

Party Identity and Political Leaders   191

TABLE 6.1 *The effect of party identity on turnout in parliamentary and presidential elections (logistic coefficient* b, *and standard error)*

	1999	2004a	2004b	2004c	2009a	2009b	2014a	2014b
Party	.460***	.274***	.292**	.456***	−.048	.534***	.090	.083
Identity	(.082)	(.080)	(.098)	(.089)	(.070)	(.140)	(.113)	(.158)

***P<.001, **P<.01, *P<.05
Control variables: national economic condition, education, Muslim religiosity, regional origin, age, urban-rural residence, and gender.

POLITICAL INFORMATION

In addition to party identity, another psychological factor that is important in the comparative literature is political information or knowledge, i.e. voters' exposure to political news, in particular via the mass media. Political information is an attitudinal element relevant for participation. Knowledge about political matters encourages participation, because political information helps citizens to understand the importance of political decisions. Political information is more cognitive than affective, but it still may be seen as a part of political attitudes (Zaller 1992, 42–43).

Norris (2011) devotes a whole chapter to exploring the literature on the relationship between "negative news" and the growth in critical citizens. She distinguishes two alternative theories, the first focusing on type of media, the second on the tone of media coverage. The first, or "video-malaise" theory, asserts that standard TV news reporting fosters "public mistrust of government and dissatisfaction with regime institutions, thus contributing toward civic disengagement." The second theory suggests that vigorous watchdog journalism can have the undesirable side effect of encouraging "a rising tide of political disenchantment" (169).

Norris' evidence, from the fifth wave World Values Survey covering almost fifty countries and comparing regular exposure to newspapers, television and radio news, and the internet, leads her to three conclusions. First, general exposure to news from all media sources "usually strengthened democratic aspirations." Second, contrary to the video-malaise thesis, "users of television and radio broadcast news proved more satisfied with democracy, not less." And finally, "regular use of all these news media … *reduced* the democratic deficit, or the size of the gap between expectations and perceived performance" (186) [her emphasis].

What can our Indonesian data contribute to this discussion? Operationally, political information in this study is the intensity with which a citizen follows political news, including campaigns, in various media: television, newspapers, radio, and the internet.[5] In Indonesia most citizens frequently or often follow the news on television, while those who follow it in newspapers or on radio are many fewer. Internet readers are few and far between but growing in number.

The association between turnout and exposure to political news via various media in general was not significant or consistent. Perhaps most interesting, as a harbinger of things to come, despite small numbers to date, is the negative connection with exposure to political news on the internet. The more a voter followed the news on the internet the more he or she failed to vote.

However, for those citizens who participate in campaign politics, the intensity with which they follow news has a powerful and consistent association. But the number of citizens who participate is small compared to voting; even rarer is participation associated with help for parties, donating money to candidates and parties, and persuading others to vote for one's preferred candidate or party. Of course, citizens who often follow the news do tend to participate directly in campaigns, support or donate to candidates and parties, and actively persuade others. In other words, the mass media play a role in raising the level of political participation beyond the mere act of voting.

It is possible that these significances are spurious. Other factors behind the intensity of following the news may play a more determining role in shaping campaign participation, assistance, donations, and persuading others. Causal candidates are party ID, interest in politics, or some demographic factor like level of education. Citizens may follow the news because they are party sympathizers or interested in politics. The effect of including these variables in the analysis will be explored below.

[5] In every survey discussed in this study respondents were asked, during the campaign period just prior to the election, how often they had followed political or governmental news like campaigns, the election of members of Parliament, the president, the issue of corruption, and so on. Respondents' answers for each form of media included every day or nearly every day (5), 3–4 days every week (4), 1–2 days every week (3), rarely/less than once a week (2), or never (1). In the 1999 survey, the answers were: very often, often, rarely, or never. What is presented in the tables are the total responses from the first and second categories whom we identified as "very often" or "often."

POLITICAL DISCUSSION

In theory, the intensity of discussing politics with others has the potential to increase citizens' level of insight, motivating them to act politically. Discussion may also become a medium of political persuasion between individuals or groups, shaping attitudes that encourage citizens to participate in elections or other forms of politics. Political discussion may also be a medium for the formation of negative attitudes toward politics, creating pessimistic citizens who conclude that there is no point in participating. These possibilities will depend heavily on the substance of the political discussions, and must be verified empirically.

Prior to the 1999 parliamentary election, approximately two in ten citizens had at some time discussed politics with a close friend and about fifteen of every 100 citizens had at some time discussed politics with a neighbor. In the 2004 survey, the measure was broadened to encompass not only political discussion with friends and neighbors but also within the family and among colleagues at work. In that year, the number of citizens who discussed politics with friends was slightly more, three of every ten citizens; also with neighbors, about two in ten. Citizens who discussed politics in the family were about three of every ten, and about two of ten discussed politics with work colleagues.

Leading up to the 2009 parliamentary election, the number of citizens who discussed politics in the family declined. We see similar results for discussing politics with friends, workmates, and neighbors. Before the 2009 parliamentary election we also asked about discussing politics with one's spouse, and the response was about two in ten. In 2014, the intensity declined further: only about one in ten voters discussed politics with their spouse, within the family, or with friends, neighbors, and colleagues at work.

In general, there was a decline in the frequency of political discussion with others over the four election cycles. This phenomenon requires its own analysis. How important is discussion for participation?

Bivariate analysis demonstrates that political discussion, measured in various ways, does not generally have a significant association with participation in elections (voter turnout). There is no difference in the number of citizens who often or never discuss politics, on the one hand, and who participate in elections on the other. Citizens come to the polling station not because they are inspired or motivated after conducting political discussions but for other reasons, including the demographic factors already discussed and the psychological factors that will be discussed below, such as interest in politics, and perhaps also because they were mobilized.

If participation is measured not as voting in elections, but as participation in campaigns, helping or donating to parties and candidates, and persuading others to vote for a preferred party or candidate, political discussion does have a significant influence. People who often discuss politics tend to participate more often in these activities. Voters who often discuss politics with colleagues, neighbors, and family members tend to participate more than those who rarely or never do. The gap is about 22 percent in 1999, 23 percent in 2004, 34 percent in 2009, and 29 percent in 2014.

As with political information, political discussion may also not have an independent direct connection with political participation. People who frequently discuss politics are perhaps those who feel close to a particular party. If that is the case, when party identity is incorporated into the analysis, the significance will disappear. We will explore this issue in the multivariate analysis below.

INTEREST IN POLITICS

As in the case of political discussion, interest in politics is believed to help us explain variation in participation (Almond and Verba 1963, Conway 2000). Citizens who are able to participate in politics because their socio-economic status is relatively high, have the relevant experience and skills, and are embedded in extensive social networks will not necessarily become involved in politics if they lack interest in or concern for public affairs (Brady, Schlozman, and Verba 1995).

Explaining political participation in terms of interest in politics has been criticized as tautological because the connection between the two is so close (van Deth 1989). Nonetheless, conceptually, attitude (interest) and behavior (participation) are two different things, so that not necessarily all those who are interested in politics will in fact participate (Campbell, Gurin, and Miller 1954, 33; Klingemann 1979, 264).

In descriptive terms, most citizens in Indonesia are not interested in politics. Across four elections only three or four of ten citizens typically expressed interest in politics or governmental affairs, and the tendency has been toward decline over time, from 40 percent in 1999 to 30 percent in 2014. Norris (1999) reports a similar phenomenon in other countries, so this is not a specifically Indonesian problem. Most people are not interested in politics even though politics or government can have a significant impact on their lives.

Does political interest affect participation? In 1999, interest did not have a consistent and significant influence. There was even a small effect in the other direction, that more people who expressed an interest in politics nonetheless did not vote. At that time, the meaning of "politics" was perhaps less associated with elections. Many of those who voted did so precisely because they were not interested in politics. Almost everybody voted, both those who were and those who were not interested. As we have argued in Chapter 5, many vote because they have been mobilized, not because they have their own psychological reason for doing so. So, interest in politics had little effect on turnout.

When participation is measured in terms of campaign activity, supporting or donating to parties and candidates, and persuading others to vote, however, interest does have a positive and significant impact. In 1999, 9 percent of those who expressed interest in politics participated in campaigns, 32 percent of those who expressed great interest did so, while among those who said they were not interested at all only 7 percent participated. We found a similar result in 2004, 2009, and 2014. A significant association was also found when participation was defined as assisting and donating to parties or candidates, and when it was defined as persuading others.

Psychological factors, that is, party identity, interest in politics, political discussion, and political information are in general significantly associated with particular forms of political participations, i.e. campaigning, assisting parties, and persuading others, but not with voting. Does this connection remain significant when political economy and sociological factors are incorporated? Multivariate analysis in Table 6.2 shows the level of consistency across all parliamentary and presidential elections.[6]

The psychological factor with the most significant influence on political participation (not only voting) is party ID. Citizens with high party ID, whatever their party affiliation, participate more in many political activities. This finding confirms many previous studies conducted elsewhere

---

[6] In the multivariate analysis, political participation as the dependent variable is an index of participation that is constructed from voting (0=did not vote, 1=voted) and ever participated in a campaign (0=never, 1=ever) for the 1999 and 2004 parliamentary elections and also the first and second round 2004 presidential elections (below), to which we added ever assisting a party or candidate in a campaign (0=never, 1=ever), and ever persuaded others to vote for a specific party or candidate (0=never, 1=ever) for the 2009 and 2014 elections.

TABLE 6.2 *Multivariate analysis of political participation for parliamentary elections*

	1999 B	Beta	2004 B	Bata	2009 B	Beta	2014 B	Beta
Constant	.808**(.087)		.739**(.125)		-.233*(.117)		-.318*(.156)	
Party Identity	.089**(.021)	.163	.181**(.041)	.154	.194**(.026)	.191	.164***(.028)	.146
Discussion	.082**(.018)	.112	.028(.018)	.065	.225**(.038)	.168	.393***(.039)	.287
Political Interest	-.062**(.018)	-.081			.208**(.024)	.222	.028(.021)	.036
Political Information	.086**(.021)	.102	.018(.032)	.025	.042(.037)	.033	.028(.042)	.020
Active in Social Organizations	.043(.026)	.039	.053*(.024)	.081	.020(.036)	.014	.680***(.116)	.147
Education	-.023**(.006)	-.106	-.005(.002)	-.014	.006(.010)	.017	-.019*(.009)	-.066
Religiosity	.078**(.022)	.085	.053(.036)	.054	.041(.022)	.049	-.034(.027)	-.032
Urban Residence	-.056*(.027)	-.050	-.109*(.044)	-.093	-.072(.045)	-.044	-.004(.036)	-.003
Age	-.004**(.001)	-.100	-.001(.002)	-.014	.003(.002)	.049	.001(.001)	.017
Male Gender	.137**(.026)	.126	.070(.042)	.060	.007(.043)	.004	.097**(.034)	.070
R-square	.123		.064		.170		.184	
N	1668		802		1368		1446	

B is the regression coefficient (with standard error) and Beta is the standardized regression coefficient.
** $p = .01$, * $p = .05$.

that party identity is an important factor in explaining participation. Other psychological factors, including interest in politics and political discussion, are also significant, but less consistently influential after incorporating party identity into the analysis. Sociological factors are less influential after weighing all the psychological factors.

The triumph of psychological factors is also visible in presidential elections (Table 6.3) after including other factors. Party identity has a significant influence, consistent across presidential elections, in increasing participation in general. Other psychological factors, that is political information and interest in politics, also have a positive and significant though inconsistent influence.

The pattern in which participation is stronger among older, less educated people who live in villages shows that mobilization rather than participation is more likely. At the same time psychological aspects, especially party identity, have a powerful influence on participation. It follows that when this identity declines the level of participation also declines, as can be seen at the aggregate level in all of the elections. It is probable that the level of participation will continue to decline consistent with the increase in level of education and urbanization, on the one hand, and the decline in level of party identification on the other.

We need to stress here that the effect of psychological factors on participation is only important with regard to nonvoting, its volume is relatively small, and it has tended to shrink. In other words, psychological factors, including party ID, do not help us explain participation in the case of voting, where the numbers are larger. And campaigning is very close to mobilization.

POLITICAL CHOICE

Are psychological factors also important in shaping political choice? The psychological factor thought to be most relevant here is party identity. How important is level of party ID for the voter's choice of party, parliamentary candidate, or president?

The association between party ID and choice of political party turns out to be very strong. Identification with a particular party and choice of that party at the election are almost identical. For that reason, if the number of people who identify with a party declines sharply the level of stability of support for that party will also decline sharply. Conversely, if the number of party identifiers increases the party's stability is strengthened. Even though the number of swing voters from election to election is

TABLE 6.3 *Multivariate analysis of political participation in the presidential elections*

	2004a		2004b		2009		2014	
	B	Beta	B	Beta	B	Beta	B	Beta
Constant	.479** (.096)		.306** (.119)		-.589** (.130)		-.136 (.198)	
Party ID	.073** (.012)	.175	.046** (.012)	.112	.188** (.028)	.187	.149*** (.036)	.135
Discussion	.042** (.016)	.082	-.028 (.017)	-.054	.236** (.040)	.183	.332*** (.044)	.292
Political Interest	NA	NA	NA	NA	.145* (.023)	.172	.060* (.027)	.083
Political Information	.112** (.023)	.127	.073** (.021)	.025	.073* (.035)	.033	.038 (.050)	.031
Active in Social Organizations	.012 (.056)	-.003	.089 (.048)	.055	.274** (.064)	.117	.326* (.148)	.073
Education	-.017** (.006)	-.086	-.037** (.006)	-.192	-.024* (.010)	-.078	-.017 (.010)	-.065
Religiosity	-.027 (.026)	-.031	.067** (.025)	.079	.032 (.026)	.034	.015 (.032)	.016
Urban Residence	-.088** (.029)	-.093	-.071* (.028)	-.075	.045 (.044)	.030	-.010 (.044)	-.008
Age	.005** (.001)	.150	.006** (.001)	.159	.004** (.001)	.076	.001 (.002)	.016
Male Gender	.071** (.028)	.074	.002 (.028)	.062	-.055 (.041)	-.037	.027 (.042)	.021
R-square	.101		.099		.194		.180	
N	1189		1200		1225		846	

B is the regression coefficient (with standard error) and Beta is the standardized regression coefficient
NA indicates no data for that variable.

198

quite large, a few parties continue to win relatively high percentages of the vote, including PDIP, Golkar, PKB, PPP, PKS, PAN, and Demokrat.

Even though in general there is a significant association between party ID and partisan choice, that association has weakened from election to election. That includes Golkar, the oldest party, generally believed to have the strongest party ID because it has had the longest time to build mass loyalty. The association was 90.5 percent in 1999, dropping to 78.6 percent in 2014. And it includes PDIP, believed to have a deeper psychological tie with the masses because it was founded by Sukarno, the most well-known nationalist and populist figure in the country's history. The association in 1999 was 91.3 percent, dropping to 79.4 percent in 2014.

The decreasing association is more significant for other parties such as PKB (from 94 percent in 1999 to 68.9 percent in 2014), PPP (88.7 percent in 1999 to 0.2 percent in 2014), PAN (87.6 percent in 1999 to 68.7 percent in 2014), PKS (90 percent in 2004 to 75.1 percent in 2014), and Demokrat (90.9 percent in 2004 to 44.4 percent in 2014). In the cases of Hanura and Gerindra the association is more stable but at a lower level. Voters for Nasdem, the newest party, show no loyalty whatsoever to the party.

It is the decline in this relationship that probably explains best why support for parties in general is not stable. Party ID is not as important as previously reported, based on data from just the 1999 and 2004 elections (Liddle and Mujani 2007). What has happened is a secular decline in the number of people who feel close to a party, so that many parties have experienced declining support, accompanied by the mobilization of voters for new parties and the number of voters who switch parties. As pointed out in previous chapters, in Indonesia there has been a huge transformation in support for political parties over the last four elections.

Partai Demokrat, not yet born before the 1999 election, was able to win a significant percentage (about 7 percent) in 2004, defeating several existing parties. In the 2009 parliamentary election, the party of Yudhoyono, then the incumbent president, experienced a huge increase to 21 percent, while older parties dropped sharply, Golkar from 22 percent (2004) to 14 percent (2009), PDIP from 18.5 percent (2004) to 14 percent (2009). In the 2014 election, however, Demokrat experienced a sharp decline in turn, dropping to 10 percent compared to 21 percent before.

How about the presidential elections? Bivariate analysis indicates that the association with party ID is strong and significant, but varies considerably among candidates. The strongest association was in 2014. All party identifiers with parties supporting Jokowi voted for him, as did identifiers with parties supporting Prabowo. In previous elections, Yudhoyono's support from the parties in his coalition was consistently very strong, 85.4 percent in the 2004 first round and 96.6 in 2009. The association was also strong in the cases of Megawati and Amien Rais (above 80 percent). The association was not strong, however, in the cases of Hamzah Haz, Wiranto, and Kalla (below 60 percent).[7]

The association was still strong, though weaker, when party identities were combined in presidential coalitions.[8] Of the voters who identified themselves with one of the coalition parties supporting Yudhoyono in the 2004 second round, 90.1 percent voted for Yudhoyono and only 9.9 percent chose Megawati. Of the voters who identified with one of the parties supporting Megawati, only 56.9 percent chose her. The rest did not divulge their choice to our survey interviewers.

This pattern may also be seen in 2009, when 84 percent of the voters who identified with one of the parties in Yudhoyono's coalition chose him, while the remainder chose Megawati. Among those who identified with one of the parties in Megawati's coalition, 89.2 percent chose Megawati and the remainder Yudhoyono. Among voters who identified with one of the parties in Jusuf Kalla's coalition, only 55.3 percent supported Kalla; most of the remainder chose Yudhoyono.

The strongest connection is visible in 2014, where those who identified with the party supporting a particular presidential candidate also tended to vote for that candidate. This occurred because in 2014 there were only two pairs of candidates, which made for a much more vigorous campaign on both sides. The journalistic perspective was also that the 2014 election

---

[7] In this analysis, the party identified with Megawati was PDIP, with Yudhoyono Partai Demokrat, Wiranto Partai Golkar, Amien Rais PAN, Hamzah Haz PPP, Jokowi PDIP, and Prabowo Gerindra.

[8] This analysis is limited to the second round of the 2004 presidential election and the 2009 presidential election because in the first 2004 round coalition activity was not yet strong because the parties that had won 5 percent or more of the parliamentary vote or more tended to support their own leader like PAN for Amien Rais and PPP for Hamzah Haz. PKB at that time had not taken a clear position because its leader, Abdurrahman Wahid, had been declared ineligible by the General Election Commission. In the second round, the coalition effort was stronger because there were only two candidates, Megawati and Yudhoyono. Yudhoyono was supported by Demokrat, PPP, PKPI, PAN, and PKS among others. Megawati's primary support was from PDIP, Golkar, PPP, and PDS. In 2009, Yudhoyono was nominated by Demokrat, PKS, PPP, PKB, and PAN. Megawati was nominated by PDIP and Gerindra, and Jusuf Kalla by Golkar and Hanura. In 2014, Joko Widodo (Jokowi) was nominated by PDIP, PKB, Nasdem, Hanura, and PKPI, while Prabowo Subianto was nominated by Gerindra, Golkar, PAN, PPP, and PKS.

was much more hotly contested, close and tense, compared to the previous election. This suggests that party ID and its effect on a presidential election cannot be separated from mobilization.

The strength of the relationship between party identity and choice of presidential candidate may tell us something about the ease with which voters change their vote when party identity declines. In addition, partisan choice cannot be completely mobilized or directed to support a party's presidential candidate because for most citizens party identity is weak. We can see this in the 2004 second round where nearly half the citizens who identified with one of Megawati's coalition partners did not then vote for Megawati. The same is true for supporters of Kalla in 2009.

Is the strength of the association between party identity and political choice independent of sociological factors, evaluations of the national economy, and leadership quality? Table 6.4 displays the very significant and consistent influence of party ID on both party and candidate choice in general. Citizens who identify with PDIP tend to choose PDIP whatever their sociological background, evaluations of the condition of the national political economy, and evaluations of the qualities of party leaders. The pattern holds for older parties such as Golkar, Demokrat, PKB, PPP, and PKS.

There are many more voters who feel close to PDIP and then vote for PDIP than those who do not feel close to PDIP. This has been true in all of the parliamentary elections. It describes the behavior of citizens who identify with other parties as well. To be sure, the effect of party identity on party choice declines substantially, in a statistical sense, after it is controlled for other theoretically important factors. Nonetheless, the effect of party identity remains strong.

The effect on presidential is not as strong as on parliamentary elections, though it remains significant after being controlled for other factors. It is especially strong and consistent for Yudhoyono's voters both when his vice presidential candidate was Jusuf Kalla in 2004 and when it was Boediono in 2009. The probability that voters who feel close to Partai Demokrat would choose Yudhoyono was 63 percent compared to those who did not in the 2004 first round, 19 percent in the second round, and 26 percent in 2009.

The effect was less strong, indeed lost significance, for voters for Megawati and Kalla in 2009 after controlling for other factors, especially leadership quality. This indicates that leadership quality has been a powerful factor in presidential elections, stronger than party identity, as Liddle and Mujani suggested in their 2007 analysis. A more consistent

TABLE 6.4 *The effect of party identity on choice of party and presidential candidate, 1999–2009 (difference in predicted probability)*

	PDIP	Golkar	PKB	PPP	PAN	PD	PKS	Gerindra	Hanura	NasDem
Parliamentary Election										
1999[1]	0.83***	0.89***	0.95***	0.95***	0.97***					
1999[2]	0.84***	0.90***	0.99***	0.94***	0.92***					
2004[1]	0.78***	0.81***	0.80***	0.59***	0.69***	0.93***	0.62***			
2004[2]	0.64***	0.80***	0.23*	0.73***	0.39**	0.82***	0.35**			
2009[1]	0.73***	0.61***	0.68***	0.57*	0.67***	0.46***	0.68***	0.62***	0.47***	
2009[2]	0.33***	0.59***	0.54***	0.67***	0.69***	0.40***	0.49****	0.34	0.95***	
2014[1]	0.88***	0.92***	0.78***	0.83***	0.57**	0.43**	0.86***	0.69***	0.35*	
2014[2]	0.71***	0.90***	0.39	0.85***	0.55**	0.42**	0.94***	0.65***	0.22	NS
Presidential Election	Megawati-Hasyim (Prabowo) [Prabowo-Hatta]	Yudhoyono-Kalla (Boediono) [Jokowi-Kalla]	Wiranto-Salahuddin (Kalla-Wiranto)	Amien-Siswono	Hamzah-Agum					
2004a[1]	0.85***	0.62***	0.52***	0.68***	0.52***					

(continued)

2004a²	0.50***	0.63***	0.40***	0.32**	0.14
2004b¹	0.70***	0.47***			
2004b²	0.17**	0.19***			
2009¹	(0.59***)	(.42***)	(0.37***)		
2009²	(0.07)	(0.26***)	(0.06)		
2014¹	[0.36*]	[0.63***]			
2014²	[0.40*]	[0.61***]			

[1] Analysis with only one independent variable (one party identity from the relevant party).

[2] Analysis of the effects of party identity (from each relevant party) after controlling for sociological factors (Muslim religiosity, ethnicity, education, urban-rural, age, and gender), political economy, and quality of leadership.

*** p = 0.001, ** p = 0.01, and * p = 0.05

association between party ID and voting for president can be seen in 2014. The contest was tighter and the mass mobilization by the parties more intensive.

To summarize: In general, there is a significant relationship between party ID and political choice. This makes it important to study what shapes party ID.

POLITICAL SOCIALIZATION

Most comparative behavior scholars believe that party identity emerges and develops as a result of a long and complex process of political socialization. The process includes early political experiences in the family and in the wider social world, in school, in exposure to political information via the mass media, and so on (Campbell, Converse, Miller, and Stokes 1960; Iyengar 1979; Wong 2000).

Early socialization in the family is believed to contribute powerfully to the formation of party identity, with children being influenced to support the party of their parents if a parent has a strong identity (Achen 2002). Conversely, a parent who is not or is less partisan tends to produce children who are also not or are less partisan. Discussing politics in the family from early youth to near-adulthood is believed to play a crucial role in the formation of party identity.

Outside the home, citizens are politically socialized through interactions with neighbors, close friends, workmates, schoolmates, and in various social groups and institutions. For the young, the strongest influences may be in school and later university, including student social and political organizations. For those who are employed, the influence may come from fellow workers in a factory or farmhands. For professionals, socialization frequently occurs in employment-related organizations to which they belong. Religious socialization often comes through churches and religious organizations to which citizens belong.

Several studies have concluded that party identity is shaped by social identity (Green, Palmquist, and Schickler 2002). Social identity is typically connected to standard sociological indicators, such as religion or religiosity, social class, ethnic or regional group, age groups, and specific organizational membership in religious organizations, labor unions and farmers' organizations, and so on (Abramowitz and Saunders 2006).

A strong relationship between social identity and the emergence and development of party identity may not be a universal characteristic of contemporary societies. It may have a greater impact in societies that have long had deeply rooted parties as in the US or Western Europe. It may or may not be strong in new democracies such as Indonesia. Even in the US, its importance is still being debated (Abramowitz and Saunders 2006).

In the US, social identity has been seen as a factor supporting stable party identities (Green, Palmquist, and Schickler 2002). At the same time, several studies have described a rather rapid rise and fall in party identity and have argued that this phenomenon cannot be explained by stable social identities. These studies have proposed a number of alternative explanations.

One approach claims a connection between rational voting and party identity. This argument returns to the rational voter perspective developed by Downs (1957). It is also associated with Key (1966), who emphasized the impact of voters' rational evaluations toward parties, candidates, the condition of the economy, incumbents' performance, and party and candidate issue positions.[9] Perceptions of political economic condition can change more quickly than social identity, and for that reason are a better source of explanation of the shifting dynamics of party identity.

In addition, still focused on psychological factors, shifting party identities may be connected to changes in the levels of citizens' affection toward national political figures such as party leaders or presidential candidates rather than sociological or political economy factors. National leaders or party figures also change more quickly than social identity, and citizens' affection toward national figures may be a better explanation, especially in new democracies with minimal experience with political parties that have been created from below (Campbell, Converse, Miller, and Stokes 1960; Barnes, McDonough, and Pina 1985; cf. White, Rose, and McAllister 1997). Affection for leaders may of course be shaped as well by partisan attitudes (McGrath and McGrath 1962; Sigel 1964). It may also be shaped by issues on which a candidate has taken a position, or by the performance of an incumbent in office.

All of these possibilities will be explored here. The relationship between discussing politics and party identity is significant.[10] The more often voters talk about politics with their parents when still young and the more often they talk about politics with other members of the family

---

[9] See also Fiorina (1981); Page and Jones (1979); Franklin and Jackson (1983); Carmines, McIver, and Stimson (1987); Luskin, McIver, and Carmines (1989); Franklin (1992); Weisberg and Smith, Jr., (1991).

[10] In the 1999 survey, responses about political discussion were only in two categories, often or rarely, so that it is difficult to compare them with data after that.

and nonfamily members, the stronger is their party identity. We can see this effect especially in the association between early socialization and party identity. The pattern indicates that party identity is shaped by socialization processes from an early age, in the family, and also by personal relationships with others such as friends. It confirms the findings of many previous studies conducted elsewhere.

Because of the strength of the effect of political socialization in the family on the formation of party identity, the increase in the number of those who engage in this socialization will increase the level of party identity; conversely, if the level decreases the number of party identifiers will decline. What has occurred since 1998, when most citizens live in a freer political climate, is apparently that there has been no increase in political socialization within the family. Indeed, the tendency has been for it to decrease. We see a similar pattern in discussion of politics with others. At the aggregate level, this decline is parallel with a decline in party identity in society.

Political socialization is also believed to occur during social interaction. All citizens live in specific social groups or contexts, which can shape their social identity, that is, their self-assessment that they belong to a particular social organization or organizations, e.g., religious, regional/ethnic, social class, professional and so on. As explained in Chapter 4, involvement in social groups positions citizens in broader networks, increasing opportunities to learn about public issues to which parties and politicians attend. In addition, placement in a social network means that citizens are within reach of politicians' and parties' radar, making it easier for them to be mobilized politically. This dimension of socialization helps citizens to form attitudes toward political parties. It is a source of party identity.

The connection needs to be given special attention in the cases of religious, labor, farmers, and fisher's organizations, which are relatively large. We also make involvement in other organizations a part of the mix, enabling us to construct a single index of social identity. The index includes involvement in sports, cultural, professional, nongovernmental, and business organizations like the Chamber of Commerce.[11]

Citizens have a religious social identity when they state that they belong to a particular religious group. Identity can also refer to intensity, that is, how strong the feeling of attachment to a religion is, which can be measured

---

[11] The social identity index consists of involvement in religious, labor, farmers, fishers, professional, sports, cultural, nongovernmental, and business organizations. Each is made up of three categories of responses: not a member (1), nonactive member (2), and active member (3). The combined scores constitute an index scaled 1–3.

by the degree to which adherents perform the duties of their religion. In our study, to reiterate, religious social identity is the religion to which the citizen adheres; for Muslims, it is also tied to the level of piety in carrying out the requirements of Islam.

The question we address is why religious social identity shapes partisanship or party identity. Religion and religiosity represent a social resource that promotes and mediates citizens' involvement in collective life so that they have an opportunity to learn more and to care about various public issues beyond the confines of the religion itself. Religion teaches us the importance of mutual help, doing good to others, developing friendships, and so on. These values encourage citizens to extend a hand, to provide assistance, to come together, all of which have value in society. Of course, these values do not have to come from religion alone. In Indonesia, however, as in the US, there is no moral institution that is more massive and enduring than religion. So, it is reasonable if religion is connected to social involvement and commitment.

This social involvement or commitment creates citizens who are more open to a range of public issues that are also attended to by political parties. The concerns of citizens that are motivated by religion meet the concerns of the parties. In addition, citizen involvement in social life motivated by religious values also places citizens in social networks where they become available for mobilization by politicians. Citizens in turn develop affection for parties. They feel that they are aware of, familiar with, comfortable with political parties that have the capability of mobilizing them. Many Indonesian citizens who are active in religious social organizations subsequently become party activists. There are even political parties that are direct expressions of the political aspirations of religious organizations, like PKB and PAN among Muslims and PDS (Partai Damai Sejahtera, Prosperous Peace Party) among Protestant Christians.

As in the case of citizens who are active in religious organizations, those who are active in social class organizations also help citizens to enter networks which make them accessible to politicians and parties, especially those with a commitment to represent class interests. Party identity formation may result from this interaction.

In the comparative literature, in addition to religious identity, social class is also considered an important form of identity in shaping party ID (Prandy 2000; White, Rose, and McAllister 1997). Social class identity can be seen in self-identification with a particular class, that is, upper, middle, or lower. But it can also be seen in involvement in organizations that are considered close to particular classes, like organizations of workers, farmers, or fishers for the lower class or business and professional organizations for middle and upper classes.

Social class organizations, like religious organizations, can become a medium for political socialization, encouraging citizens to become involved in issues that are connected to public interests, placing them in social networks where politicians and parties will mobilize them. From this process citizens develop an affection for political parties.

Among Indonesian voters, is it empirically the case that social identity helps form party identity? The data indicate that for most Indonesians party identity is indeed significantly associated with membership or activity in a religious social organization. Citizens who are active in religious organizations like NU and Muhammadiyah, Qur'anic study groups, the Catholic or Protestant churches, and so on tend to feel close to particular political parties. Chapter 4 has demonstrated that level of religiosity has a significant relationship with involvement in religious social organizations. Citizens who identify with a party tend to be involved in religious social organizations, and that involvement is rooted in a high level of piety.

Social class also encourages the emergence of party identity. Citizens who are active in labor unions, farmers' and fishers' organizations tend to feel more positively toward a political party. The effect is weaker, however, than in the case of religion.

Looked at as a whole, involvement in various social organizations helps raise the level of affection for political parties and the emergence and strengthening of party identity. The more active citizens are in organizational life, and the more organizations they join, the stronger the tendency to identify with a political party and for that identity to strengthen.

Does the connection between social identity and party ID remain significant when other factors are included in the analysis? Multivariate analysis shows that social identity does in fact have a significant effect on party identity, and this effect is very consistent whatever the voter's demographic background (Table 6.5). Citizens who are active in social organizations tend to have a party ID regardless of whether their education is high or low, whether they live in villages or cities, on Java or outside Java, and whether they are young or old.

For Indonesians, as for voters in advanced industrial democracies, party identity is shaped by social identity. It is also true, however, that not all party identity can be explained by social identity. Religion- and class-based social identities are relatively more stable, while party identities have declined sharply in the last fifteen years. This suggests that social

TABLE 6.5 *Multivariate analysis (regression) of the effect of social identity on party identity*

	2004a B (Std. Error)	2004b B (Std. Error)	2004c B (Std. Error)	2009a B (Std. Error)	2009b B (Std. Error)	2014a B (Std. Error)	2014b B (Std. Error)
Constant	1.633*** (.239)	1.508*** (.275)	.878*** (.270)	.601*** (.160)	-.067 (.214)	.433** (.152)	-.019 (.199)
Social Identity	.076+ (.040)	.532*** (.152)	.590*** (.123)	.341*** (.096)	1.126*** (.146)	.607*** (.107)	.808*** (.136)
Religiosity	.168** (.065)	.206** (.068)	.165** (.065)	.038 (.033)	.035 (.031)	.019 (.025)	.046 (.029)
Economic Condition	-.042 (.033)	-.084* (.037)	.038 (.040)	.038 (.022)	-.034 (.027)	-.009 (.020)	-.022 (.025)
Education	-.036* (.016)	-.005 (.017)	-.045* (.076)	.003 (.010)	.014 (.012)	.007 (.008)	.015+ (.009)
Urban Residence	-.090 (.077)	-.190* (.079)	.154* (.076)	.185*** (.044)	-.071 (.053)	.083* (.035)	.066 (.042)
Resident on Java	.174* (.074)	.172* (.078)	.157* (.076)	.050 (.042)	-.118* (.052)	-.089** (.033)	.034 (.040)
Age	.000 (.003)	-.004 (.003)	-.007* (.003)	-.001 (.002)	.004* (.002)	.000 (.001)	.001 (.002)
Male Gender	.119*	.004 (.077)	.077 (.076)	.149*** (.041)	.084 (.049)	.067* (.032)	.034 (.040)
N	908		945	1641	981	1501	871
R-square	.051	.047		.038	.083	.038	.059

***p = .001, **p = .01, *p = .05, +p = .1

209

identity, while a part of the total picture, is not strong enough to explain the dynamics of party identity.

Several studies have discovered more dynamic factors that help us to explain party identity. The rational voter perspective offers an issue-based dynamic, especially concerning economic issues, the positions of parties on those issues, evaluation of the performance of incumbents in executive office, and evaluations of the performance of ruling parties (Downs 1957; Page and Jones 1979; Fiorina 1981; Franklin and Jackson 1983; Carmines, McIver, and Stimson 1987; Luskin, McIver, and Carmines 1989; Franklin 1992). Other studies have shown that changes in party identity are connected to the popularity of leaders, which is in turn connected to evaluations of the performance of incumbents and perceptions of a country's macroeconomic condition (MacKuen, Erickson, and Stimson 1989; Weisberg and Smith, Jr., 1991).

These arguments have been developed mainly in the context of American elections, where party identity is connected to the two major parties, Republican and Democrat. Voters who do not identify with one or the other of these two major parties are usually labeled independents.[12] In other words, the measurement of party identity is directly connected to the two parties which dominate the American political landscape. These measures have also been used to test the rational voter argument.

If this argument of voter rationality is correct, we would expect that in the 1999 parliamentary elections positive evaluations of the national economic condition would increase the number of Golkar party identifiers, because Golkar was in power. Conversely, negative evaluations should have increased the level of party identification for PDIP, PKB, PPP, and PAN, all of which were out of power.

In 2004, PDIP was the main incumbent party, and the opposition was led by Partai Demokrat and PKS. Positive economic evaluations should have increased PDIP party ID and decreased it for the main opposition parties. In 2009, Demokrat and Yudhoyono were the main incumbents, while PDIP, Hanura, and Gerindra were the chief opposition. Positive evaluations of the national economic condition should have

---

[12] In US National Election Surveys, the question is usually formulated as follows: "Are you a Republican, Democrat, or independent?" If the response is Democrat or Republican the follow up questions asks how strong is the support. Combined responses to these questions produce a party ID variable on a scale of 1–7, in which 1 is strong Republican and 7 strong Democrat.

strengthened party identity for Demokrat and weakened it for PDIP, Hanura, and Gerindra. In 2014, it was expected that positive evaluations of the national economic condition would increase identifications with Demokrat, which represented the incumbent, compared to PDIP, which had now become the opposition.

Connected to evaluation of the national economic condition, the rational voter perspective also regards as important for party identity the issue positions of each party and its leader, including job approval of incumbents. Voters who evaluate positively the issue positions of each party and leader tend to identify with that party. Voters who feel satisfied with the performance of a ruling party and its leader also identify with that party. And voters who evaluate positively the performance of the government or the head of government tend to strongly identify with the party in power. As argued in Chapter 5, the rational voter model assumes two contesting poles, incumbent and opposition.

The data indicate that evaluations of national economic condition have a positive and significant relationship with party identity for the party in power, but are less consistent for other parties.[13] Most voters had difficulty determining which is the opposition party, except during the first round 2004 and the 2009 presidential elections, where the economic effect is significant for PDIP and Demokrat, the main antagonists. Party identity for the coalition parties in 2004 and 2009 was not much influenced by the national economic condition. This also shows that there is no party ID incentive in terms of evaluations of the national economic condition in joining a progovernment coalition, except for the dominant party in the coalition.

In 1999, Partai Golkar party ID was protected by positive evaluations of the national economic condition. Voters recognized that Golkar was the ruling party. In 2004, the ruling party was PDIP; positive evaluations of the national economic condition strengthened PDIP identity. In 2009, the ruling party was Partai Demokrat; positive economic evaluations strengthened voters' identification with Demokrat and weakened their identification with PDIP. However, that effect can no longer be seen in 2014, when the Demokrat party suffered a significant decline from 21 percent to 10 percent.

---

[13] National economic condition is the evaluation of the voter as to whether the national economy now is in general much better, better, no change, worse, or much worse than last year.

The rational voter perspective claims that party identity is closely tied to positions on issues and evaluations of incumbents' performance that are more dynamic over time than other factors. Our main finding is that voters' evaluations relate more significantly to party identity for the party in power than for opposition parties.[14]

As we have already stated, the argument about the relationship between governmental performance and party identity assumes that there are two diametrically opposed camps in an election. In 1999, evaluations of the national economic condition and the performance of the Habibie government were strongly associated with Partai Golkar identity, since Golkar was the party of the incumbent President Habibie. In 2004, PDIP and Megawati were the ruling party and incumbent president, and positive evaluations of Megawati's performance strengthened identification with her party.

In 2009, Yudhoyono and Partai Demokrat were in power, Megawati and PDIP in opposition. Positive economic condition and performance evaluations of Yudhoyono strengthened identification with Demokrat and weakened it with PDIP. The effect on other parties was mostly not significant, primarily because those parties were not clearly identified in the minds of the voters as governing or opposition parties.

---

[14] The political economy measure is not the same across our surveys because government performance is connected to various actual issues as they emerge at the time of parliamentary and presidential elections. For the 2004 parliamentary election, we did not ask about government performance. In 1999, the political economy evaluation consisted of several items: the implementation of government under President Habibie, Habibie's performance in resolving problems of corruption and economic crisis, strengthening the rule of law, resolving horizontal conflict, and the condition of the national economy. For the 2004 presidential election, the questions were about the national economic condition, national politics, rule of law, social order, the performance of President Megawati in reducing the level of poverty, unemployment, resolving social conflict, combating corruption, and terrorism. In 2009, the questions included evaluation of the national economic condition, national politics, rule of law, security and order in society, combating corruption, unemployment, and poverty, improving education and health services and of Yudhoyono's performance in general. In 2014, the political economy variable was an index constructed of several items: evaluation of the national economic condition now compared to last year (1=better, 0=worse), the Yudhoyono government's performance in controlling the prices of basic commodities (1=good, 0=bad), in reducing poverty (1=good, 0=bad), in reducing unemployment (1=good, 0=bad), in eradicating corruption (1=good, 0=bad), and satisfaction with President Yudhoyono's performance (1=satisfied, 0=unsatisfied). Positive responses for each of these items were coded 1 and negative 0. For every survey, therefore, except the 2004 parliamentary election, we constructed an index with a scale of 0 to 1 (the closer to 0 the more negative the evaluation).

In 2004, in fact, almost all of the parties were in the ruling coalition except for Demokrat and PKS. PKS was still known as PK, before it changed its name to PKS to contest the 2004 elections. Yudhoyono had been a member of Megawati's cabinet, but had resigned not long before the parliamentary election in order to strengthen his recently established Partai Demokrat. PK/PKS was understood to be outside of Megawati's coalition, more in the camp of Amien Rais than Megawati. For his part, Amien Rais' relationship to the government was also unclear, as was that of his party, PAN. PAN was formally a member of Megawati's coalition, but prior to the parliamentary election nominated Amien Rais for the presidency. The position of all of the other parties, like PPP, PKB, and Golkar, was unclear as well.

In 2009, the coalition position of most parties was once again unclear, other than Demokrat and PDIP. Golkar, led by Jusuf Kalla, announced its opposition to the Yudhoyono government even though Kalla was the sitting vice president. There was inconsistency, to put it mildly, in Golkar's position in relation to the government! In return, Golkar was punished by the voters, who abandoned it in droves for Partai Demokrat, strengthening the latter's party ID, and to Yudhoyono, who was reelected to a second term as president.

To be sure, examined more closely it was not negative evaluations of the performance of the government but other factors that reduced Golkar identity. PDIP, as the opposition that year, was clearly punished by the positive evaluations of the performance of the government, which weakened PDIP identity and subsequently the number of its voters in the 2009 parliamentary election. The effect was the same on Megawati's presidential candidacy.

The rational voter effect was not consistent from election to election, across categories of gender, age, residence on or off Java, rural-urban, level of education, Muslim religiosity and activity in social organizations (Table 6.6) especially in 2014 when the incumbent party, Partai Demokrat, declined sharply. Social identity and specifically regional residence did remain important in forming party identity.

It was not primarily these factors, however, but rather voter rationality that influenced the shifts in party identity, since social identity and regional residence are relatively stable compared to evaluations of incumbent performance or national economic condition. The relative numbers of voters on Java and outside Java, and also of citizens who identify with religious and class organizations such as NU, Muhammadiyah, churches,

TABLE 6.6 *Multivariate analysis (regression) of party identity*

	1999 (ID-Golkar)	2004b (ID-PDIrP)	2004c (ID-PDIP)	2009a (ID-PD)	2009b (ID-PD)	2014a (ID-PD)	2014b (ID-PD)
Constant	1.447***	4.248***	1.845***	1.546***	.835**	.534***	.944***
	(.146)	(.311)	(.217)	(.157)	(.318)	(.154)	(.200)
Economic Condition	1.277***	.996***	1.140***	.524***	1.020***	.007	.026
	(.095)	(.157)	(.115)	(.078)	(.163)	(.020)	(.025)
Social Identity	.063	-.761***	.455***	.289**	.868***	-.569***	-.803***
	(.049)	(.180)	(.111)	(.099)	(.231)	(.108)	(.137)
Education	.017	.005	-.044**	.007	.011	-.003	-.014
	(.011)	(.021)	(.014)	(.010)	(.018)	(.008)	(.009)
Urban Residence	-.121*	-.003	.161*	.079	-.125	-.078*	-.053
	(.056)	(.096)	(.067)	(.045)	(.085)	(.035)	(.042)
Muslim Religiosity	.001	-.249**	-.124*	.071*	.091	-.025	-.030
	(.041)	(.082)	(.057)	(.035)	(.048)	(.025)	(.030)
Residence on Java	-.406**	.145	.254***	-.168***	-.030	.088**	-.046
	(.050)	(.092)	(.067)	(.044)	(.084)	(.033)	(.041)
Age	.001	.005	-.005	.000	.002	.000	-.001
	(.002)	(.004)	(.003)	(.002)	(.003)	(.001)	(.002)
Male Gender	-.047	.081	.014	-.043	-.097	-.054	-.050
	(.048)	(.093)	(.068)	(.042)	(.079)	(.032)	(.040)
N	1801	964	997	1375	1036	1501	871
R-square	.139	.082	.145	.059	.067	.031	.057

***p = .001, **p = .01, *p = .05

labor unions, professional organizations, and so on, did not change much over the fifteen-year period between the first and most recent elections.

To what extent are voters influenced by evaluations of the quality of party leaders and by party campaign mobilization? Several comparative studies show that the quality of a party leader or presidential candidate can influence shifts in party identity (Weisberg 2002; Allsop and Weisberg 1988). Other studies have reversed the causal arrow, however, concluding that it is party identity which shapes evaluations of the quality of leaders and incumbent governments (Miller and Shanks 1996; McGrath and McGrath 1962). Our first voting behavior studies (Liddle and Mujani 2007; Mujani and Liddle 2010) found evidence that the causal arrow runs from leadership to partisan identity.

LEADERSHIP QUALITIES

In the context of new democracies where party institutionalization is weak, the leader may become a magnet attracting individuals to vote for the party and indeed to identify with it (Barnes, McDonough, and Pina 1985; White, Rose, and McAllister 1997; Colton 2000). When a well-known leader forms a party, and becomes its principal figure, the appeal of the party will probably be strongly influenced by the appeal of the leader. There is thus a high probability that leadership qualities play a powerful role in determining not only the individual's choice of vote but also his or her party identity.

Even in advanced democracies, leaders continue to be considered an important part of the explanation of voting behavior (Campbell, Converse, Miller, and Stokes 1960; Miller and Shanks 1996; Bean and Mughan 1989; Bean and Kelley 1988; Graetz and McAllister 1987; Miller and Miller 1976; Butler and Stokes 1974; Stokes 1966). In studies of the effect of leadership qualities on voting and partisanship, the concept is understood as the perceived qualities of the leader according to the voter. Specific qualities include competence, integrity, firmness, empathy, and likeability (Miller and Shanks 1996; Bean and Mughan 1989; King 2000; Colton 2000).

In 1999, we defined leadership quality minimally as the likeability of the major party leaders who competed in the election.[15] In 2004 and 2009,

---

[15] The question was: "Is there a national or party leader whom you like?" Those who answered affirmatively were then asked: "Who is that leader? Please name him or her." In 2004 and 2009, leadership qualities were specified, including competence, integrity, and empathy.

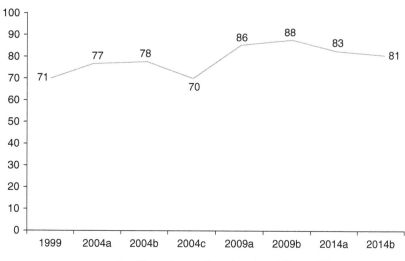

FIGURE 6.2 There is a preferred national figure (%)

the definition was expanded to include several dimensions as indicated above. Figure 6.2 portrays the affection trend of voters for party leaders. In 1999, 71 percent of voters said that there was a national or political party leader whom they preferred, a figure that increased to 77 percent in 2004.

We found similar percentages in the first-round presidential election in July 2004 (78 percent) and the second round in September (70 percent). In the 2009 parliamentary and presidential elections respectively, 86 percent and 88 percent preferred a particular leader.[16] In the 2014 elections the affection decreased, but was still very high compared to the affection toward political parties (see the party ID trend).

In general, Indonesian voters express affection for specific political figures. That affection is consistent from election to election. Despite the numerical uniformity, voters' affection is rich in variety. Depending on the figure preferred, the level of preference ranges widely and changes from

---

[16] In 2009 and 2014, we changed the format of the question. We no longer asked if there is a leader who is preferred, but rather offered specific names of party leaders and asked how much they were preferred or unpreferred on a scale of 1–10, with 1 the least preferred. For this reason, it is difficult to compare the results of this survey directly with previous surveys. We use it anyway, by choosing the leaders who received a score of 6–10 as an approximation of those leaders who are preferred by the voters. The leader with the highest rating is Yudhoyono.

election to election. It is almost certainly this variation that best explains the shifts in party identity and voting behavior described earlier in this chapter.

In 1999, of the voters who said there was a preferred figure, the largest number named Megawati (48 percent), then Habibie (19 percent), Abdurrahman Wahid (12 percent), and Amien Rais (11 percent), with the remainder scattered among a number of leaders. In 2004, the most popular figure was Yudhoyono, who was preferred by 41 percent in April, 46 percent in July (at the time of the first round) and 49 percent in September (the second round). After Yudhoyono, Megawati was the most-preferred figure at the time of the parliamentary election with 15 percent. This percentage did not change much at the time of the July (19 percent) and September (20 percent) rounds in the presidential election. Compared to 1999, Megawati's level of preference was much lower in 2004. Unfortunately, the questions asked in our 2009 and 2014 surveys were sufficiently different that we cannot make a direct comparison.

Before examining the association between leadership quality and party ID, we will look at the association with voting for party or parliamentary candidates and for presidential candidates. Table 6.7 shows the association between leadership likeability, as one form of measurement of leadership quality, and voting for party or parliamentary candidate and for president.[17] Regardless of the specific measure, leadership quality as a concept is associated very strongly with voting for party and parliamentary candidates. This means that the more voters like a particular figure of a party, the higher the probability they will vote for that figure's party. The converse is also true.

The leadership effect on party choice declines, however, after being controlled for other theoretically relevant variables, especially party identity and political economy. The Megawati effect on PDIP in these four elections was still significant and substantively strong after being controlled for other factors. The pattern repeats in the cases of the relevant leaders of other parties. The leadership effect was not significant for PKB and PPP after the 2004 elections, however. Muhaimin Iskandar, who had taken over the leadership of PKB, was not as popular as Abdurrahman Wahid. A similar phenomenon can be seen in PPP, where Suryadarma Ali,

---

[17] In the logistic analysis, the effect of an independent on a dependent variable is analyzed by comparing one party with another as the reference category. There are nine political parties that are analyzed and for that reason 72 dependent variables with their references. We display only those that reference Partai Demokrat.

TABLE 6.7 *The effect of leadership quality on choice of party and presidential candidates, 1999–2014 (difference in predicted probability)*

	PDIP	Golkar	PKB	PPP	PAN	PD	PKS	Gerindra	Hanura	NasDem
Parliamentary Election										
1999[1]	0.79***	0.65***	0.70***	0.55***	0.60***					
1999[2]	0.37***	0.42***	0.19***	0.27***	0.11***					
2004[1]	0.36***	0.36***	0.34***	0.14***	0.16***	0.11***	0.42***			
2004[2]	0.24***	0.38***	0.20***	0.06*	0.13**	0.01	0.23*			
2009[1]	0.52***	0.30***	0.12*	0.08	0.15**	0.35***	0.37***	0.23**	0.10*	
2009[2]	0.25***	0.13**	0.02	NS	0.04	0.26***	0.11*	0.09	0.07	
2014[1]	0.36***	0.30***	0.14*	0.10*	0.25***	0.17***	0.27**	0.30***	0.16***	0.07*
2014[2]	0.26***	0.22***	0.09	-0.01*	0.32***	0.24***	0.34**	0.30***	0.18***	0.03
Presidential Election	Megawati-Hasyim (Prabowo) [Prabowo-Hatta]	Yudhoyono-Kalla (Boediono) [Jokowi-Kalla]	Wiranto-Salahuddin (Kalla-Wiranto)	Amien-Siswono	Hamzah-Agum					
2004a[1]	0.55***	0.44***	0.40***	0.42***	0.24***					
2004a[2]	0.44***	0.51***	0.49***	0.26***	0.04					

(continued)

2004b[1]	0.70***	0.53***	
2004b[2]	0.61***	0.33***	
2009[1]	(0.84***)	(0.86***)	(0.70***)
2009[2]	(0.52***)	(0.81***)	(0.61***)
2014[1]	[0.90***]	[0.91***]	
2014[2]	[0.93***]	[0.89***]	

[1] Analysis with only one independent variable (one leadership quality of the leader of the relevant party).
[2] Analysis of the effect of leadership quality after controlling for sociological factors (Muslim religiosity, ethnicity, education, urban-rural, age, and gender), political economy, and party identity.
NS = not significant in the analysis without the control variables, so no further analysis was conducted. $***p = 0.001$, $**p = 0.01$, and $*p = 0.05$.

who had replaced Hamzah Haz as the party head, was not as popular as his predecessor.

The leadership effect on Gerindra and Hanura was also not so strong in 2009, perhaps because they were new parties, as Demokrat had been in 2004. In 2014, however, the effect was very strong after a long period of socialization. Following this pattern, the leadership effect was weak on Nasdem, a new party in 2014. Apart from these variations, in general the effect of leadership was very strong on legislative elections for nearly all of the parties after controlling for other factors, especially party ID.

The leadership effect can also be seen in the voting for presidential candidates, where it is stronger and more consistent than in the parliamentary elections. For the most part, evaluations of the quality of leadership are closely related to voting for presidential candidates. The more positive the evaluation of a leader's personal qualities, the higher the probability the voter would choose that candidate. This effect is very significant across the presidential elections even after being controlled for other factors, especially party identity and political economy.

Among voters who liked Yudhoyono, 51 percent chose him in the 2004 first round, 33 percent in the second round, and 81 percent in the 2009 presidential election. The pattern is similar for Megawati, Wiranto, Amien Rais, Jusuf Kalla, Jokowi, and Prabowo in the relevant elections. The perceived quality of Hamzah Haz was the only one whose effect was not significant in the presidential elections after including other factors, especially party identity.

Though the association between the personal qualities of the candidates and voting for a president are very close, we cannot claim a causal relationship. As with the other factors we have studied, a different research design is required to determine causality. At least, however, we have affirmed that the connection is very strong.

To this point, we have established that party identity has a strong influence on voting behavior, that is, on party and candidate choice. Also, that party identity is closely tied to voter rationality. Studies of other countries, as we have already pointed out, have found that party identity is shaped by evaluations of the personal qualities of leaders. The rise and fall of partisan attitudes and voting for parties is caused by the rise and fall of voters' affection for leaders and changes in the leaders themselves. We found that the more voters like the leader, the more they tend to identify with that leader's party. This is true across the board, including Megawati and PDIP, Amien Rais and PAN,

Habibie, Akbar Tandjung and Jusuf Kalla with Golkar, Yudhoyono with Demokrat, and so on.

How independent is this effect? Is it still influential after voter rationality, social identity, and other demographic factors are incorporated in the analysis? Our multivariate analysis shows that it is indeed (Table 6.8).[18] Voters' affection (likeability) continues to strengthen party identity significantly, positively, and consistently, regardless of voters' evaluation of governmental performance, social identity, Islamic religiosity, regional residence, age, urban-rural residence, and gender. The impact of the quality of the incumbent is not epiphenomenal to his or her performance in office, whether positive or negative, but is instead a factor in its own right.

However, in the 2014 elections the relationship between leadership and party ID weakened for most parties. Only in the case of PDIP is it consistently strong. This change is apparently connected with the sharp drop in party ID in 2014. Voters who claim to be closer to a particular party numbered only 14 percent after the legislative election and 9 percent after the presidential election. The largest number of voters felt close to PDIP.

What is the effect of leadership comparisons by the voters? In the 1999 election, how did Megawati compare to other leaders, like incumbent President Habibie at that time, and how did Yudhoyono compare to his

---

[18] The dependent variable in this analysis is party identity measured as a feeling of closeness to the party connected to its leader, both measured on a scale of 1–5, in which 1 is not close and 5 is very close. To see the effect of Megawati's leadership qualities, for example, the dependent variable is closeness to PDIP (on a scale of 5). For the 1999 election, party identity was constructed from three variables: feeling close to a particular party (yes or no), if "yes" which party, and finally how close (very close, somewhat close, or slightly close). For example, to construct PDIP party identity, the respondent who answered "no party to which he or she felt close" was given a score of 3, a respondent who answered "very close to PDIP" was scored 5, a respondent who answered that he or she felt close to another party was scored 2, a respondent who was very close to another party was given a 1, and so on, to form a PDIP identity on a scale of 1–5 (1=very far, 3=neutral, and 5=very close). This method was used for other parties as well. In the 1999 election the Golkar leader evaluated was Habibie, in 2004 it was Tandjung, in 2009 Jusuf Kalla. In the 2004 first round the Golkar figure was Wiranto, and the PDIP figure was Megawati. The relevant PPP figure was Hamzah Haz in 1999, the 2004 parliamentary election and the first round of the 2004 presidential election, and Suryadarma Ali for the 2009 parliamentary election. Amien Rais was the PAN leader for all of the elections except the last (in which it was Soetrisno Bachir). Their respective influence was about the same. Yudhoyono was the Demokrat leader evaluated, while the PKB leader for 1999 and 2004 was Abdurrahman Wahid and for the 2014 election Muhaimin Iskandar. For PKS, we evaluated both Hidayat Nurwahid and Tifatul Sembiring but their influence was similar. The Gerindra and Hanura leaders were Prabowo Subianto and Wiranto respectively.

TABLE 6.8 *Regression analysis of the effect of leadership quality on party identity (regression coefficient and standard error)*

	1999	2004a	2004b	2004c	2009a	2009b	2014a	2014b
Megawati	.614***	.504***	.339***	.262***	.091***	.121***	.035***	.028**
	(.023)	(.049)	(.053)	(.051)	(.008)	(.013)	(.008)	(.010)
Yudhoyono		.273***	.283***	.340***	.067***	.128***	.009	.023
		(.041)	(.072)	(.042)	(.011)	(.022)	(.008)	(.012)
Amien Rais	.330***	.371***	.228***		.052***			
	(.016)	(.049)	(.046)		(.007)			
Hamzah Haz	.379***	.186**	.276***		.048***			
	(.033)	(.066)	(.047)		(.009)			
Akbar Tandjung	.383***	.279***	.294***		.071***	.103***		
	(.023)	(.054)	(.054)		(.009)	(.015)		
Abdurrahman Wahid	.448***	.385***			.036***			
	(.201)	(.050)			(.009)			
Hidayat Nurwahid		.227***			.063***			
		(.058)			(.009)			
Wiranto					.041***		.000	-.006
					(.007)		(.009)	(.011)
Prabowo Subianto					.068***		.019*	.004
					(.007)		(.009)	(.010)
Jokowi							.042***	.029**
							(.009)	(.011)

(continued)

Aburizal Bakrie	.009	.041***
	(.009)	(.012)
Hatta Rajasa	−.006	.019
	(.011)	(.012)
Surya Paloh	−.008	−.018
	(.011)	(.015)
Muhaimin Iskandar	.014	−.003
	(.017)	(.021)
Anis Matta	.007	.023
	(.018)	(.022)
Suryadharma Ali	.023	.042*
	(.016)	(.018)

Control variables: voter rationality, social identity, education, Muslim religiosity, urban-rural residence, Java-non-Java residence, age, and gender.

competition at the time of the 2004 and 2009 elections? Is a party leader more liked because of sociological factors, superiority in campaign skills, or because he or she is a government leader as was Megawati in 2004 and Yudhoyono in 2009? In order to answer these questions, we must look first at the role of the mass media.

MASS MEDIA

In order to feel affection for a party leader, voters must be exposed to that leader. They must have enough information to feel whether he or she is worthy of being liked or disliked, loved or hated. No instrument is more important in assisting this exposure than the mass media. In a large country with hundreds of millions of people it is impossible for public figures to interact directly with more than a few voters.

In Indonesia, the reach of mass mobilization in campaigns in the form of public meetings and rallies might attract as many as a quarter of all voters, but this takes place prior to legislative, not presidential elections. In legislative elections, there are many more political actors involved in the mobilization process, both at the local and at the national levels. In presidential elections, the percentage of voters who have ever followed campaigns directly has never been more than 10 percent. At the same time, public exposure to news and campaign information via the mass media is pervasive. Citizens who have ever followed a campaign via watching TV may be as many as 87 percent, reading newspapers 41 percent, and listening to the radio 49 percent. The mass media, especially TV, therefore have the greatest potential for helping the voter to know, for better and worse, parties and candidates.

The effect of mass media exposure on affection for party leaders varies, both substantively and in intensity, and the causes of this variation may be multiple. We found that the association is diverse. In the 2004 parliamentary election, the strongest relationship between voters who followed the campaigns and party leaders was with Yudhoyono, then Abdurrahman Wahid and Amien Rais. In the presidential election of the same year, the relationship was strongest for Yudhoyono, followed by Megawati. In the 2009 parliamentary election, it was strongest for Yudhoyono followed by Amien Rais, and in the presidential election of the same year it was strongest for Yudhoyono, then Megawati, then Jusuf Kalla. In 2014, the strongest association between campaigning via mass media and leader affection

TABLE 6.9 *Multivariate analysis of the effect of advertising on affection for leader (regression coefficient with standard error)*

	2004a	2004b	2009a	2009b	2014a	2014b
PDIP Leader	.235*** (.051)	.214*** (.035)	.689* (.286)	.503*** (.104)	.534** (.167)	1.256*** (.133)
Demokrat Leader	.240 (.177)	.123*** (.025)	.631*** (.107)	.258*** (.062)	.376 (.234)	
Golkar Leader	.247*** (.066)	.135** (.043)	.627*** (.183)	.362** (.106)	.649*** (.127)	
PAN Leader	.580*** (.110)	.117** (.044)	2.732*** (.570)		.157 (.472)	
PPP Leader	.564*** (.162)	.081 (.052)	−.005 (.673)		.587 (.943)	
PKB Leader	.468** (.153)		.114 (.654)		.375 (.667)	
PKS Leader	.178 (.121)		.012 (.207)		−.745 (1.127)	
Gerindra Leader			.588*** (.139)		.634*** (.130)	.963*** (.140)
Hanura Leader			−.772 (.756)		.437*** (.126)	
NasDem Leader					−.011 (.270)	

Control variables: evaluations of national economy, social identity, education, Muslim religiosity, urban-rural, region, age, and gender.

was for Jokowi, followed by Prabowo. Both were presidential candidates that year.

Does the greater strength of the connection between exposure to the party or candidate campaign of Partai Demokrat and Yudhoyono, on the one hand, and affection shown toward Yudhoyono as a leader, on the other, demonstrate that the intensity of exposure to Demokrat advertisements is higher compared to advertisements of other parties, PDIP for example? The facts only sometimes support this interpretation. In the 2004 legislative election, more voters were exposed to PDIP ads than to

Demokrat ads.[19] Most of these ads featured the party leader, Megawati or Yudhoyono. In 2009, Demokrat and Yudhoyono ads were indeed most numerous, while in 2014 there were more ads from Golkar, Gerindra, and Hanura, not from PDIP, which won that election.

It is nonetheless clear that there is a significant relationship between party advertisements and affection for the leader of that party (Table 6.9). That effect was most consistent for PDIP, Golkar, and Gerindra, and inconsistent for other parties. In 2014, not all parties enjoyed a significant association between their mass media ads and affection for a particular leader. Where there was consistency, it was tied to the intensity of the advertising. Gerindra is a party that advertises a great deal; its leader became a vice presidential candidate in 2009 and a presidential candidate in 2014. PDIP always has had a presidential candidate, but Demokrat has not. In 2014 Demokrat made no presidential nomination, while Golkar and Hanura, even though their leaders did not become presidential candidates, aired the most ads because their leaders were owners of TV stations.[20]

CONCLUSIONS

Indonesian national politics, in its first two democratic decades, has been marked by substantial changes in the behavior of its voters, as we saw in Chapter 3. Turnout in parliamentary and presidential elections declined sharply, from 93 percent in the 1999 parliamentary election to 75 percent in the 2014 parliamentary election, and from 80 percent in the first round of the 2004 presidential election to 71 percent in 2014. The pattern of political choice has also been transformed. Four parliamentary elections have produced four different parties receiving a plurality of the vote. In the presidential elections, candidates who have been supported by the largest party or by a coalition of parties with the most votes have not themselves always received the most votes.

---

[19] In the 2004 legislative election, 57 percent, 13.4 percent, 31 percent, 2.9 percent, 2 percent 1.5 percent, and 1 percent of the voters reported to have been exposed to PDIP, Golkar, PAN, Demokrat, PKS, PKB, and PPP ads respectively. The frequency of following party or presidential candidate advertisements in other media (newspapers, radio, and internet) was too small to be analyzed by party.

[20] In 2014, the largest percent of voters said they had seen Hanura ads on TV even though that party got only 6 percent of the vote. The number of Hanura ads cannot be separated from Hary Tanoesoedibjo, one of the top party leaders and also owner of RCTI, the most popular TV station.

What accounts for these phenomena, which have made politics and in particular the party system unstable and less representative, and which have in turn reduced the effectiveness and efficiency of government because of the power of diverse interests to pull it in conflicting directions? The principal cause of the fall in turnout and the changes in party strength is the very weak or continuing decline in party identity, a factor with an enormous effect on voting behavior. Because the connection between the two is so strong, when party identity weakens, so does turnout, and political choice becomes unstable.

The actions of political leaders have been both the main cause of these negative changes and the greatest hope for positive reform, though we should not exaggerate the prospects for the latter. Many party leaders have not been able to attract the support of the masses of voters, causing a weakening of the psychological bond between voters and parties. In this situation, nonparty figures with great appeal to voters have emerged and rapidly built new parties and patterns of party identification. The rapidity of these changes of course raises a question as to how long these new patterns are likely to continue.

The low appeal of the first generation of party leaders – Megawati for PDIP; Habibie, Akbar Tandjung, Jusuf Kalla, and Aburizal Bakrie for Golkar; Amien Rais, Sutrisno Bachir, and Hatta Rajasa for PAN; Hamzah Haz and Suryadarma Ali for PPP; and Abdurrahman Wahid and Muhaimin Iskandar for PKB – reduced the attractiveness of their parties for the voters. Their lack of appeal was due in part to their subpar governmental performance, in the eyes of the voters, which also led to reduced votes for many parties. Prime instances are Habibie and Golkar, defeated by PDIP in the 1999 election, and also Megawati and PDIP, defeated by Yudhoyono and Partai Demokrat in 2004 and 2009, and Demokrat defeated by PDIP in 2014.

The poor performance of the early party leaders created an opportunity for the emergence of a new figure who had not been a leader of one of the existing parties or of a prominent nongovernmental organization: Susilo Bambang Yudhoyono. In a short time, as a relatively skillful political communicator, Yudhoyono built a new party, Demokrat, and won a substantial percentage of votes, 7 percent, in the 2004 parliamentary election. Yudhoyono was considered by voters to be more personally qualified at the time: more likeable, more competent, more empathetic toward the common people, more honest, with higher integrity, and friendlier. These personal qualities were recognized and appreciated by growing numbers of citizens as Yudhoyono himself reached out to the voters via the mass media prior to the 2004 parliamentary election.

The relatively high regard in which Yudhoyono was held personally made him the first president to be directly elected in the history of Indonesia. He defeated candidates supported by larger parties (Megawati and Wiranto) and one who was believed to have the support of a top mass organization, Muhammadiyah (Amien Rais). Since 2004, the public has understood that parties are not that important in direct presidential elections beyond their legal mandate to nominate candidates.

After five years in power, President Yudhoyono underwent a new test: how well his popularity had withstood the challenges of incumbency. Megawati had faced the same test in 2004. In contrast to Megawati, however, and also to then-President Habibie in the 1999 election, Yudhoyono and Partai Demokrat were still highly regarded by the voters in 2009, much more highly regarded than any of the alternative candidates.

The effect was not only that Yudhoyono was reelected but that his party massively increased its vote, from 7 percent to 21 percent. Yudhoyono's campaign effort was an important element as well, but underneath it was the voters' appreciation for what the government had done during the previous five years. Government programs in response to the rise in international fuel prices and the 2007–8 global financial crisis were positively evaluated. Other crucial issues, like maintaining public security and combating corruption, had also been handled satisfactorily by the Yudhoyono government in the minds of many voters. Not least important, there were no other candidates who were judged potentially superior by voters. Many critical public intellectuals had charged that Yudhoyono's performance was worse than promised, which may have been true, but voters failed to find a candidate who in their eyes was more likely to perform better.

Leadership and personal qualities also dominated the 2014 elections. The new president, Joko Widodo or Jokowi, was not a party chair or even a top leader of a party. He was only a party cadre who ran successfully for office as mayor of a small city and was then elected governor of one of the most important provinces and capital city, Jakarta. Like Yudhoyono, he became nationally known relatively rapidly. In the short space of two years he became the most-liked national figure, heavily constraining PDIP to nominate him, not Megawati, the party's chair, for the presidency. Jokowi not only won the presidential election that year, he also boosted the vote for PDIP in the legislative election.

The victory of PDIP in 1999, the victory of Yudhoyono and the Demokrat party in 2004 and 2009, plus the success of Jokowi and PDIP in 2014 holds up a mirror to an electorate and a polity undergoing rapid change. PDIP was the primary opposition party against Golkar, which had been the political machine of Suharto's authoritarian New Order until it collapsed in 1998; Demokrat and Yudhoyono were the opposition or main alternative in 2004. Between 2004 and 2009, Yudhoyono's government did well in the eyes of the public.

By 2014, however, the Demokrat brand had become badly tarnished by corruption and the arrest and conviction of several leaders. In the 2014 legislative election, the Demokrat vote plummeted because of the party's record of corruption. PDIP, the main opposition party, became once again the largest party. In addition, Yudhoyono, by far the most important Demokrat leader, was not eligible to run for reelection and his party chose to nominate no other candidate.

These events show us an open, rational, and critical electorate. Voters are increasingly afloat, not tied to parties or social identities. They change their attitudes and their political choices when they negatively evaluate the performance of the party in power, and when they are unsatisfied with the leader who is at the head of government. What determines their subsequent choice is their evaluation of the current government and their view of other leaders whom they know and believe or at least hope may be able to perform better. If there are no better leaders, they tend to choose the lesser evil or abstain from voting. Even a carpenter, whose background is no different from most ordinary Indonesians, can become president and enlarge the party that supports him. This can only happen in a world where the voters are rational, open, and critical, which is what Indonesia is becoming.

7

Conclusion

Critical Democrats as Rational Voters

Indonesia is one of the world's newest democracies, its people having overthrown the three-decades-long, Suharto-led New Order dictatorship in 1998. Since that time, four democratic elections have been held at the national level, in 1999 (for Parliament), 2004, 2009, and 2014 (for Parliament and president). These elections, examined through public opinion surveys, have provided the basis for our evaluation of the current state and future prospects of the Indonesian democratic project.

CRITICAL DEMOCRATS

Indonesian voters, as reported in our surveys, consider the 1999 and subsequent elections to have been conducted freely and fairly. Moreover, they have a strong commitment to democracy as the best system for their country even though they recognize that it is not perfect. This strong positive commitment is closely connected in turn to perceptions of how democracy is implemented. The higher the perception of democratic performance, the stronger the citizen's commitment to democracy; conversely, if democratic performance is perceived to be low, the commitment declines.

While most citizens feel satisfied with how democracy is being implemented, the better-educated tend to be negative in their evaluations of democratic performance. They have a commitment to democratic values, and that commitment is accompanied by demands for better implementation of democracy. They are critical democrats, "critical citizens" or "dissatisfied democrats" in the terminology of Pippa Norris (1999,

2011). Quoting Norris: "This group aspires to democracy as their ideal form of government, yet at the same time they remain deeply sceptical when evaluating how democracy works in their own country" (2011, 5). Because Indonesians are becoming more educated, we predict that citizens' commitment to democracy will become greater, but so will their dissatisfaction.

POLITICAL PARTICIPATION

What explains the critical democrat phenomenon in the Indonesian case? In Chapter 1, we identified political participation and political choice as the main foci of our research attention, comparable to voting behavior studies in other democracies. Concerning participation, we found and have described a sharp decline in the level of turnout in legislative and presidential elections since Indonesia returned to democracy. In theoretical terms, this decline reflects a growing collective action problem. It constitutes evidence of a growing number of free-riders who benefit from democratic institutions without contributing to their maintenance by voting during elections.

Rational voters are voters who calculate cost and benefit for themselves alone. An action is regarded as a benefit by the voter if he or she can obtain that benefit to the maximum extent possible by paying the smallest cost. If one can enjoy the benefit of having a government and public policies without having to pay a cost in the form of registering to vote and going to the polling station on election day, why should he or she take those actions? The official and the policy are after all public, that is, can be enjoyed by everyone. For that reason, the rational voter tends not to participate in elections.

Empirically, the Indonesian voter is indeed becoming more rational. This is indicated by the decline in the number of citizens who feel that voting in an election is a civic duty. Though it remains true that a majority of Indonesians vote, the trend is negative, and strongest among the younger voters who live in cities, have a higher level of education and are more exposed to the mass media. These demographic factors impact negatively on political participation. Unless other factors intervene, the increase in urbanization and higher levels of education among young Indonesians will quicken the pace of decline in participation.

These other factors might include a law requiring all citizens to vote or psychological factors such as a restrengthened party identity, comparable to the early years of the democratic transition, or the emergence of new political leaders who inspire hope and optimism. If these factors are not present the probability is that the polling booths will become increasingly empty. The power of the Indonesian elite will rest more on a hollowed-out shell of popular sovereignty that is seen by voters as less and less legitimate.

POLITICAL CHOICE

The tendency for Indonesian voters to become increasingly rational in choosing their governments is even more visible when we examine who rules, or who gets a mandate to rule from the people, among Indonesian elites. When choosing a party or candidate, people engage in a cost-benefit calculation and do not choose for primordial reasons as has been frequently argued by participants and scholars. Religion, ethnic group, and social class are not the most important factors for the people in deciding to which elite to give a mandate to lead them.

Religion: Muslim voters for the most part do not choose Muslim parties or presidential candidates whom they consider more pious or santri Muslims. Even though a large majority of voters (88 percent) are Muslims, the total vote obtained by Muslim parties has never reflected the strength of this majority. The strong tendency indeed is for fewer and fewer Muslims to vote for ostensibly Muslim parties. The combined strength of those parties reached its peak at 44 percent in the 1955 democratic election. In 2014, the total popular strength of Muslim parties (PKS, PPP, PKB, and PAN) with seats in Parliament was only about 30 percent, and that figure includes the non-Islamist PKB and PAN, built on Nahdlatul Ulama and Muhammadiyah respectively. Without PKB and PAN, political Islam in Parliament is represented only by the Muslim Brotherhood-inspired PKS and the traditional patronage based PPP, with 13 percent of the voters.

A number of studies claim that many Indonesian Muslims, especially among the ethnic Javanese, are only nominal, "identity-card" Muslims or *abangan* whose culture is more animist and Hindu than Islamic. This was asserted to be the cause of the relatively small support for Islamic parties. "Identity-card" Muslims are born as Muslims and claim to be Muslims but never or rarely carry out the obligations of their religion such as praying five times a day and fasting during the month of Ramadhan. If we use these latter indicators, which are employed in surveys everywhere in the world, Indonesian Muslims are in general not identity-card or *abangan* Muslims. They are mostly *santri*, pious Muslims who carry out their obligations. More recent anthropological studies have also found that Indonesian Muslims are not nominal Muslims.

For those who have studied the social development of Indonesian religion over an extended period, changes are certainly visible. Examples include women's dress, religious programs in the media, especially TV which reaches a huge audience, the presence of mosques or prayer rooms in government and private offices, and so on. In short, there are many signs that Indonesian Muslims today are pious, not nominal. Most carry out the basic rituals of their religion, as do pious practitioners of religion everywhere.

At the same time, the strength of political Islam as measured by support for Islamic parties or presidential candidates is numerically far below the size of the *santri* population. Both *santri* and non*santri* voters choose religious and nonreligious parties and presidential candidates (to the extent to which they can evaluate the religious views of presidential candidates, not always an easy matter in Indonesia!), in about the same proportions. Religion has not been an important consideration for most voters in determining choice of party or presidential candidate since democratization. Indeed, there are signs of political secularization: Indonesian Muslims are religious in their social behavior but not in their electoral behavior. The number of pious Muslims is expanding but support for Muslim parties is shrinking.

Why has this political secularization occurred? On the demand side, secularization should not be taking place because most Indonesian voters are Muslim and religious. Because they are religious, if there are parties or presidential candidates that are more religious they should tend to vote for those parties. But that is not the reality. They are indeed religious but do not choose parties or presidential candidates who are religious or are thought to be the most religious. In general, they do not choose Islamist parties like PKS or PPP; they also do not choose presidential candidates who are perhaps regarded as more Islamist or just more santri like Amien Rais, Hamzah Haz, or Jusuf Kalla. Instead they choose secular parties like PDIP, Golkar, Partai Demokrat, and Gerindra, the top four parties in 2014. They choose presidential candidates who they may consider less santri, like President Yudhoyono, Megawati, or Joko Widodo.

If seen from the supply side, electoral secularization is easier to understand. What do the parties offer the voters? All parties, including Islamist parties, offer similar programs without an exclusively Islamic context. There is no single Islamic issue or program that is monopolized by a single party or candidate. Islamist parties have not offered programs successfully claimed to be exclusively Islamic compared to non-Islamic programs offered by non-Islamist parties.

All parties make promises to improve popular welfare, provide clean government, strengthen the rule of law, fight corruption, and so on. Islamist parties have not been able to persuade voters that their programs connected to these issues are Islamic and differ in substance with what is offered by other parties. There is no local understanding of a concept of, say, Islamic prosperity, that differs with non-Islamic prosperity that Islamist parties have been able to sell to the voters. If "Islamic prosperity" only means prosperity that is created in service to God, the same can be claimed by politicians from non-Islamist parties. The meaning of "Islamic" in political or public discourse thus becomes blurred.

Secularization at the mass-voter level has also occurred because party leaders and political elites in the post-New Order period do not fore-ground religious or symbolic differences between Islamist and nationalist or secular politics. The debate about the foundation of the state, whether based on Islam or Pancasila, the religiously pluralist state doctrine first introduced by Sukarno in 1945, no longer colors national politics as in the 1950s when Muslim parties captured their highest share of the vote in the history of the republic.

Though today a number of parties incorporate Islam as their basic doctrine, this is often translated in their programs in ways that make it more inclusive, so the Islamic dimension no longer colors political discussion at the mass level. Even though PPP and PKS are known to be Islamist parties, for example, in practice they have chosen for vote-getting purposes not to restrict their identity to religion. As a result, they differ little from secular parties like PDIP, Golkar, or Partai Demokrat.

Nonetheless, the symbolic or ideological vagueness of Islamist parties probably helps them attract voters as long as the nonreligious programs of the secular parties are not vaguer. According to an experimental survey conducted by a team of scholars including two of the present authors, the Islamic factor remains important in determining partisan choice at the mass voter level if the nonreligious factors, especially the economic program that is offered by the party or presidential candidate, are also vague (Pepinsky, Liddle, and Mujani 2012). The failures of Islamist parties and candidates indicate that economic programs offered by other parties and candidates are more appealing.

Moreover, elite political behavior has tended to be rational. While it is true that nearly all Indonesian voters are Muslim, most non-Muslim elites prefer to join secular parties, especially PDIP, rather than a Christian party. This arguably promotes political secularization and reduces Islamist political sentiment. If Indonesian religious demography were different, say 40 percent Christian and 50 percent Muslim, then politics tinged with religion would probably become stronger, as famously argued by Horowitz (2000). In addition, because of the small size of the non-Muslim population, non-Muslim political elites tend to avoid participation in national politics, which further helps minimize religious influence. The relative unimportance of religion in national electoral politics must be understood in that demographic context.

This is not to say that religion does not continue to be a political issue, even at the national level, or that Islamists do not often press their case. Most recently, in late 2016, Islamist groups accused the incumbent governor of Jakarta, a Protestant and Sino-Indonesian, of blasphemy against Islam and were able to draw hundreds of thousands into the streets to protest. In April 2017, that governor was defeated in his bid for reelection in a runoff against a candidate who was supported by Islamists, including radical groups that until now had been on the margins of national politics.

Postelection, several respected survey organizations reported that religious identity and religious political orientations significantly explain the outcome (*Tempo* April 24, 2017; Mujani 2017). This confirms our book's main finding about religion that until now religion has not been important because the contestants in presidential elections have been adherents to the same religion (Islam). Religion is not important when it is understood as a variant of Muslim religiosity, that is santri (pious) versus abangan (nominal). The case of the election of the Jakarta governor, where the candidates were not all Muslim, differs from the national pattern.

In Chapter 1, we stated that "Throughout the democratic period there have been many instances of violations of religious freedom, committed by the state and by citizens, both individually and as organized groups." To us, as to many Indonesians and outsiders, these violations constitute one of the greatest threats to the quality of democratic life. In this book, we have shown scientifically that in eight national parliamentary and presidential elections over fifteen years the vast majority of Indonesian citizens have been open, rational, and critical in their voting behavior, not motivated by religious or other primordial sentiments. Pious Muslims, specifically, have been less inclined over this period to vote for either candidates or parties perceived as more Islamic. We hope this is a sufficient contribution to the Indonesian debate and also to the broader debate about the role of religion in political life in other Muslim-majority countries.

Ethnicity: The pattern of religious demographic reality is also reflected in ethnic and regional diversity. Ethnic affinity is not important, or not as important as believed until now, in post New Order national electoral politics. The source of this unimportance is on the one hand the ethnic diversity of Indonesian voters and on the other the presence of an ethnic group that is proportionally much larger than the others, even though not a majority, which is the Javanese at about 40 percent.

After the Javanese are the Sundanese, about 16 percent, followed by hundreds of groups, none of which has more than 4 percent of the total population. In this situation, it is difficult for a party or presidential candidate to claim to represent ethnic groups other than the Javanese because in actuality a party leader or presidential candidate comes from a specific, necessarily small, ethnic group that cannot be aggregated into a larger group.

PPP's Hamzah Haz, for example, cannot claim to represent "outer island" ethnic groups, because his tiny ethnic Banjar group from South Kalimantan is not part of any larger group identified primordially. Golkar's Jusuf Kalla, a presidential candidate in 2009 and currently serving as vice president under President Joko Widodo, cannot represent outer island ethnic groups because he is tied to a specific group in South Sulawesi, the Bugis, whose size is also less than 3 percent and cannot be assimilated to any larger group. In short, there is no ethnic or primordial reason why a member of one ethnic group other than the Javanese or the Bugis, for example, should feel more represented by Jusuf Kalla than by Megawati, Yudhoyono, or Jokowi, all Javanese.

This large imbalance between the Javanese and the rest and the broader pattern of great ethnic diversity makes ethnicity insignificant in determining mass political behavior at the national level. This is also why most presidential candidates are Javanese, and compete against other Javanese, so that ethnicity becomes unimportant, or at any rate less important than has been previously claimed.

In short, national elite politics is supraethnic. There is no party or presidential candidate that openly identifies with a particular ethnic group because that identification would be of no benefit. All parties and politicians advance a vision of Indonesia as a unitary state that trumps any ethnic or regional affiliations. This elite behavior, rooted in the country's revolutionary origins and fertilized continuously since independence, reduces the influence of ethnic sentiments in voting behavior at the national level.

Social Class: Class, a sociological factor that has long been considered important in shaping Indonesian voting behavior, disappears in our analysis. One source of this invisibility is probably our definition of social class, which is confined to socioeconomic status indicators, that is level of education and income and type of employment. But subjective self-identification with a certain social class has also not been influential in shaping voting behavior. Another measure, common in the Western European and Latin American literature, is the tendency to position oneself ideologically on the left or right. We have not incorporated this distinction in our surveys because in our judgment left and right designations are too complex and/or culturally foreign to be understood by most voters in Indonesia.

The lack of importance of social class in shaping post-New Order voting behavior is probably due as well to the absence of mobilization of classes by political parties. This may be due in turn to the fact that mobilizing on the basis of social class was banned throughout the New Order after the destruction of the communist party in the late 1960s. Labor, farmer, and other workers' organizations were tightly controlled by the government for three decades.

In the current democratic period, all parties claim to represent the interests of the lower class or "little people" (*wong cilik*). This group of voters cannot, however, be monopolized by any party, including the PDIP, which has always claimed most vociferously to be the party of the little people. As a result, members of this class are spread proportionally among all parties. Because the lower class is by far the largest in Indonesia, the party that gets the most votes in an election also gets the highest proportion of votes from members of this class. We see this effect for PDIP in 1999, Golkar in 2004, Partai Demokrat in 2009, and again PDIP in 2014. Each of these parties obtained the most votes in one of the three elections, and each simultaneously got the most votes from lower-class voters.

If sociological factors, that is religion, ethnicity, and social class are not important or are less important than often claimed in shaping Indonesian voting behavior, what factors are more important?

Political Economy: We have argued throughout this book that political economy is a key factor. In our definition, political economy is the performance of the government as perceived by voters in their household and national economic life. These voters evaluate the performance of national leaders and the success or failure of the government in overcoming problems facing the nation. Positive evaluation of the national economic condition has a significant influence on evaluation of the party or president currently in power; conversely, negative evaluation has a significant positive influence on support for the party or candidate most clearly positioned as the opposition.

The influence of political economy is not significant for parties or presidential candidates who are perceived ambiguously as to whether they are actually in power or a part of the opposition. Positive national economy evaluations in 1999 had a positive influence on support for Golkar, which was then in power, and conversely a negative influence on PDIP, at the time the clearest opposition party. More voters at that time evaluated the national economic condition negatively under Habibie, and for that reason Golkar was defeated in the election by PDIP.

In 2004, positive economic evaluations had a positive and significant influence on PDIP and presidential candidate Megawati, the incumbent president. But they had a negative influence on Partai Demokrat and presidential candidate Yudhoyono who was most clearly positioned as the opposition candidate. The position of other parties was ambiguous, because almost all of them were in Megawati's government. More voters offered a negative evaluation of the economy at that time, so PDIP and Megawati were defeated. Partai Demokrat had just been founded and Yudhoyono had recently left Megawati's cabinet, a step that angered Megawati, who saw Yudhoyono as her main challenger.

In 2009, the voters who evaluated the economy positively tended to choose the party and candidate in power, Demokrat and Yudhoyono, and not to choose the party and candidate who were most clearly in the opposition, PDIP and Megawati. In that election, most voters evaluated the economy positively and tended to choose the party and presidential candidate already in power. The political economy model did not, however, help to explain the variations in choice of the many parties and candidates who were between the poles of those in power and in opposition. In 1999, there was a total of forty-six parties contesting the election. In 2004 it was twenty-two, in 2009 thirty-six, and in 2014 twelve parties.

In 2014, Partai Demokrat was the main governing party, and President Yudhoyono was the de facto leader of that party. The Indonesian constitution limited him to two terms, so he was not a candidate for reelection. About two years before the 2014 election, corruption scandals, widely reported in the media, engulfed the party leadership. PDIP, Gerindra, and Hanura were the out-of-power parties, not a part of Yudhoyono's coalition. They were all in the opposition, but PDIP was the party whose position against the government was most clear.

Voters in 2014 struck a blow against Partai Demokrat because of its recent reputation for corruption, reducing its vote percentage by half. At the same time PDIP, Gerindra, and Hanura enjoyed a new swell of support. Voters punished Demokrat for its corruption and shifted their votes to the opposition parties, especially PDIP. In this context, when Yudhoyono was no longer a candidate for president and Partai Demokrat failed to nominate any other candidate of its own, the presidential candidates were all from the opposition: Jokowi from PDIP and Prabowo from Gerindra. The political economy argument, so relevant in previous elections, was not applicable in 2014.

Our alternative explanation highlighted the leadership qualities of the presidential candidates, not differences in their platforms or economic programs, because the two had similar programs, difficult for voters to distinguish. We operationalized the quality of leadership as level of preference for the relevant leader, voters' evaluations of the leader's integrity (not corrupt and can be believed), level of empathy (concern for others), and competence (intelligent and capable of resolving problems faced by the nation).

The combined score for all of these items had a significant influence both on choice of party and of leader, and also on choice of a presidential candidate, regardless of the sociological background, political economy evaluation, and even level of self-identification of the voter with his or her party. Because of the strength of the relationship between the perception of the quality of leadership and political choice, we are persuaded that a change in party leadership or a change in the configuration of the national political leadership is the main cause of large shifts in the partisan map from one election to the next.

Prior to the 1999 election, Megawati was the best-known national political figure with the strongest and longest track record. Without Megawati, who had been sidelined by the New Order regime, the then-PDI received only about 3 percent of the 1997 vote. When the New Order fell, and she emerged as the PDIP leader, Megawati's party was able to win the largest vote (34 percent) in the 1999 election. Other reformers, particularly Abdurrahman Wahid of PKB and Amien Rais of PAN, had a much weaker track record in opposing Suharto, the New Order, and Golkar.

By the time of the 2004 elections, the era of Amien Rais and Abdurrahman Wahid, such as it had been, was over. Megawati's position was similar. Her performance and that of her government, in office from 2001 to 2004, failed to fulfill the very high hopes of the citizenry at the time, causing her support and that of her party to fade.

With declining support for the main protagonists of reform, others emerged, including retired Army Generals Wiranto and Yudhoyono, two figures associated with the New Order. When Suharto announced his resignation as president, in a ceremony that was televised to the nation and the world, Wiranto was at his side, promising that the armed forces would protect the personal security of the former New Order ruler. Wiranto further affirmed his connections with New Order politics when he was nominated as Golkar's candidate in 2004, since Golkar was the New Order's main political vehicle for most of its three decades in power. Wiranto was not, however, able to boost popular support for Golkar. Though it received the most votes of any party in the 2004 election, its percentage was still less than its modest showing in 1999.

Though a product of the New Order, Yudhoyono took a different approach. Initially known only to a small circle of members of the political elite and observers, he was one of a few army officers committed to civilian supremacy in the last years of Suharto's rule. After democratization, Yudhoyono joined the cabinet of President Abdurrahman Wahid, in power from 1999 to 2001. When Wahid proposed a presidential decree that would dissolve Parliament, reminiscent of a similar action in 1959 by President Sukarno (marking the overthrow of the country's first democracy), Yudhoyono disagreed and eventually left the cabinet. His action was widely praised by the public, and indeed may have marked a transition point in Indonesia's democratic consolidation.

When Wahid was replaced by Megawati, Yudhoyono once again became a cabinet member. At the same time, he founded a new political party, Partai Demokrat, based on his own leadership. Megawati was angered and Yudhoyono withdrew from her cabinet at a time when her popularity was at its lowest. Extensive and mostly favorable media coverage helped boost his public recognition and support. By the time of the 2004 parliamentary election, his party was capable of amassing a large vote, larger than that for parties like PAN which had a longer track record and deeper roots in society. Yudhoyono himself soon overcame Megawati and several other candidates in the first direct presidential election in Indonesian history.

The first Yudhoyono administration was evaluated positively by the voters, as was his own leadership. As the incumbent president, he developed a network, including Partai Demokrat, to explain and promote his ideas and policies. No alternative leaders emerged other than the old players, Jusuf Kalla and Megawati, both of whom once again ran for president. In the eyes of the voters, Jusuf Kalla was and remained throughout the campaign in the shadow of Yudhoyono. He was unable to attract voters either to Golkar or to himself. Support for Golkar declined sharply and for Kalla even more sharply.

Megawati did better. But voters by this time knew her well, both her personal strengths and weaknesses and those of her performance as president. Her opportunity to build her party and impress the voters with her executive ability had come during her service as president, from 2001 to 2004. She did not succeed in the first direct presidential election, and by 2009 her reputation was poorer and her political resources were still fewer.

Finally, changes in national leadership shape changes in political attitudes at the mass level, toward both the existing party leaders and the parties. Party identity which can in comparative theory become the psychological foundation for stable voting behavior turns out in the Indonesian case to be weak at best. The strength of leadership appeal, on the one hand, and the weakness of party identity, on the other, has resulted in an unstable electoral pattern that in turn makes the party system increasingly fragmented and volatile, party strengths rising and falling with the popularity of particular leaders.

National politics has become increasingly complex and the formulation and implementation of government policy increasingly difficult because of the many elite interests which must be negotiated and accommodated. Not all increases in the amount of elite negotiation at the elite level improve the quality of the decision process. Much time is wasted in the process of producing final decisions. For their part, the mass of voters has become increasingly dissatisfied and cynical about politics, especially the more educated voters who are more exposed to the media and whom we have identified as critical democrats. Fortunately, to this point, these more educated citizens remain loyal to democracy even though they are disappointed in the way it is implemented day to day. How long will their disappointment continue and what will its consequences be?

OVERCOMING INDONESIA'S "DEMOCRATIC DEFICIT"

For Norris (1999, 2011), the growing numbers of critical citizens in many countries contribute to a problematic "democratic deficit," "constituting an important cause of civic disengagement, encouraging an erosion of conventional participation among citizens. At worst, fragile regimes lacking a broad and deep foundation of legitimacy among the mass public are widely believed to face serious risk of instability and even breakdown" (2011, 20).

How serious is the problem in Indonesia and what can be done to combat it? First, it is necessary to emphasize that Indonesia is a new democracy and that our analysis is based on four elections over a fifteen-year period, long enough to establish trends but short enough to keep us cautious about extrapolating too far.

Those trends, however, as we have documented throughout this book, are worrisome. On the participation side, there has been a secular decline in turnout, strongest among the younger voters who live in cities, have a higher level of education and are more exposed to the mass media. On the choice side, party identity has declined precipitously and the party system is increasingly fragmented and unstable, its current condition and probable future prospects hostage to the rise and fall of particular leaders. Government policymaking has suffered as a result.

At the same time, there are at least two rays of hope present or implicit in our findings, one in the growth of civil society and the other in emerging national leadership. Politically active independent civil society organizations have a long history in Indonesia, dating back at least to the 1912 founding of Muhammadiyah, the chief organization of Muslim modernists, and the 1926 founding of Nahdlatul Ulama, the dominant organization among Muslim traditionalists. Their positive consequences for the establishment and maintenance of democracy have been chronicled in this book and in earlier works (Mujani and Liddle 2004; Mujani 2007).

Perhaps more importantly, as an augur of the future, is the emergence and growth of a wide range of civil society groups, beginning in the mobilization to overthrow Suharto at the end of the New Order (Aspinall 2005). While these groups are active in many fields of public policy, they are particularly visible in the struggle against corruption, promoting and defending the activities of the national Corruption Eradication Commission (KPK, Komisi Pemberantasan Korupsi).

Established during Megawati's presidency, the KPK has been received with ambivalence or outright hostility from the national police and other government agencies, and many Members of Parliament. Its present prominence as a corruption-fighter is due directly to the strong support it has received from mobilized civil society groups (Liddle 2013). At the same time, it is clear that these activities have largely been restricted to the national level, and that Indonesia's economy remains too undeveloped to provide the resources necessary to create a truly vibrant civil society sector in the near future.

Finally, presidential political leadership may be paradoxically a prime cause of major challenges to democratic and governmental performance, as we have seen, and at the same time one of the best potential sources of positive change within that system. It is worth recalling that, as recently as 2003, Susilo Bambang Yudhoyono was a new figure on the national political scene who inspired hope in tens of millions of voters.

Megawati Sukarnoputri played a similar role not only in the anti-New Order mobilization of the 1990s but in the first years of democratic reform. While many aspects of the performance of the two presidents are of course open to criticism, it is also true in our view that both contributed positively to the transition and consolidation of democracy. Not less importantly, they restored the commitment to economic growth that was the singular achievement of the Suharto presidency.

Though still too early to evaluate, the rise of Joko Widodo (Jokowi) as president in 2014 replacing Yudhoyono can be read optimistically in terms of the voters' choices and Indonesian democracy. The voters responded positively to the candidacy of a carpenter, demonstrating that they were not tied to parties and primordial factors like religion and were hopeful that a new government would lead to a better Indonesia. When they were offered a limited choice, between Jokowi, a common citizen with a positive record as mayor and governor, and Prabowo Subianto, a figure who reflected the most repressive characteristics of Suharto's authoritarian New Order, they chose Jokowi.

What accounts for Jokowi's meteoric rise and elevation to the presidency? Of course, his own political skills are crucial. But at least two characteristics of the Indonesian electorate, clearly visible in our data and analysis, are also playing an important and positive role (see also Mujani and Liddle 2013). The first is voters' high degree of attentiveness through the media, especially TV, to politics, and governmental performance nationwide. There may be few countries in the world, even with developed economies, in which voters are so attentive to the rise of new leaders. Second is the voters' strong preference and demand for capable governmental leadership and integrity. In short, Indonesian voters continue to display a high degree of rationality, openness, not to mention a critical cast of mind, as described in Chapters 5 and 6 of this book, which hopefully will stand them in good stead as they confront the challenges ahead.

APPENDIX

Data, Method, and Model

DATA AND METHOD

This book is based largely on data from several national surveys of voters conducted by the authors several days after parliamentary and presidential elections in 1999, 2004, 2009, and 2014. There was one survey in 1999 (after the parliamentary election, the sole election that year), three in 2004 (after the parliamentary and each round of the presidential election) two in 2009 and in 2014 (after the parliamentary and the single round presidential election).

In 2014, the surveys were conducted by Saiful Mujani Research and Consulting (SMRC), in 2004 and 2009 by LSI (Lembaga Survei Indonesia, Indonesian Survey Institute, lsi.or.id). In 1999, the survey team, consisting of scholars from the University of Indonesia, was led by R. William Liddle and Saiful Mujani, then both at Ohio State University. The 1999 survey was funded by the National Science Foundation (Grant #9975671) and the Mershon Center at Ohio State University. The 2004 surveys were made possible by a grant from the Japan International Cooperation Agency. The 2009 surveys were funded by the LSI foundation, while the 2014 surveys were the corporate social responsibility of SMRC.

In all our surveys the population and unit of analysis consist of Indonesian citizens with the right to vote, which according to law is all citizens aged 17 or older or who are married. The sample size for each of the surveys differs, depending on our experiences in the field and available financial resources. In the 1999 survey the total sample was 2,488 respondents, while in the subsequent surveys the size was 1,200. The samples from populations of more than 100 million voters were chosen through probability sampling, in which every member of the voting population had an equal chance to be selected as a respondent. We did not use the simple random sampling technique, which requires a list of the names and addresses of all 100 million plus voters, which does not exist in Indonesia. Moreover, sampling in this way would require us to interview respondents spread uniformly across the country, again at great expense. Indonesia is a large and still developing country, more than 3,000 miles from east to west, with access to many regions difficult or impossible.

To reduce the level of error and also the expense of conducting the surveys, we used a complex sampling procedure called multistage random sampling, where population clusters and stratification are used simultaneously in drawing the sample. The cluster technique helps us to disaggregate the population into smaller groups so that we can reduce the number of surveyors put in the field, but this technique has the disadvantage of increasing the margin of error. Conversely, the use of stratification limits the amount of error but is not an efficient use of human resources. With this combination we hope that the selected samples both reflect accurately the population and approach the level of error in simple random sampling.

In our complex sampling procedure, the population of voters is stratified in three ways. First, sample provinces are chosen proportionally from all provinces based on population data from the BPS (Badan Pusat Statistik, Central Statistical Body). Second, the population is divided proportionally between those who live in the rural areas (*desa* or village in the BPS enumerating scheme) and cities (*kelurahan* or urban ward), with a rural-urban ratio of 58:42 for 1999 and 56:44 for the subsequent surveys. Third, the population of voters is divided by gender, again following the BPS ratio of 50:50.

In each selected province we further selected randomly a number of villages and urban wards from the official government list and further selected eight respondents for the 1999 survey and ten respondents for the subsequent surveys. In 1999, the total number of villages and wards chosen was 250, while in all subsequent surveys it was 120.

After a village or ward was chosen, the next step was to list the RT (*rukun tetangga*, a grouping of neighbors, the lowest level of neighborhood organization, headed by a popularly elected member of the RT) or equivalent unit. From the RT list were chosen four RT in 1999 and five in subsequent surveys (if there were only five RT or fewer all were included). In every selected RT two households (KK, *kepala keluarga*) were chosen. In the selected KK, all of the members of the family who have the right to vote (age 17 or older or married) were listed. In each KK either all males or all females were chosen. If in a given KK males were chosen, then females would be chosen in the next KK. This technique was adopted to achieve the desired 50:50 gender proportion.

After the names of the members of the household were listed (from oldest to youngest), one individual was selected as the respondent. That person was asked if he or she was willing to be a respondent and to be directly interviewed. The trained interviewers were mostly male and female students at local universities. Interviewers were instructed to dress conservatively and to address interviewees respectfully.

For quality control, we followed a supervision procedure consisting of monitoring and spot checks to determine that the survey had been carried out properly. In the 1999 survey spot checks were conducted for 60 percent of the respondents. In subsequent surveys 20 percent were directly spot checked but an additional 50 percent were monitored via cell phone. These checks turned up no significant concerns.

MISSING VALUES

In public opinion surveys based on individual respondents it is common to find respondents who do not answer, state that they don't know or don't understand, and so on, with regard to specific questions. These responses cannot be processed and we regard them as missing values. In multivariate analysis, missing values create a problem because they reduce the total number of respondents whose answers can be analyzed. To determine whether the reduction in the sample size has a significant influence or not, we conducted an analysis with the existing sample and then compared it to a sample in which the missing values were replaced with the mean. For the arguments that we develop in this book, whether we use the existing sample or one in which the missing values have been replaced with the mean, there is no significant effect.

STATISTICAL MODELS

In this book several statistical models have been introduced depending on the theoretical need, from the simplest, descriptive statistics, to bivariate analysis and multivariate analysis in order to understand the relative effect of each independent variable on the dependent variable. In our multivariate analysis, we have used two regression models, regular linear regression and logistic regression. The first was used to analyze data where the dependent variable is continuous, like the political participation index and the party identity index. The second was used for analysis of data where the dependent variable is a categorical or nominal variable like ever having voted in an election, the choice of a party, and the choice of a president. The values of variables like these cannot be analyzed with regular regression models because they are not continuous.

In this book we rely heavily on a logistic regression model. This model is relatively new in the study of Indonesian politics and should perhaps be explained in greater detail. Because the choice of a party or candidate represents a nominal variable with many categories, we used Multinomial Logistic Regression based on Long (1997). After the logistical analysis was carried out, we then analyzed the effect of one independent variable relative to another independent variable on the dependent variables using difference in predicted probabilities. These calculations were based on the *Stata Post-Estimation Commands* program of Long and Freese (2005), while the organization of the output used the work of Ben Jann (2005, 2007).

Glossary

Abangan, syncretistic Javanese whose culture contains animistic and Hindu in addition to Islamic elements.

Aliran, stream or current in Indonesian partisan politics. Originally used to refer to a party system representing both cultural and socioeconomic class cleavages.

DPD, Dewan Perwakilan Daerah, Regional Representative Council, a legislative body representing the provinces but with limited powers.

DPR, Dewan Perwakilan Rakyat, People's Representative Council, Parliament.

Gerindra, Partai Gerakan Indonesia Raya, Greater Indonesia Movement Party, the electoral vehicle of retired Major General Prabowo Subianto, a prominent figure since the late-Suharto era. Founded in 2008.

Hanura, Partai Hati Nurani Rakyat, People's Conscience Party, the electoral vehicle of retired General Wiranto, Suharto's last armed forces commander. Founded in 2006.

HMI, Himpunan Mahasiswa Islam, Islamic University Students' Association, the leading organization of Muslim university students and an important network for aspiring politicians throughout the independence period.

ICMI, Ikatan Cendekiawan Muslim Indonesia, Indonesian Muslim Intellectuals' Association, an influential lobby for Muslim modernists at the end of the Suharto era.

Kaum Marhaen, people like Marhaen. A label for ordinary people, first used in a speech by the nationalist leader Sukarno to describe a farmer who was oppressed by Dutch colonial rule.

Kiai, Indonesian term for Muslim religious scholars and teachers (ulama in Arabic).

Kopassus (Komando Pasukan Khusus, Special Forces Command), an elite army unit once commanded by 2014 presidential candidate Prabowo Subianto.

KPK (Komisi Pemberantasan Korupsi, Corruption Eradication Commission), established by Parliament and president in 2002 during the Megawati presidency, the main corruption fighting body in democratic Indonesia.

Kostrad (Komando Cadangan Strategis Angkatan Darat, Army Strategic Reserve Command), the main basic combat unit of the Indonesian army, once commanded by Wiranto and Prabowo Subianto, democratic-era presidential candidates.

KPU, Komisi Pemilihan Umum, General Election Commission.

Mahkamah Konstitusi, Constitutional Court, one of the most important political institutions created as a part of the post–1998 democratization process.

MARA, Majelis Amanat Rakyat, People's Mandate Council, a predecessor to PAN founded by Amien Rais.

Masjumi, Majlis Syuro Muslimin Indonesia, Council of Indonesian Muslim Associations, a 1950s-era political party identified with modernist Islam and the social and educational organization Muhammadiyah.

MPR, Majelis Permusyawaratan Rakyat, People's Consultative Assembly, the super-Parliament mandated by the original 1945 Constitution, but reduced today to a joint session of Parliament and the Regional Representative Council.

Muhammadiyah, followers of Muhammad, a modernist Islamic organization created in 1912. Originally and still predominantly situated in urban areas, its leaders were inspired by Middle Eastern reformism that called for a return to the Qur'an and Hadith (sayings or traditions of the Prophet Muhammad). They developed social and educational programs that competed with, but also emulated, Christian missionary activities. On the one hand, Muhammadiyah has fiercely opposed superstitious beliefs and practices that in its view run counter to the rational interpretation of the Qur'an that it advocates. On the other hand, calling for a return to the Qur'an and Hadith has given room for the rise of a puritanical and literalist strand within the organization.

Nahdlatul Ulama or NU, Awakening of the Traditional Religious Leaders, Indonesia's largest traditionalist Muslim social and educational organization, created in 1926. Founded in response to developments in the Middle East that threatened established religious practices and religious authorities, such as the conquest of Mecca by the fundamentalist Wahhabis (founded by the eighteenth-century cleric, Muhammad ibn Abd al-Wahhab). Prior to its establishment, many traditional Islamic scholars sent a delegation to the Saudi family to protest the Wahhabis' plan to demolish the tomb of the Prophet Muhammad. They were also concerned about the impact of Wahhabism and Islamic reformism in Indonesia. Today, NU seeks to preserve the classical Islamic jurisprudential schools (madhab) and to protect traditional Islamic practices such as grave visitations (ziarah), celebration of the Prophet's birthday, and other local practices from the puritanical zeal of the reformists.

PAN, Partai Amanat Nasional, National Mandate Party, created by Muhammadiyah in 1999.

Parmusi, Partai Muslimin Indonesia, Indonesian Muslims Party, a New Order-era successor party to Masjumi, subsequently fused into PPP.

Partai Golkar, Functional Groups Party, the Suharto-era electoral vehicle turned into a democratic political party in 1999.

Partai NasDem, Partai Nasional Demokrat, National Democratic Party, the personal electoral vehicle of Surya Paloh in the 2014 presidential election.

PBB, Partai Bulan Bintang, Crescent Moon and Star Party, an Islamic party and self-described inheritor of the mantle of Masjumi, the principal modernist Muslim party of the 1950s.

PD, Partai Demokrat, Democratic Party, the electoral vehicle of Susilo Bambang Yudhoyono.

PDI, Partai Demokrasi Indonesia, Indonesian Democracy Party, a Suharto-era party created as a forced fusion of the secular nationalist and Christian parties of the 1950s.

PDIP, Partai Demokrasi Indonesia Perjuangan, Indonesian Democracy Party of Struggle, led by Megawati Sukarnoputri, daughter of founding father Sukarno. Formed by Megawati and other former Suharto-era PDI leaders in 1998.

PDS, Partai Damai Sejahtera, Prosperous Peace Party, a Protestant party in the current democratic period.

Perti, Pergerakan Tarbiyah Islamiyah, Islamic Educational Movement, a 1950s-era political party.

PKB, Partai Kebangkitan Bangsa, National Awakening Party, a contemporary political party created by Nahdlatul Ulama leaders.

PK, Partai Keadilan, Justice Party, an Islamic party created by Muslim Brotherhood inspired activists in 1999, formally dissolved after the 1999 elections (see also PKS).

PKI, Partai Komunis Indonesia, Indonesian Communist Party, a 1950s-era political party banned in 1965.

PKS, Partai Keadilan Sejahtera, Prosperous Justice Party, the continuation of PK.

PNI, Partai Nasional Indonesia, Indonesian National Party, a colonial era and 1950s political party representing secular nationalism and close to national founding father and first President Sukarno.

PRD, Partai Rakyat Demokratik, Democratic People's Party, a neo-Marxist party, employing many of the symbols and slogans of the banned Indonesian Communist Party, created to contest the 1999 parliamentary elections.

PRRI, Pemerintahan Revolusioner Rakyat Indonesia, Indonesian People's Revolutionary Government, a separatist movement in the 1950s in parts of Sumatra and Sulawesi.

PPP, Partai Persatuan Pembangunan, Development Unity Party, a political party created during the Suharto era as a forced fusion of all Islamic parties.

PSI, Partai Sosialis Indonesia, Indonesian Socialist Party, a democratic socialist party active in the 1950s.

PSII, Partai Sarekat Islam Indonesia, Islamic Association Party of Indonesia, a 1950s-era political party.

Priyayi, Javanese aristocrats.

Reformasi, reform, an Indonesian term for the democratic period after 1998.

Santri, a devout Muslim, contrasted with abangan.

Sembilan bahan-bahan pokok (sembako), nine basic commodities, promised to voters in campaigns.

Syariah (Arabic), Islamic law.

Tarbiyah (Arabic), education. An Islamist movement on Indonesian university campuses which began in the Suharto New Order period and provided the base for several political parties in the current democratic period.

Tim sukses, success team, a political candidate's campaign advisors.

References

Abramowitz, Alan J. and Kyle L. Saunders. (2006). Exploring the Basis of Partisanship in the American Electorate: Social Identity vs. Ideology. *Political Research Quarterly*, 59(2), 175–187.

Achen, Christopher H. (2002). Parental Socialization and Rational Party Identification. *Political Behavior*, 24(2), 151–170.

Allsop, Dee and Herbert F. Weisberg. (1988). Measuring Change in Party Identification in an Election Campaign. *American Journal of Political Science*, 32(4), 996–1017.

Almond, Gabriel A. and Sidney Verba. (1963). *The Civic Culture: Political Attitudes and Democracy in Five Nations*, Princeton, NJ: Princeton University Press.

Anderson, Benedict R. (1996). Elections and Participation in Three Southeast Asian Countries. In R. H. Taylor, ed., *The Politics of Elections in Southeast Asia*. New York, NY: Cambridge University Press.

Asian Barometer www.asianbarometer.org

Aspinall, Edward. (2005). *Opposing Suharto: Compromise, Resistance, and Regime Change in Indonesia*, Stanford, CA: Stanford University Press.

Aspinall, Edward and Marcus Mietzner, eds., (2010). *Problems of Democratisation in Indonesia: Elections, Institutions and Society*, Singapore: Institute of Southeast Asian Studies Press.

Azwar, Rully Chairul. (2008). *Politik Komunikasi Partai Golkar di Tiga Era: Dari Partai Hegemonik ke Partai Berorientasi "Pasar"*, Jakarta: The Indonesian Institute and Grasindo.

Badan Pusat Statistik (Central Statistical Body) https://bps.go.id

Badan Pusat Statistik. (2010). *Penduduk Indonesia Hasil Sensus Penduduk 2010*. Nomor Katalog: 2102001 (data processed)

Barnes, Samuel H., Peter McDonough, and Antonio Lopez Pina. (1985). The Development of Partisanship in New Democracies: The Case of Indonesia. *American Journal of Political Science*, 29(4), 695–720.

Barnes, Samuel H., M. Kent Jennings, Ronald Inglehart, and Barbara Farah. (1988). Party Identification and Party Closeness in Comparative Perspective. *Political Behavior*, 10(3), 215–231.

Baswedan, Anies. (2004). Political Islam in Indonesia: Present and Future Trajectory. *Asian Survey*, 54(4), 669–690.

Bean, Clive and Jonathan Kelley. (1988). Partisan Stability and Short-Term Change in the 1987 Federal Election: Evidence from the NSSS Panel Study. *Politics*, 23, 80–94.

Bean, Clive and Anthony Mughan. (1989). Leadership Effects in Parliamentary Elections in Australia and Britain. *American Political Science Review*, 83, 1165–1179.

Blais, Andre. (2000). *To Vote or Not To Vote: The Merits and Limits of Rational Choice Theory*, Pittsburgh, PA: University of Pittsburgh Press.

Boileau, Julien. (1983). *Functional Group Politics in Indonesia*, Jakarta: Centre of Strategic and International Studies Press.

Brady, Henry E. (1999). Political Participation. In John R. Robinson, Phillip R. Shaver, and Lawrence S. Wrightsman, eds., *Measures of Political Attitudes*, San Diego, CA: Academic Press.

Brady, Henry E., Kay L. Schlozman, and Sidney Verba. (1995). Beyond SES: A Resource Model of Political Participation. *American Political Science Review* 89, 271–294.

Bratton, Michael, Robert Mattes, and E. Gyimah-Boadi. (2004). *Public Opinion, Democracy, and Market Reform in Africa*, New York, NY: Cambridge University Press.

Brug, van der, Wouter, Cees van der Eijk, and Mark Franklin. (2007). *The Economy and the Vote: Economic Conditions and Elections in Fifteen Countries*, New York, NY: Cambridge University Press.

Burns, Nancy, Kay L. Schlozman, and Sidney Verba. (2001). *The Private Roots of Public Action: Gender, Equality, and Political Participation*, Cambridge, MA: Harvard University Press.

Butler, David and Donald Stokes. (1974). *Political Change in Britain: The Evolution of Electoral Choice*, London: Macmillan.

Campbell, Angus, Gerald Gurin, and Warren E. Miller. (1954). *The Voter Decides*, Evanston, IL: Row and Peterson.

Campbell, Angus, Philip E. Converse, Warren E. Miller, and Donald Stokes. (1960). *The American Voter*, New York, NY: John Wiley.

Carmines, Edward G., John P. McIver, and James A. Stimson. (1987). Unrealized Partisanship: A Theory of Dealignment. *Journal of Politics*, 49, 376–400.

Clarke, Harold D., Nitish Dutt, and Allan Kornberg. (1993). The Political Economy of Attitudes toward Polity and Society in Western European Democracies. *Journal of Politics*, 55, 998–1021.

Colton, Timothy J. (2000). *Transitional Citizens: Voters and What Influences Them in the New Russia*, Cambridge, MA: Harvard University Press.

Conway, M. Margaret. (2000). *Political Participation in the United States*, Washington, DC: Congressional Quarterly Press.

Cribb, Robert. (1990). *The Indonesian Killings of 1965: Studies from Java and Bali*, Clayton, Vic.: Monash University Centre of Southeast Asian Studies

Crouch, Harold. (1978). *The Army and Politics in Indonesia*, Ithaca, NY: Cornell University Press.

Damanik, Ali Said. (2002). *Fenomena Partai Keadilan*, Bandung: Mizan.

Deth van, Jan W. (1989). Interest in Politics. In M. Kent Jennings and Jan W. van Deth, eds., *Continuities in Political Action*, New York: Walter de Gruyter.

Diamond, Larry and Richard Gunther. (2001). *Political Parties and Democracy*, Baltimore, MD: Johns Hopkins University Press.

Downs, Anthony. (1957). *An Economic Theory of Democracy*, New York, NY: Harper and Row.

Durkheim, Emile. (2014). *The Division of Labor in Society*, Glencoe, IL: Free Press.

Emmerson, Donald. (1976). *Indonesia's Elite*, Ithaca, NY: Cornell University Press

Evans, Geoffrey. (1999). *The End of Class Politics? Class Voting in Comparative Context*, New York, NY: Oxford University Press.

Feith, Herbert. (1957). *The Indonesian Elections of 1955*, Ithaca, NY: Modern Indonesia Project, Southeast Asia Program, Cornell University.

Feith, Herbert. (1962). *The Decline of Constitutional Democracy in Indonesia*, Ithaca, NY: Cornell University Press.

Ferejohn, John A. and Morris P. Fiorina. (1975). Closeness Counts Only in Horseshoes and Dancing. *American Political Science Review*, 69, 920–925.

Ferejohn, John A. and Morris P. Fiorina. (1974). The Paradox of Not Voting: A Decision Theoretic Analysis. *American Political Science Review*, 68, 525–536.

Fiorina, Morris P. (1981). *Retrospective Voting in American National Elections*, New Haven, CT: Yale University Press.

Franklin, Charles H. (1992). Candidate Influence over the Voter's Decision Calculus. Paper presented at annual meeting of the Midwest Political Science Association, Chicago.

Franklin, Charles H. and John E. Jackson. (1983). The Dynamics of Party Identification. *American Political Science Review*, 77, 957–973.

Freedom House. (2016). https://freedomhouse.org/report/freedom-world/2016/indonesia

Gaffar, Afan. (1992). *Javanese Voters: A Case Study of Elections under a Hegemonic Party System*, Yogyakarta: Gadjah Mada University Press.

Geertz, Clifford. (1960). *The Religion of Java*, Glencoe, IL: Free Press.

Geertz, Clifford. (1965). *The Social History of an Indonesian Town*, Cambridge, MA: MIT Press.

Gerber, Alan S., Gregory A. Huber, and Ebony Washington. (2010). Party Affiliation, Partisanship, and Political Beliefs: A Field Experiment. *American Political Science Review*, 104, 720–744.

Graetz, Brian and Ian McAllister. (1987). Party Leaders and Election Outcomes in Britain, 1974–1983. *Comparative Political Studies*, 19, 484–507.

Green, Donald P. and Ian Shapiro. (1994). *Pathologies in Rational Choice Theory: A Critique in Application in Political Science*, New Haven, CT: Yale University Press.

Green, Donald P., Bradley Palmquist, and Eric Schickler. (2002). *Partisan Hearts and Minds: Political Parties and the Social Identities of Voters*, New Haven, CT: Yale University Press.

Hadiz, Vedi. (2010). *Localising Power in Post-Authoritarian Indonesia: A Southeast Asian Perspective*, Stanford, CA: Stanford University Press.

Hasan, Riaz. (2002). *Faithlines: Muslim Conceptions of Islam and Society*, Oxford: Oxford University Press.

Hill, Hal. (2012). The Best of Times and the Worst of Times: Indonesia and the Economic Crises. In Anne Booth, Chris Manning, and Thee Kian Wie, eds. *Land, Livelihood, the Economy and the Environment in Indonesia: Essays in Honour of Joan Hardjono*, Jakarta, Indonesia: Yayasan Pustaka Obor Indonesia, pp. 279–301.

Horowitz, Donald. (2000). *Ethnic Groups in Conflict*, Berkeley, CA: University of California Press, 2nd edition.

Huntington, Samuel P. (1993). *The Third Wave: Democratization in the Late Twentieth Century*, Norman, OK: University of Oklahoma Press.

Inglehart, Ronald. (1997). *Modernization and Postmodernization: Cultural, Economic, and Political Change in 43 Societies*, Princeton, NJ: Princeton University Press.

International Foundation for Electoral Systems. (1999). *IFES Survey of the Indonesian Electorate*. www.ifes.org

International Foundation for Electoral Systems. (2005). *Public Opinion Survey Indonesia 2005*. www.ifes.org

International Foundation for Electoral Systems. (2010). *IFES Indonesia Electoral Survey 2010*. www.ifes.org

International Foundation for Electoral Systems. (2015). *Indonesia Post-Election National Survey 2014*. www.ifes.org

International IDEA, accessed April 4, 2017: www.idea.int/data-tools/question-view/521

Iyengar, Shanto. (1979). Television News and Issue Salience: A Reexamination of the Agenda-Setting Hypothesis. *American Politics Quarterly*, 7, 395–416.

Jann, Ben. (2005). Making Regression Tables from Stored Estimates. *The Stata Journal*, 5(3), 288–308.

Jann, Ben. (2007). Making Regression Tables Simplified. *The Stata Journal*, 7(2), 227–244.

Jennings, M. Kent and Gregory B. Markus. (1989). Political Involvement in the Later Years: A Longitudinal Survey. *American Journal of Political Science*, 32, 302–316.

Kaase, Max and Alan Marsh. (1979). Political Action: Theoretical Perspective. In Samuel H. Barnes and Max Kaase, eds. *Political Action: Mass Participation in Five Western Democracies*, Beverly Hills, CA: Sage Publications.

Key, V. O. (1966). *The Responsible Electorate*, Cambridge, MA: Harvard University Press.

Kiewiet, Roderick. (1984). *Macroeconomics and Micropolitics: The Electoral Effect of Economic Issues*, Chicago, IL: University of Chicago Press.

King, Dwight Y. (2003). *Half-Hearted Reform: Electoral Institutions and the Struggle for Democracy in Indonesia*, Westport, CT: Praeger.

King, Anthony. (2002). *Leaders' Personalities and the Outcomes of Democratic Elections*, New York, NY: Oxford University Press.

Klingemann, Hans-Dieter. (1979). The Background of the Ideological Conceptualization. In Samuel H. Barnes and Max Kaase, eds., *Political Action: Mass Participation in Five Western Democracies*, Beverly Hills, CA: Sage.

Komisi Pemilihan Umum (KPU). (2004). *Pemilu 2004 dalam Angka dan Gambar Peristiwa*.

Komisi Pemilihan Umum (KPU). (2014). *Buku Data dan Infografik Pemilu Anggota DPR dan DPD RI 2014*.

Lazarfeld, Paul, Bernard Berelson, and Hazel Gaudet. (1948). *The People's Choice: How the Voter Makes Up His Mind in a Presidential Campaign*, 2nd ed., New York, NY: Columbia University Press.

Leege, David C. and Lyman A. Kellstedt. (1993). *Rediscovering the Religious Factor in American Politics*, Armonk, NY: M. E. Sharpe.

Lewis-Beck, Michael S. (1998). *Economics and Elections: The Major Western Democracies*, Ann Arbor, MI: University of Michigan Press.

Lewis-Beck, Michael S., Helmut Norpoth, William G. Jacoby, and Herbert F. Weisberg. (2008). *The American Voter Revisited*, Ann Arbor, MI: University of Michigan Press.

Liddle, R. William. (1970). *Ethnicity, Party, and National Integration: An Indonesian Case Study*, New Haven, CT: Yale University Press.

Liddle, R. William. (1973). *Political Participation in Modern Indonesia*, New Haven, CT: Yale University Southeast Asia Studies.

Liddle, R. William. (1996a). *Leadership and Culture in Indonesian Politics*, Sydney: Allen and Unwin.

Liddle, R. William. (1996b). A Useful Fiction: Democratic Legitimation in New Order Indonesia. In R. H. Taylor, ed., *The Politics of Elections in Southeast Asia*, New York: Cambridge University Press.

Liddle, R. William. (2013). Improving the Quality of Democracy in Indonesia: Toward a Theory of Action. *Indonesia*, 96, 59–80.

Liddle, R. William and Saiful Mujani. (2007). Leadership, Party, and Religion: Explaining Voting Behavior in Indonesia. *Comparative Political Studies*, 40 (7), 832–857.

Liddle, R. William and Saiful Mujani. (2013). Indonesian Democracy: From Transition to Consolidation. In Mirjam Kunkler and Alfred Stepan, eds., *Democracy & Islam in Indonesia*, New York, NY: Columbia University Press.

Lijphart, Arend. (1979). Religious vs. Linguistics vs. Class Voting: The "Crucial Experiment" of Comparing Belgium, Canada, South Africa, and Switzerland. *American Political Science Review*, 73(2), 442–458.

Lijphart, Arend. (1999). *Patterns of Democracy: Government Forms and Performance in Thirty-Six Countries*, New Haven, CT: Yale University Press.

Linz, Juan J. and Alfred Stepan. (1996). *Problems of Democratic Transition and Consolidation: Southern Europe, South America, and Post-Communist Europe*, Baltimore: John Hopkins University Press.

Lipset, Seymour Martin. (1959). Some Social Requisites of Democracy: Economic Development and Political Legitimacy. *American Political Science Review*, 53, 69–105.

Long, J. Scott. (1997). *Regression Models for Categorical and Limited Dependent Variables, Thousand Oaks*, Beverly Hills, CA: Sage.

Long, J. Scott and Jeremy Freese. (2005). *Regression Models for Categorical Outcomes Using STATA*, 2nd edition, College Station, TX: Stata Press.

Luskin, Robert C., John P. McIver, and Edward G. Carmines. (1989). Issues and the Transmission of Partisanship. *American Journal of Political Science*, 25, 494–511.

Malik, Husni Kamil. (2013). Pemutahiran Data Pemilih dan Penyusunan Daftar Pemilih. www.dpr.go.id/doksetjen/dokumen/mingwan-seminarKisruh-DPT-G olput-atau-diGolputkan-1432262112.pdf, accessed April 4, 2017.

Mallarangeng, Andi A. (1997). Contextual Analysis of Indonesian Electoral Behavior. A Dissertation Submitted to the Graduate School, Department of Political Science. DeKalb, IL: Northern Illinois University.

Matusaka, John. (1995). Explaining Voting Turnout Patterns: An Information Theory. *Public Choice*, 84, 91–117.

McDonough, Peter, Doh C. Shin, and Jose Alvaro Moises. (1998). Democratization and Participation: Comparing Spain, Brazil, and Korea. *Journal of Politics*, 60, 919–953.

McGrath, Joseph E., and Marion F. McGrath. (1962). Effects of Partisanship on Perception of Political Figures. *Public Opinion Quarterly*, 26(2), 236–248.

MacKuen, Michael B., Robert S. Erickson, and James A. Stimson. (1989). Macropartisanship. *American Political Science Review*, 83(4), 1125–1142.

McVey, Ruth. (2006). *The Rise of Indonesian Communism*, Sheffield: Equinox.

Mietzner, Marcus. (2015). *Reinventing Asian Populism: Jokowi's Rise, Democracy, and Political Contestation in Indonesia*, Honolulu, HI: East West Center Press.

Milbrath, Lester W. (1965). *Political Participation*, Chicago, IL: Rand McNally.

Miller, Warren E., and J. Merrill Shanks. (1996). *The New American Voter*, Cambridge, MA: Harvard University Press.

Miller, Arthur H. and Warren E. Miller. (1976). Ideology in the 1972 Election: Myth or Reality-A Rejoinder. *American Political Science Review*, 70, 832–849.

Mishler, William and Richard Rose. (1997). Trust, Distrust, and Skepticism: Popular Evaluation of Civil and Political Institutions in Post-Communist Societies. *Journal of Politics*, 2, 418–451.

Mortimer, Rex. (2006). *Indonesian Communism under Sukarno: Ideology and Politics, 1959–1965*, Sheffield: Equinox.

Mughan, Anthony. (2000). *Media and the Presidentialization of Parliamentary Elections*, London: Palgrave Macmillan.

Mujani, Saiful. (2007). *Muslim Demokrat: Islam, Partisipasi Politik, dan Budaya Demokrasi Indonesia Pasca Orde Baru*, Jakarta: Gramedia.

Mujani, Saiful. (2017). *Agama dan Rasionalitas Pemilih: Kasus Pemilihan Gubernur DKI Jakarta 2017*, Jakarta: SaifulMujani Research and Consulting.

Mujani, Saiful and R. William Liddle. (2004). Indonesia's Approaching Elections: Politics, Islam, and Public Opinion. *Journal of Democracy*, 15(1), 109–123.

Mujani, Saiful and R. William Liddle. (2010). Personality, Party, and Voter. *Journal of Democracy*, 21(2), 35–49.

Mujani, Saiful and R. William Liddle. (2013). *The Electability of Political Parties and Candidates: The 2014 Indonesian Elections*, Presented at United States Indonesia Society (USINDO), Washington, DC, December 4, 2013.

National Democratic Institute. (1999). *Post-Election Statement No.3*, Jakarta: National Democratic Institute.

National Democratic Institute. (2004). *Advancing Democracy in Indonesia: The Second Democratic Legislative Elections since the Transition*, Washington, DC: National Democratic Institute.

Nie, Norman H., Sidney Verba, and Jae-on Kim. (1974). Political Participation and the Life Cycle. *Comparative Politics*, 3, 319–340.

Nie, Norman H, Jane Junn, and Kenneth Stehlik-Barry. (1996). *Education and Democratic Citizenship in America*, Chicago, IL: University of Chicago Press.

Noer, Deliar. (1973). *The Modernist Muslim Movement in Indonesia 1900–1942*, Kuala Lumpur: Oxford University Press.

Norris, Pippa, ed. (1999). *Critical Citizens: Global Support for Democratic Governance*, Oxford: Oxford University Press.

Norris, Pippa. (2002). *Democratic Phoenix: Reinventing Political Activism*, Cambridge: Cambridge University Press.

Norris, Pippa. (2011). *Democratic Deficit: Critical Citizens Revisited*, Cambridge: Cambridge University Press.

Olsen, M. E. (1972). Social Participation and Voting Turnout: A Multivariate Analysis. *American Sociological Review*, 37, 317–33.

Olson, Mancur. (1965). *The Logic of Collective Action: Public Goods and the Theory of Groups*, Cambridge, MA: Harvard University Press.

Page, Benjamin I. and Calvin C. Jones. (1979). Reciprocal Effects of Political Preferences, Party Loyalties, and the Vote. *American Political Science Review*, 73, 1071–1098.

Parry, Geraint, George Moyser, and Neil Day. (1992). *Political Participation and Democracy in Britain*, Cambridge: Cambridge University Press.

Pepinsky, Thomas B., R. William Liddle, and Saiful Mujani. (2012). Testing Islam's Political Advantage: Evidence from Indonesia. *American Journal of Political Science*, 56(3), 584–600.

Powell Jr., Bingham. (1982). *Contemporary Democracies*, Cambridge, MA: Harvard University Press.

Prandy, Kenneth. (2000). Class, the Stratification Order, and Party Identification. *British Journal of Political Science*, 30(2), 237–258.

Przeworski, Adam and Michael Alvarez. (2000). *Democracy and Development*, New York, NY: Cambridge University Press.

Putnam, Robert D. (1993). *Making Democracy Work: Civic Traditions in Modern Italy*, Princeton, NJ: Princeton University Press.

Putnam, Robert D. (2000). *Bowling Alone: The Collapse and Revival of American Community*, New York, NY: Simon and Schuster.

Resosudarmo, Budy and Arief Anshory Yusuf. (2009). Survey of Recent Developments. *Bulletin of Indonesian Economic Studies*, 45(3), 287–315.

Riker, William H., and Peter C. Ordeshook. (1968). A Theory of the Calculus of Voting. *American Political Science Review*, 62, 25–43.

Rosenstone, Steven J. (1982). Economic Adversity and Voter Turnout. *American Journal of Political Science*, 26(1), 25–46.

Rosenstone, Steven J., and John Mark Hansen. (1993). *Mobilization, Participation, and Democracy in America*, New York, NY: Macmillan.

Samadhi, Willy Purna and Nicolaas Warouw, eds., 2009. *Building Democracy on the Sand: Advances and Setbacks in Indonesia*, Yogyakarta and Jakarta: Demos and PCD Press.

Scarbrough, Elinor. (1995). The Materialist-Postmaterialist Value Orientations. In Jan W. van Deth and Elinor Scarbrough, eds., *The Impact of Values*, Oxford: Oxford University Press.

Schwarz, Adam. (1994). *A Nation in Waiting: Indonesia in the 1990s*, St. Leonard, Australia: Allen & Unwin.

Shin, Doh C. (1999). *Mass Politics and Culture in Democratizing Korea*, Cambridge: Cambridge University Press.

Sigel, Roberta S. (1964). The Effect of Partisanship on the Perception of Political Candidates. *Public Opinion Quarterly*, 28(2), 483–496.

Soekarno. (1927). *Nationalism, Islam and Marxism* (Translated by Karel Warouw and Peter Weldon), Ithaca, New York: Modern Indonesia Project, Southeast Asia Program, Cornell University.

Stokes, Donald E. (1966). Some Dynamic Elements of Contests for the Presidency. *American Political Science Review*, 60, 19–28.

Strate, John M., Charles J. Parish, Charles D. Elder, and Coit Ford. (1989). Life Span Civic Development and Voting Participation. *American Political Science Review*, 83, 443–464.

Sullivan, John L., Michael Shamir, Patrick Walsh, and Nigel S. Roberts. (1985). *Political Tolerance in Context: Support for Popular Minorities in Israel, New Zealand, and the United States*, Boulder, CO: Westview.

Sullivan, John L., James Pierson, and George E. Marcus. (1982). *Political Tolerance and American Democracy*, Chicago, IL: University of Chicago Press.

Suparlan, Parsudi. (1982). Pengantar. In Clifford Geertz, ed., *Abangan, Santri, dan Priyayi dalam Masyarakat Jawa*, Jakarta: Pustaka Jaya

Suryadinata, Leo. (1992). *Golkar dan Militer: Studi tentang Budaya Politik*, Jakarta: LP3ES.

Tandjung, Akbar. (2008). *The Golkar Way: Survival Partai Golkar di Tengah Turbulensi Politik Era Transisi*, Jakarta: Gramedia.

Tempo, No. 3813/May 18–24, 2009. Jakarta, Indonesia.

Tempo, No. 3815/June 1–7, 2009. Jakarta, Indonesia.

Tempo, No. 4609/April 24–30, 2017. Jakarta, Indonesia.

Tocqueville, Alexis de. (2000). *Democracy in America*, Garden City, NY: Anchor Books.

Topf, Richard. (1995). Electoral Participation. In Hans Dieter Klingemann and Dieter Fuchs. eds., *Citizens and the State*, Oxford: Oxford University Press.

Verba, Sidney, Kay L. Schlozman, and Henry E. Brady. (1995). *Voice and Equality: Civic Voluntarism in American Politics*, Cambridge, MA: Harvard University Press.

Verba, Sidney, Norman H. Nie, and Jae-On Kim. (1978). *Participation and Political Equality*, Cambridge: Cambridge University Press.

Verba, Sidney and Norman H. Nie. (1972). *Participation in America*, New York, NY: Harper and Row.

Weisberg, Herbert. (1999). Political Partisanship. In John P. Robison, Phillip R. Shaver, and Lawrence S. Wrightsman, eds., *Measures of Political Attitudes*, San Diego: Academic Press.

Weisberg, Herbert F. (2002). Partisanship and Incumbency in Presidential Elections. *Political Behavior*, 24(4), 339–360.

Weisberg, Herbert F., and Charles E. Smith, Jr., (1991). The Influence of the Economy on Party Identification in the Reagan Years. *The Journal of Politics*, 53(4), 1077–1092.

Wertheim, W. F. (1980). *Indonesian Society in Transition*, Westport, CT: Greenwood.

White, Stephen, Richard Rose, and Ian McAllister. (1997). *How Russia Votes*, Chatham: Chatham House Publisher.

Widyawati, Nina. (2014). *Etnisitas dan Agama sebagai Isu Politik: Kampanye JK-Wiranto pada Pemilu 2009*, Jakarta: Obor.

Winters, Jeffrey A. (2011). *Oligarchy*, Cambridge: Cambridge University Press.

Wolfinger, Raymond E., and Steven J. Rosenstone. (1980). *Who Votes?*, New Haven, CT: Yale University Press.

Wong, Janelle S. (2000). The Effects of Age and Political Exposure on the Development of Party Identification among Asian American and Latino Immigrants in the United States. *Political Behavior*, 22(4), 341–371.

Zaller, John. (1992). *The Nature and Origins of Mass Opinion*, Cambridge: Cambridge University Press.

Zucco, Cesar Jr., and David J. Samuels. (2010). The Roots of Petismo in Brazil. Washington, DC. American Political Science Association Annual Meeting paper.

Name Index

Subject Index

abangan, 77, 78, 248
  in PKI, 84
  in presidential elections, 90
  ritual practices of, 84
  santri and, 87, 90, 91–92, 93–94,
    139–140, 232–233
Abdurrahman Wahid, 40, 48, 50–51,
  53–54
advertising, 225–226
affection, for leaders, 205, 221, 225
age. *See also* younger voters
  of citizens, 124–125
  in evaluation, of performance, 22
  Hasyim, Megawati and, 128–129
  in parliamentary elections, 125, 127–128
  in Partai Golkar, 127
  in PDIP, 127–128
  in political
    participation, 124–130
    parties, 126–127
  in presidential elections, 128–130
aliran, 84–85, 88, 248
Amien Rais
  on Boediono, 66–67
  in ICMI, 63
  Muslim voters for, 88
  in PAN, 49–50, 63–64
  Siswono and, 63–64
Asian Barometer Wave 2 Survey, 10–12

basic commodities, 154
behavioral component, of religiosity, 77–78
Boediono, 66–67, 100

campaigns, 155
  donating money to, 32
  legislative contestants in, 30
  mass media in, 32–33
  as mobilization, 29, 33
  participation in, 25–26, 29–33
    by Christians, Muslims, 76–77
    education and, 113
    rural-urban difference in, 104–105
  presidential
    contestants in, 30–31
    strategy in, 55
  symbolic issues in, 154–155
campus, 46
candidate pairs
  Boediono, Yudhoyono as, 57, 66
  catch-all parties and, 64
  Hasyim, Megawati as, 56–59
  Kalla, Wiranto as, 67–68, 179
  Kalla, Yudhoyono and, 61–63
  Megawati, Prabowo and, 68–69
  political parties and, 57
  in presidential elections, 65–66
    of 2004, 56
    of 2014, 70–71
    of 2009, 66
  Rais, Yudohusodo as, 63–64
  Salahuddin, Wiranto as, 59–61
candidates
  Javanese, 99, 236
  as santri, 233
capital, 150
catch-all party

participation, political (cont.)
  by farmers, 112
  gender in, 121–124
  income in, 111
  information in, 191, 192
  interest in, 194–197
  Islamic elements to, 79–80
  in Java, 95–96
  logistic regression of, 133
  mobilization in, 104
  of Muslims, 76
  other, 79
  in parliamentary elections, 196
  party identity and, 189–190
  in presidential elections, 198
  psychological factors in, 195–197
  rationality in, 149
  religion in, 75–76, 80–81
  religiosity in, 77–79, 131, 132–134
  rural-urban difference in, 104–110
  SES in, 95
  social class in, 113–115
  social organizations in, 81–83
  sociological factors of, 130–131,
      147–148
  sociological model on, 75
  voting in, 25–26
parties. *See* leaders; political parties
partisanship, 20, 96, 108, 116–117. *See also*
    choice
party identity
  affection, for leaders in, 205
  in choice, 185, 197–204, 218–219
  decline in, 199
  dynamics of, 187–189, 210
  economy in, 210–212
  governmental performance in, 212–213
  leaders in, 215, 217–220, 222–223
  measuring, 186–187
  multivariate analysis of, 214
  Norris on, 186
  opposition and, 210–212
  in parliamentary elections, 187–189, 190
  PDIP and, 185
  political
    attitudes and, 184–185, 241
    discussion in, 205–206
    participation and, 189–190
    socialization in, 204, 206
  in presidential elections, 199–201
  in psychological approach, 184–186

rational voter theory on, 210–211
religious organizations in, 208
social class in, 207–208
social identity and, 204–205, 208–210
social organizations in, 207
in United States, 185–186, 210
in voter turnout, 189–190, 191, 227
PBB. *See* Partai Bulan Bintang
PD. *See* Partai Demokrat
PDI. *See* Partai Demokrasi Indonesia
PDIP. *See* Partai Demokrasi Indonesia
    Perjuangan
PDS. *See* Partai Damai Sejahtera
Pemerintahan Revolusioner Rakyat
    Indonesia (PRRI), 71–72, 250
performance, governmental, 18
  in commitment, to democracy, 16, 18
  corruption in, 171, 173
  economy in, 169–171
  evaluation of, 18, 22, 23–24, 169–174,
      237–238
  of Habibie, 170
  of Indonesian democracy, 12–13, 14, 15
  of leaders, 227–228
  of Megawati, 170–171, 173
  in partisan choice, 171–172
  in party identity, 212–213
  PDIP and, 171
  political parties and, 172–173
  presidential elections and, 212–213
  regression in, 19
  of Yudhoyono, 171–172, 173
permissible rituals, 78–79, 131
Perti, 44, 250
pious Muslims
  fasting, praying by, 78–79
  in Partai Golkar, 43
  in PK, 46
  political party and, 87–88, 235
  as santri, 84, 87, 88, 232–233
PK. *See* Partai Keadilan
PKB. *See* Partai Kebangkitan Bangsa
PKI. *See* Partai Komunis Indonesia
PKS. *See* Partai Keadilan Sejahtera
PNI. *See* Partai Nasional Indonesia
political
  attitudes, party identity and, 184–185, 241
  behavior, social class in, 102–104
  discussion
    in parliamentary elections, 193
    in participation, 193–194

CPSIA information can be obtained
at www.ICGtesting.com
Printed in the USA
LVHW03*2032130618
580611LV00006B/204/P